T0162464

Rhode Island Notebook
Gabriel Gudding

DALKEY ARCHIVE PRESS
CHAMPAIGN · LONDON

Library of Congress Cataloging-in-Publication Data

Gudding, Gabriel.
Rhode Island notebook / Gabriel Gudding. -- 1st ed.
p. cm.
ISBN-13: 978-1-56478-479-7 (alk. paper)
ISBN-10: 1-56478-479-7 (alk. paper)
I. Title.
PS3607.U336R56 2007
811'.6--dc22
                                    2007026629

Partially funded by a grant from the Illinois Arts Council,
a state agency, and by the University of Illinois, Urbana-Champaign

www.dalkeyarchive.com

Printed on permanent/durable acid-free, recycled paper and bound
in the United States of America

For my daughter
when she is much older
and comes to see
the road

herself

Rhode Island Notebook

His spirit responds to his country's spirit...
he incarnates its geography and natural life and rivers and lakes.
Mississippi with annual freshets and changing chutes, Missouri and
Columbia and Ohio and St. Lawrence with the Falls and beautiful
masculine Hudson, do not embouchure where they spend themselves
more than they embouchure into him....

He spans between them also from east to west and reflects what is
between them.

Walt Whitman
(1855)

We flew throughout the summer and fall and the start of winter. At
first the whiteness gave way to the green of summer, and then gold
covered the fields and forests, and then the whiteness again.

Anatoli Berezovoy, Soviet Cosmonaut,
Commander of the Soyuz T-5
(1985)

Begin thou, unforgetting C____, for all the ages are in thy keeping,
and all the storied annals of the past.

Statius, *Thebaid*, 10, 630 ff (trans. Mozley)
(Roman epic C1st A.D.)

As you put out for Ithaca
hope the voyage is a long one
rich in exploration, full with discovery.

Laistrygonians and Cyclops
enraged Poseidon—don't be scared of them:
you won't meet such things on your way
so long as you keep your thoughts raised high
....   —you won't encounter them
unless you bring them along inside you
unless your mind sets them up in front of you.

Hope the journey is a long one.
...
Hold Ithaca firmly in mind.
Arriving there is what you are meant for.
Be careful not to hurry the journey even a little.
Better it lasts for years
so you are old when you reach the island,
rich with all you found on the way,
and expecting nothing from Ithaca.

Ithaca gave you this miraculous journey.
Without her you would not have set out.
She has nothing left to give you now.

And if you find her poor, you won't have been fooled by Ithaca.
Wise as you will have become, so full of experience,
you will have understood at last
what all these Ithacas mean.

Constantine Cavafy
(1911)

Continents

PROLOGUE..xi

Notebook Made While Driving 18 Hours from Illinois to
Rhode Island, Labor Day Weekend 2002, in One Go,
Stopping to Gas Only and to Urinate my Pee 1

9.20.02 – 9.22.02 5
9.27.02 – 9.29.02 29
10.9.02 – 10.11.02...45
10.25.02 – 10.27.02..59
11.8.02 – 11.10.02..68
11.29.02 – 12.01.02..71
12.7.02 – 1.17.03 76
1.24.03 – 1.27.03 94
2.14.03 – 2.19.03 109
2.26.03 – 3.2.03 135

THE BRIDGE.. 163

3.7.03 – 3.17.03 165
4.10.03 – 4.14.03 194
5.11.03 – 5.14.03 213
6.17.03 – 6.20.03 231
8.29.03 – 9.2.03 268
10.30.03 – 11.4.03..281
12.20.03 – 12.24.03...303
2.19.04 – 2.23.04 320
4.12.04 – 4.17.04 347
7.5.04 – 7.10.04 366
10.15.04 – 10.19.04...377
12.17.04 – 12.21.04...392

APPENDIX.. 406

PROLOGUE

And what, friends, is called a road? If there is, friends, an island, akin to a river, resembling a fence, used in the purpose of swiftly moving bodies and goods, a hallway lined in names, an aisle through counties, a duct in webs, a gangway to seeds, a traveling of beings, a river composed of islands, a place of simultaneous attraction and repulsion, a place for the finding of place, an area of exchange like unto an immense abacus. This, friends, is called a road.

And what, friends, is a car? If there is, friends, a metal corpuscle, a small room in which one cannot walk, a kind of peregrine room, a metal corpuscle battened to wheels, with an interior fitted with instruments used to control its movement, purposed to haul bodies from place to place with minimal exertion on the musculature of those bodies, being thus a small room on wheels that metallizes the human body, being a small mobilized building, a portable shack, conveying of hairdos, children, coins, drinks and fuels across the air and into the surface of hills and athwart old and dull and glittering rivers. This, friends, is called a car.

And what, friends, is called a daughter? If there is, friends, a little girl, impressionable, precious, complex, in need of love, desiring of security, warmth, kindness, giving of kindness, who is brave, who witnesses storms in awe and in fright, who enjoys big trees, has seen the fighting of her parents, owns a teddybear, goes with a teddybear, carries a white stuffed polar bear throughout her childhood, who is five, who is six, who is nine, who makes little camps in livingrooms, or in the backs of great cars, who is as an enfoldment of joy and whose life, despite her parents' efforts, is still surrounded by the causes of death, who is ten, who still finds grief, whose small hands are growing away, whose large eyes are growing away, whose funny way of talking is growing away. This, friends, is called a daughter.

And what, for us, is called a long-distance relationship? If there are friends, or any two people separated purposefully by a distance, whose history of interaction is characterized by misunderstanding, frequent fighting and interpersonal pain, such that the factors of their differences of age, culture, their styles of temperament and the scripts they were taught (in which they may seem imprisoned) have exercised them to a distance, of say eleven hundred miles, and who, despite compatibilities, and because of incompatibilities, find themselves frustrated yet willing to try. This, friends, is called a long-distance relationship.

And what, at last, is called a notebook? If, friends, there is a road through emptiness, a sea sewn to a spine, placed on tables, laps, or on the passenger seat of a car, used for palliation in a wash of disappearances, in haphazard recording of minutiae, road conditions, the recording of road condition and aggregates of thought that occur while driving on a condition, the invitation of emotion and radio, the notation of sign, a setting down of compendious or incidental note, in the grammars of back and forth going, the traveling from period to period, the coming from west to west, a sending between, a going in weather, whether between Illinois and Rhode Island, whether Normal and Providence, or between any several places normal, providential, for the purposes of trying to be happy, or of saving one's relationship, with one's estranged partner, or of seeing one's small daughter, during a separation, or of seeing her during a divorce, or of seeing her, during her swift youth after a divorce, or of driving to participate, even briefly, in the life of a sadder and less buoyant daughter, a little daughter, who is brave, who puts her chin up, who is kind, who only wishes to be happy, whom one cannot find a job near, for the recording of any elemental time of alienation, for the chronicling of any emotional pain, evoked by any unnatural distance, from a small daughter, one might love, with all one's understanding, such that, by a collection of scrawl, in an accrual of insight, some use be invited, to recollect painful things, that they may not become misery, and the refusal, to be steered by pain, or to recollect, and in fact insist, the living, with awareness, to joy, to recollect this way, for a daughter, when she is grown, or for oneself, or for anyone else, who may have found, to whatever degree, in this place of orphans, this endless humility, in our sorrow for lost homes. This, friends, is called a notebook.

Notebook Made While Driving 18 Hours from Illinois to Rhode Island, Labor Day Weekend 2002, in One Go, Stopping to Gas Only and to Urinate My Pee

Departing after teaching English 247, 2:30 PM, bright sky, HWY 74 east.

Those poor raccoons.

From that rock song I learned "every rose has its thorns."

The Ford Expedition is an abomination. Great day teaching at ISU today except for the one kid hunched at his desk: the sand-dollars of sleep hanging under his eyes kept clacking in the small breezes of his mouth weather. I woke him and explained that eye-sleep constitutes a type of guano.

Jazz is pervert music. Maurice Scharton died two days ago, crashed thru car windscreen. I did not know him many people spoke of his pigtail.

From that rock song I learned Ooh Shadoobay.

Inexplicable erection between Dayton and Columbus. Very hard, very very hard.

Buicks. These cars are for white elder couples. The Buick design-engineers of the late 1980s modeled their conveyances upon Ethan Allen furniture. The model straining to pass my efficient Toyota resembles a teak coffee table. That Ohio Buick is occupied by people who appear to be Christians. They have very loose skin. A coffee table on wheels driven by a pair of coasters.

1. "When your brother is shot out of the cannon, is he conscious the whole time?"

2. "I hope so."

Shoulder smeared with the meat-frosting of an antelope. Up inside the antelope one sees blood and feces and chemicals frozen under the horns. One sees bubbles in the eyes, the flight of the brown-red eggs. I see all of this while passing the ripped carcass at 70 miles an hour. At this speed my vehicle will achieve 46 miles per gallon. At 62 miles an hour I achieve 50 miles per gallon if I don't use the air conditioner.

We will know what is inside Jerry Lewis if we continue on this road. The road we are presently on is Hwy 80 East Jerry I am coming.

I remember her breasts. Staring at her breasts was like spending 2 nights inside a kazoo.

East of Akron, out of tedium, I begin to sing "Slowly balding, slowly balding, slowly balding,
You are slowly balding and your children are balding apace.
No one else in the world is balding except your family. Wife is balding.

The vaginas of your women are balding,
the penises of your men are balding,
Your wife is stretching out. Shrungen, balden, stretchle wife. Your whole family is really bald and stretched out now.
Soon your children bald will go off to college balden, shrungen, stretchle.
Bald, slowly slowly bald. Balding slowly. Slowly shrung. Ooh shadoobay."
The sun sets beneath Akron.

When driving long distances a person enters a kind of snakedance psychosis and I really do feel at this point like I have been rewired with the ligaments of a baboon. In the twilight, bird almost hits windshield, cartwheels off in the slipstream. It is a matter of natural record that a stork can deliver its own enema. Your mother's meatloaf looked like stonehenge that night. She set it right down there between the butter plate and the jam tray, the meatloaf so hard and cold a baby fog settled over the dinnerware. The stonehenge meatloaf lay there in minuscule immensity. There was embarrassed silence for your mother. I stood up with deliberation and undid my buckle, I bent over and wishing to please your mother, placed a small wedge of meatloaf between the cheeks of my buttocks. I smiled and said, "This tastes very good." Somehow this caused an uproar.

Comfort Inn my toosh. Country Rd 533 Brookville. "I got a peaceful easy feeling." What if The Lord hid your soul in the fundament of a hen and you chose to recover it after finding out which hen contained it? How would you proceed? Or say your soul is lodged in a goat lip and you have identified the goat in question. Do you call a chaplain or a person of animal lip knowledge. Now that I am employed I hope I can avoid the direct attention of psychiatrists. Big cliffs 709 miles from Bloomington/Normal.

Pulling over in Clarion Pennsylvania to sleep, tilt seat back fall asleep seat belt on, wake 4:30 AM Eastern time, pee and drive. Clarion is one half the distance between Normal and Providence.

My advice is demonstrate incompetence in every ancillary job you undertake. Demonstrate this incompetence in every subsidiary feature of your personality, leaving a reserve mastery in the heart of your gifts. People who are strategically ineffective in this manner are left alone to do their work. If you are incompetent in the right way, no one will wish to improve upon you. Truly independent beings are incompetent by design. For instance now I am in New York and the geese are collectively independent: here are some now and they are refusing to fly in

3

W's and V's. They are flying in P's and O's.

The succeeding is my response to a fellow driver in mid Connecticut. Earnest Driver I am putting the end of a wrench in your navel, am putting the concomitant pain of a duck in each of your heels, a half a duck's pain to either heel, a full duck's pain to the pair of your feet. Into your knees I lodge the ache of a goose, into your hips I fix the soreness of an emu, into your chest I plant the suffering of an ostrich, and at the top of your head, in your ditch of reason, I button the anxiety of an hummingbird, just a fleck of misery there to goad.

Your obvious bosoms reach outward. Many prows and ships come to us like your breasts, by two's. Many ships do however come by three's and four's. The point being your obvious bosoms reach outward substantially bearing the cargo of your nipples. I have put my drafts and versions on your bosoms, but the wind blew them off. I eschewed the top of your head as a place to put my versions as there is a heavy weather out of your mouth. I adore you. This rattletrap of a dock adores you, and the old hard fish under this rigid dock adores you. I the rigid dock am sailing to rendezvous with the entire fleet of your body parts, each part bearing its cargo of boobies. And I am the dock am bearing my rigidity, my rigid wood, my immense creosote members, my masculine pylons and stiffened beams. I adore you you adore you. Life is to be dealt with over and over.

On top of your baby, I put a flat baby. The flat baby is sorrowful and smells of old wings. I am trying to extinguish your baby with a flat baby. Suffering is conservative. Endurance is progressive. Life is to be dealt with over and over. Ooh shadoobay.

D, I shall garland you with the epigraphs of far away books. And failing that, kiss you.

9.20.02 – 9.22.02

[anabasis]

2:10 PM 9.20.02 Out in
the sportscars of
the asteroids
are no sad fathers
no little wools, no sheep, no great doors:
are no daughters, nor wolves
the daughters fear, nor are
daughters on a plate of moon
to wonder
how their fathers are.

Put this book now
large format Strathmore
sketch pad
on passenger seat go to Rhode Island am
farting in farflung junior faculty
parking lot at Illinois State University
on bright day September-hot my
little five & one 1/2 yr old
daughter C___ alive in[1]

Providence in kitchen now
as her mother
Omega and sister R are
I in Normal Illinois turn left

---

1 Because a request was made, as the book was going to press, that my daughter's proper name not be mentioned, she is identified by C___ throughout—or, where appropriate, by one of her nicknames, which are Goofy, Sweetpea, or Princess Mary Animalia.

onto Main fr
College in Normal just
finished teaching for
week in Normal I think of
Black Elk and his
horses how he thought
of coming thunderstorms
as friends is this ink black or green?

A partner is
in Providence, a daughter
and a partner's
daughter in Providence, outer wall of
heaven I in norm, custom
center, this
quotidian: silence, our
fighting, gender, culture
(am American, D
Icelandic) the very tallow of the hay corn
in Illinois indifferent to all this
Hwy 74 2:25 PM.
Try maintain 70 mph

Friday now, a bright sun
will drive all night arrive tomorrow
at noon returning Sunday be
sad at it by end: 36 hrs driving in
3 days of being

Brevis esse laboro
obscurus fio[2]

---

2 "The appetite for coherence is the main cause of our exorbitant and unnatural fear of things."
—Jean Dubuffet, letter to Christophe Guilmoto, 7 April 1979, Prospectus IV, p. 626

Bad fight
last trip.
We move now to your anus, the magician.
How you bombed me in the pimple.

It was unusual Lois who bombed me in the
pimple

from high in the cold mountains

She was somewhere in the timber wood

in a dirty cabin of the purplest mtn.

She whistles to her dog there.

That is the home of the lady
who bombed me in the pimple.

85.8 m Welcome to Indiana
Crossroads of America.
What about her caused her to walk
purposely into

What had caused her to walk w/
terrible deliberation

past the dark farm of her strong and angry
                                        daughter
down then cross the digitalis peppered hill
over two string-like creeks and
a yarn-like ditch, past
a clot of 4 sleeping ducks and under

the blonde-green dreadlocks of a shivering
willow

the flaps of skin on my head I call
my ears

drinking from a bright can
I realized after driving 210.9 miles that the reason
I was upset was not b/c the steering wheel
still seemed misaligned despite the 59 dollars
but
that my scrotum had been folded tightly under
my perineum. Whatever warm thought-induced
anaesthesia had erased or edited the messages
dispatched from my distressed scrotum across
western Illinois, whatever mental epidural
had thrown its body against the door of my
medulla oblongata as I drove, the Thermopylae
of my spinal cord, this protective force had
been overrun and I was now in pain

tussus feculence dottles. Urinic
Why had she bombed my pimple. It was not an
ornery pimple. Had I some redoubt on it?
Some
consolate outpost busy with typists.
What but the white
basilica of the pus-bleb rode the broad bailey
of my pimple?

sebum. The slick field of sebum
spreading into the plains of my face
I am a rack of twine

in a hat of hair
I have morally harmed myself
Basically to live thru lust is to live thru sorrow,
the Klipot of lust
is a matrix
of Sorrow but it's weird that we don't see
how lust is at heart a sorrow

the Kilpot, or Kelipa, acc to the Kabbala
is the shell that conceals a holiness
I quit drinking 12 days ago, after
really bad fight w/ D
Brookville OH 267.4 m Exit 21
itty majiggers
6:43-6:54 Gas Stop
          @ 276 m
Was Lois, the odd lady who bombed
my pimple, devoid of good regard
for me? Was there an indefatigable
contumely against acne?
          339 m to Junction 270 N
Whom among us shd have our
pimples bombed!
                    emotional incontinence
                    flaccid diction
"tactical overdeployment" of the
          word "love" D F Wallace
which, I submit, …
          hypertonically
what lonely, odd, intricately paisled
cosmology wd cause her to
deploy
to induce

Why was not my pimple antipodal to
her lonely purple mortar-bearing mtn?

Punitive use of ordnance against
    my pimple

As if a bell had rung deep in my face
and my jaw vibrated w/ it
my jaw's reverberation from the bell
that had rung coldly beneath my
bone (zygoma) the vibration's paths became
                                complex
when they entered the 6 flaps of
skin that delimit the front and sides
of my face namely my ears, the
2 circular flaps of epidural constitutive of
my nostrils, & the 2 intricate
flaps of muscle that are
the facial labia. beneath my nostrils

a mouth being a toothed bubble. exordium

Had the bombing reduced the ability of
my face to display affect?

Catachretic b.s.

the weighty boom of the shell as it
burst on my pustule
reverberated
around the topography of my head.

The mortar shell landed at the

very top of the conical pimple
w/ a sonorous boomlet
cutting away the top & leaving a
small caldera a semi-solid lake
of blood and long-anchored pus.

My crazy illness of booze
and crying so heavily that
had I built a levy upon my cheek
it would have drowned the Cortusa of my chin

Adolescence's prevailing theme's
the eruption of pimples, the
elongation of groin, extension
of nipples forward, hips
sideways, buttocks backward
and tongues & lips go clucking
& wooing forward toward other lips & tongues
Sleep fr. 2:30–7 AM EST at 672 m

the tongue, that flip arbiter of
want and language. that
deft electrical flap. That
welcome mat of the head.

Autumnal buttocks their
pear-like sag

That locomotive cd put an eye out.

22 hrs later, Saturday, I Exit in Prov
12:58 PM EST 1094.8 m
Arrive at the home of T& S & C 1097.2

Their (our?) house so near
the Brown University campus

[katabasis]

8:32 AM Fill on gas get
2 old fashioneds, the Old
Fashioned is an unadorned plain
wheat donut 9.22.02 Sunday

St John of the Cross sd
in the dark night of the soul
most turn back

Katabasis[3] : a journey of the Dead
made by the living. I feel this whole
dumb road is just going to crumble: I won't
be able to make it: This division between us,
she in Providence, heaven I
in Normal, the custom, rule, a mean,
I in median, an I-land: Road
Island—1 m from D&S&C. All
My life I have been on I-sland. My
grandmother Frances
used to make old fashioneds when
she owned a diner in Moorhead Minnesota

Pythagoras sd he'd a memory
of visiting Hades in a past life. Sd he

---

3 Anabasis is a Greek word meaning Advance or the march up country. Katabasis conversely means
retreat, and is sometimes used to describe a protagonist's descent into hell. It is a term applied to
the descents of Virgil and Dante, and Christ, not to mention Elvis, and it also applies to Alice and
Bugs Bunny.

saw Homer hanging in a tree. Sd he saw
Hesiod bound in chains. Because they dis
respected the gods. Epistemon in *Gargantua*
went to Hades. And came back to report
he'd seen Achilles begging in the street
and Hector working in a kitchen scraping
pots. He also reported he saw King Arthur
cleaning grease out of hatbands and
Cleopatra selling onions. And that Helen
sold her crotch for drachmas.

Orpheus, Hercules, Theseus
Aeneus, Virgil, Dante
followed same road
carrying fowl

They stopped
in diners, sunlit ones
on way downward under home
through honey lights, under mud light
into loam, best cup
of coffee ever had was
driving south Hwy 95 out of Providence
on gelid Sunday was happy
was prahfessr and going
to make it right
The first sip taken 21.3 m S of
city. Speed 71 mph in cloudless sky.

40 m fr. m's door CT border. 9:10 AM EST

[SE CT
Large white spider on windshield

in the lee of the wipers been there
since Prov. probably fell fr. a tree
Above C's driveway 55.9 m from Prov.
It hunkers there in the clear bellowing of the air
Is it oblivious, is it deaf?][4]

---

4 *May 2005:* Few thoughts when expressed at once so banal and profound: WE ALL GONNA DIE. A truism concrete in fact yet useless in account, being as it is an axiom hard to realize. The utterance of this phrase in boisterous company sometimes is followed with a chain of exclamation points and the unproductive ejaculation "Aaaghghg!" That is to say, it is a truth so beyond us as best to work as a joke.

I assert that death is a class of destruction. No great news there. But, looked at one way, death, though a rather complete and maybe even "no nonsense" kind of destruction, is at heart a comic destruction.

And I think Whitman, though not himself a comic writer, knew this. Let me explain.

Comic destruction is never merely destructive; it has a levity to it, as if it will be followed by an improving and restorative force. Death to me is like this. Cartoons, also, are like this: If Wylie Coyote is crushed by a boulder, he comes back flattened for some time but eventually is restored fully to a two dimensional approximation of a three dimensional being (instead of a two dimensional approximation of a two dimensional being which he was while he was flattened and walking around like a wafer with legs, not necessary for me to go on like this).

My point is I have had glimpses of my death when I have been able to achieve a calmness in meditation via the complete surrender to (and awareness of) what is in me, namely: jillions of little explosions, pin-sized gusts of warmth, tiny sciroccos of jiggling electrical clouds blowing here and there in my muscles—a constant roistering of change manifest as a flickering constellation of tiny atom-sized explosions all throughout my musculature, and in my eyes combusting and wavering fields of colors roseate, cyan, saffron, rubiate, pucid, vernal ... these racks and sets of conflagrations all throughout my body as if I were a dim backboard thrust into a storm of light.

And I strongly sense that death is merely the continuation of this conflagration without me (or with me in a different form). It's just a new stage of constant combustion and restoration. And as such it strikes me as fundamentally comic and joyous.

And though Whitman is obviously not "funny," I suppose I would hesitate to label him deadly serious because his emotional mode is so buoyant, so full of gratitude, so joyous and welcoming and generous and big-spirited—embracing, encompassing, hugging, beaming—that I do not think of him as "serious."

But he is not "funny" either. He is not making jokes. Yet his spirit has something about it that shares deeply of a kind of unexpressed comedy.

Maxine Chernoff once remarked on an affiliation between comedy and empathy: she said that comedy at its best is deeply empathic. To my sensibility this rings quite true, even in comedy's most violent and hectic forms (eg, Farce), there is a deep empathy with the simultaneity of the absurdity, joy, and pain that is our lot in this world. And Whitman is almost empathy personified. So though he is not funny, his empathy makes him a cousin to the comedian. Whitman's empathy is a cousin to the democratizing aspects of the comic mode at its best—but without being "expressed" as comedy.

There is an inclusiveness to Whitman's character that is consonant with that ideal inclusive society that all comedy (according to Northrop Frye) tends toward: a forgiveness of pain, suffering, and of those who caused, and keep causing, it.

I am sorry that much of what some folks call serious poetry reads as a misfortunate kind of whinging—about, frankly, the wide fact that we suffer. I must say that many poets who have written from a mode of high seriousness (and I'm talking since like early 20c—Pound, Eliot (not kitty cat Eliot)) do, I find, read as melodramatic. Melodrama, as well all know, occurs when there's no real (or sufficient) rationale for the emotion; it seems outsized and inappropriate.

And such is the case with the general palette of emotional responses used by many contemporary writers: We witness a bizarre collection of cultural responses to the suffering inherent to life as a body of knee-jerk emotive reactions: nostalgia, self-pity, the unconvincingly bittersweet lyric. In fact, the older I get and the more used I become to the idea that I'm going to die, the more melodrama I keep spotting in art, movies, tv, poetry. There are of course hundreds of refulgent exceptions: A few of whom I've re-read recently are Joanne Kyger and Bernadette Mayer. Such writers can tow us toward insight and deeply appreciative and productive modes of affect and insight.

At risk of sounding a little harsh, I find that so much writing seems to, well, whine and bemoan suffering. In fact whole journals seem given over to certain affective habits: Poetry Magazine, eg, is curiously invested in the marriage of light surrealism and nostalgia. What I love however about Whitman is that he is not doing any of this; and neither is he cracking jokes. Like Kyger and Mayer, Whitman's emotive moves have deep authority precisely because his emotions are not about Self so much as they are about self-in-relation. In relation to death's past, death's future, and to the living Other.

I think it is evident that he knew at a very deep experiential level (and not merely intellectually)—and one can sense this I think in the comprehensiveness of his empathy—that death comes to all of us. Not just to oneself.

He is full of empathy. He is full of true gratitude, deep acceptance, and a deeply welcoming groove that makes me want to love him A LOT. There is something about the quality of his awareness that does not bemoan or whine. It is soft, welcoming, and deeply aware.

It is admirable.

["The life of the poet is one
of ease, happiness, constant joy,
freedom"
—(actually said by) Maxine Hong Kingston
        on NPR 91.3 FM 59.2 m fr. Prov.
Does she know what
the poets do? Is it Hong Kingston herself or
her ideas that sound vapid: open throat
whisper. Something tasteful
about her: Taste
holds, maintains, guards
a deep and basic
mendacity. We lie to ourselves
about the aesthetics found in culture work
and I think Maxine Hong Kingston
is doing this now]

["We all have it." "Poetry is everywhere
all around us." acc. to C. Hong
Kingston on NPR flogging her book
To be The Poet Harvard UP Kingston sounds
, strangely, smug. Not
to say that we don't all "have it," but that
what is "had" is in fact not "had," as if one cd
own a talent to be marketed in the sense of
C B McPherson's possessive individualism. I
am

concerned these books, and this is one of a hundred
such books surrounding "poetry," sell *not poetry*
but
sow instead a sense of deficiency
at not being a poet—under the guise of

proclaiming the democratic ubiquity of
the poetic spirit—these books are legion since
Hughes Mearns's *Creative Youth* and *Creative
Power.*
Since in fact Friedrich Schlegel's
Dialogue on Poetry and Literary Aphorisms.

Exit 69 Hwy 9 N. 70 m fr. Prov.
Can't stand the voice of Garrison
Keillor. It is saccharin as if it has no mucus
Also Eileen Hansen why she do a fake laugh]

Some thunder blabbered deeply.

"There is the tree," Herodotus said,
"glittering darkly with wrens.
Can you get the thunder out of it?"

I paused. Maybe it was a test, I don't know.
He was an old man. They bug me. Pouty
wrinkled bald sponge dog toys resembling babies
looking from the neck up somehow scrotal
but thinking themselves sacerdotal.

Sir, I cannot extract lightning from sky nor
thunder from tree,
I've come to take you from this place.
"This is my home," He said. He asked,
"Is this not my home Helicarnassus?"
I said, "No Sir, this is a shitty place. I can't
really describe what this place is. It's just really
shitty."
I am an historian, He said. How can I not

know how I got to a place?

He stood up, the water giggled about his ankles.
His calves were puttied with mud. He didn't
have any pants on. His dong was small and
blue. "Sometimes, Sir, we fall asleep, the driver
makes an error." "I have died?" he asked.
I don't think so Sir. I think you just fell. Your
backside looks dented, we all heard a thud
and set out to find you.
Our libraries heard the impact
                    from deep across the world
It was sort of a fart-thump.

So we have come down here to the fundament
of the library with this
search party. I gestured to my search party.
"I am in the basement of a library?" No Sir:
we have come through the footnotes of
John Hodgson-Hinde's
A History of Northumberland, 1820. We spent
165 pages in that particular footnote. No one
knows how you got here.

"Where am I forgodsake? And assuming you
got me out of this place," he said,
"where would I go?"
I paused. "You're in my book," I said. He
rolled his eyes. "What's it about?"
It's about driving, Sir. What's it called, he said.
"Nevermind," I said, "Let's Go."

And Herodotus refused. He said,
"You need a chicken;
that's the rule."

I almost punched him. Suzanne was about
to lose it. Luckily I had brought the chicken
with me. I ordered Suzanne to pluck it,
but Herodotus said
he liked his chickens with feathers. I stepped
forward with the chicken. My wrist thickened
about the thin neck of the chicken. I swung it
high, held it above my head, as if to slam it into his
head. He blinked lightly, rabbinically. My heart
felt like a kayak banging in an ice floe. Dude
wants his payment, I thought. Even in Hades,
dude wants his due.

It is a duck, He said gently. No Sir, A chicken,
I said. A duck! he said. A chicken I said. Duck
he said chicken I shouted.

Gently he said duck.

It is a chicken, I asserted. My anger put
bile under my throat, my by now really
rug-like tongue pushed against my teeth.
Still I held the fowl high, loosened my
mouth and began to chant,

"So Here, Herodotus, dear physician,
who have fallen so down to his Dark,
take please as prize, as pity, as token,

this glorious uproarious *chicken*.

For you who have fallen on your end
have fallen a long way to drop.

And may this chicken
beckon you up."

The chicken flattened on the table.

Herodotus
did not move
did not get up, said instead

"Think I'll stay here,
you barking pup:
at the bottom
of *your* book,
the one *you* wrote,
you stupid schmuck—

it's home enough."

Suzanne began to bawl. Judy said hell. I
sneezed. We turned and strode. The road
did not look familiar, nothing
looked familiar. We heard the chicken
behind us being rent with popping. We heard
from behind us
a stupid laughing, a cackling, we said heck
with this
and strode. A dimness
came upon us as we rose

from that place. Margaret, Margaret
your fine hair behind us, I remember how
lovely
how lovely
are our loved ones' noses.
107 m. 91 S to 691 W

TOM
TAD
TIM

And here I am at Higganum
at Haddam & Higganum

Is not that a saint or sadness hanging
in that rack of cloud? It looks
like a mandorla in the sky
above prim, historical Connecticut. Or
is it a pipe organ?

What is that lodged in the cloud
above prim, historical, Connecticut?
Some kind of penitentiary just
inside NY border Caramel NY
160 m fr. Prov. 11 AM EST
Wrong: that was a factory.

183 m fr. Prov. here's the penitentiary
Peekskill NY ? New 9D Junction to
Weppinger Falls Beacon
        Exit 11
185 m Hudson River bridge over
"The Hamilton Fish

Newburgh Beacon"
A fart: ventloquism
DONUT CHYME.
DONUT. CHYME. BOLUS. FECES. DUNG.
SOIL Wheat. Donut Chyme Bolus
FECES DUNG SOIL WHEAT DONUT
CHYME BOLUS FECES DUNG SOIL
Wheat DONUT This assuming we
make donut fr. wheat. What if we make
donut from feces scooping it directly
from the rectum Feces DONUT CHYME
BOLUS FECES DONUT NO this wd
short circuit the AGRICO-DIGESTIVE Cycle
Snipping the mobius loop of nutrition
and splicing out photosynthetic regeneration of
nitro-carbonic compounds.
Beverly is the only proper name
that I can think of at the moment that
cd serve as an ADVERB
     225 fr. Prov. PA Border
       Hwy 84
DAVID FOSTER WALLACE IS TURGID
NAY BOMBASTIC: "Luminous intensity
of the light"? yeah he wrote that

I suspect that a "respect for authority"
is merely a respect for socio–economic
capital. This "respect for authority" bears
a concomitant & converse disrespect for
those w/out socio–economic capital.
The idea, furthermore, of a "moral authority" is
contradictio de adjectivo. True morality
cannot be buttressed w/ doctrine nor

scaffolded w/ law. Executive & legislative
power can sometimes be allied w/ morality
but that is not
license to confuse the two.

MLA registration. Insurance. Call Mom re
sitting
Lackawanna historical society.
Of interest to the women of Jenkins
are the men of Wilkes-Wray
Missing D deeply.

7.412 gallons 1:19-1:30 stop to fill on. Had
to wash car by hand in front b/c truck
got diesel oil on car via its
exhaust maybe

Ears are like an early kind of
seashell stapled to
sides of our heads
Lewisburg PA 365 m fr. Prov.
near Exit 210 80 w

The left & right versions of the
seashell are the male & female sexes
of the species and yr head
is the mechanism they use to mate
Yr head is in fact a pod utilized
to facilitate the mating of yr ears.
They are copulating right now, behind yr
face, somewhere just above—& slightly
behind yr. throat.

My jaws are ransacking yr lips.
393 m fr. Providence those impressive
immense cut-cakes of cliffs.
It is not even my lips that are
searching & rummaging over yrs
It is my whole jaw. My very head is
frisking yr head searching the 2
fleshy grenadiers posted at the gatehouse
of yr talk yard.
        exit 48 Hwy 80 w Exit 2 miles
        Emlenton PA 529 m fr. Prov.
        4:36 PM EST.
     Ave speed since departure 66 MPH

After gassing up in Drums, PA at
1:25 PM (the time is now 5:02 PM) I
ground the starter for the 1st time
C___ said yesterday she doesn't
like my beard. Very high whine to
the tires 560 m fr. Prov, 12 M fr
Ohio border. 1st strong signs of autumnal
chromatic metamorphoses in the leaves:
a few minutes west of Youngstown OH
Pale yellow in what appear to be alder
ocherous reds too just west of
bridge over Meander Reservoir.

649 m fr. Prov. Junction Hwy 71 S.
        6:25 PM EST Columbus 101 m

Send dead flies to Julie Cripe, her parents
X-tian, Margaret aka Molly Vitorte, Wm
& Christine, Pierre Joris, Ron

Padgett, My parents, Jean, Cheryl
Terry, Denise Carolyn, Rita Pougiales
Sara, Sarah, Bill Ransom, Nancy
Taylor (hiring dean at Evergreen)
Bill Arney, Gabrielle Raley, Poch, &
all in Market 2001-2002 folder

STOP TO PEE at 676 m rest stop 71 S
(1st pee today at 1:27 PM) 6:55 PM

That was an utterly ill-designed
reststop fr the ingress pt to the
egress and the bathroom was

small rains
throughout
Ohio
Dotty not
Splattery rains

Dot-inducing rains 1-3 millimeter dots
Bug splats rare those that do
appear on windscreen are fr lepidopterae
(the wing dust colors them) (No apians or
dragonflies, no dipterae or
mosquitoes). Sun crisply & orange in the
east south east 55 m N of Columbus Just
above the tree line occluded by the crests of
many low hills.

7:20 EST Sun flickering through the
trees & low roadside bushes Overhead
sky still very bright pink & blue &

gray electrical vanilla Headlights
bright beads string behind me in the
rearview mirror An entire bank of
immense trees appears on eastern
side of HWY & is stoutly bearing up
against a huge wave of flamingo pink
fire splashed off the sunset.[5] The reflection
fr. the lit bank of trees is at once
pink & green. 7:30 quick glimpse of the
sun as it trips into
a dark thin fuzzily dentate line of trees &
falls into the horizon.
Dusk has begun.

I like the voice of Etta James.

Faith & Justice Radio Show
95.1 FM Columbus

Often at night I dream
of the little yam of yr womb

Also I dream of lands
with hilly counties and cold rivers
and really dark desks at windows
and people giving me
wooden boxes
filled with vintage pens

847 m fr. Prov. IN/OH border

---

5 Je suis le piéton de la grand'route par les bois nains; la rumeur des écluses couvre mes pas. Je vois
longtemps la mélancolique lessive d'or du couchant. fr. *Les Illuminations,* Rimbaud, IV.

What is an emergency but a
sudden, aversion-based need
to move things along quickly. It is a
calendrical problem

10:21 STOP TO URINATE 895 m
                    fr. Prov.

10:25 on hwy again
      4 minute stop

Also send dead fly to Jordan Davis

A season is a thing follows a round
with heads of clouds and hawks behung:
. a clock of cloud, each thing camming
to each thing: the cloud of a rain day
fitting on the pond, the
cloud of a shining day
hung to frame a sun.

I make 74 W 937 m 10:05 pm central time

My favorite instrument is the pipe organ.

Back in Connecticut
the Cathedrals resemble toaster ovens
A chapel is an eagle bakery

1009 m = IL Border 11:05 PM CT

11:15 PM PEE STOP 1020 m

11:19 PM on road again
Salt Kettle Rest Area, IL

3.97 million blocks of stone
2.5 tons each on average
in the Great Pyramid
fr. 12–16 tons at bottom to
  ½ ton at top

artbell.com
gizapower.com

must buy toothbrush

Wm Rosenberg he was 86, founder of
Dunkin' Donuts
died today 9.21.02 in Cape Cod

1093 Exit into BL, IL
    exit 135

Buzz Aldrin, 72 yrs, punches
37 yr old man debunker of moon
landing

1096.6 m fr. Prov arrive Normal

9.27.02 – 9.29.02

[anabasis]

Friday 2:11 PM 9.27.02 Parking lot
at ISU overcast Just finished teaching

It is a wonder I can do anything.

My heart feels like an eagle too long hung
in the sky's angles

Traffic JAM 2:14 College Ave
ODO: 22233 Reverse course, round blocks
Mulberry & College 2:21 PM
Some kind of Homecoming parade
blocking the road Homecoming traffic at
Illinois State: I have no home. Strange
here that we call such
harsh things as schools "Homes"
and "Our Mother"

I pass the Wittenberg Lutheran Youth Center
in Normal
Illinois

Who goes but youth
and glorious small Christians

their limbs are warm, the girls have
little doves, the boys grow baby turkeys

there is no talk of Auntie Christ

no talk of boobies or of ding dongs there.

I want to run in and shout
"I have a ding dong and held the boobies!"

but I stay in the traffic, and the centuries
go joyous on

Drive to see D and Melpomene and C___: *their* home
2:35 PM HWY 74 Junction 22240 odo
I quit drinking 9.8.02. Regarding aleotoric
Nature of notebook written in car See C S Peirce
on "tychism": Chance, whim, what the very
moment lays on us is by definition
reasonable. Not only reasonable but alive
glowing, afire: In qua ratio perfecta insit:
and it "lives through all life,
extends through all extent"

Satura. The sun has shown up
again 40 m origin of Kaskaskia
River email Kent Johnson [6]
61.2 m I strike a yellow butterfly
w/ fender. Kickapoo St. Park.
Middle Fork Vermilion River 69.7 m
Potomoc, IL. 1st bug splat at the
dell of the Vermilion River 73.2 m 3:41 PM
near exit 210 HWY 74 east 2nd splat

---

6 "In brief, he became, from an Idiot and a Clown, to be one of the most complete Gentlemen in Cyprus...."—*Anatomy of Melancholy,* Part 3, Sect. 2, Memb. 3.

3:44 PM clear 1 x 5 centimeters.

It's like a tattered bird at some
            edge of the clappy old kosmos
has been staring at me since I was little
My life has about as much import
as a butterfly
            launching from a grave of a guinea pig

2 more clear splats noticed lower
right quadrant. I name them Boris
and John. Wabash College next right.
Lebanon, IN 122.6 m 4:24

There is a desperation
in what we call "music."
It is used to fill the Emptiness
—   the Emptiness which is
to wise people nurturant—
but which most see
as threatening and barren.

5 PM Traffic Jam of Indianapolis
Thank God for Barbara Ehrenreich
Rush hr Indy. Around 5:05 pm I
make 70 east. Joseph Nathan
Kane of Famous First Facts died
3 day's ago. He was 103 years old.
Cows moving fast. "Bullet Hole Gunshop
& Archery Range" Wilkinson IN RT. 109

TOM RAPER WORLD'S LARGEST
RV & MOBILE HOME DEALER
OPEN EVENINGS. WHYY in Philadelphia.
John? Africa of <u>MOVE</u> was SHOT TO DEATH
TODAY. IN/OH border 246 M 6:21 PM
God Bless the Iraqi People Sunset 6:35 PM

I should not have said those things to you
                              in the sunset
What a load of hell that was I said to you as the
sun fell back away from the world
I should not have said that.

We burned the eagle w/ Petroleum, pumpin
2 bullets into its tiny knees. We took a
nutcracker to its beak. Great Miami River
280.0 M fr Normal.

I am in fact a hardware store: capable
of being practical and valuable to others.

We beat the eagle. Its 2 eyes were kitchens
in which I cd see perspiring scullions
skittering. Maybe there were
the ghosts of mice trapped in its
head. Beyond all value I found
the look on its forehead after we
cracked its beak w/ the nutcracker.

Columbus Ohio 7 pm
Tommy began whipping the eagle

w/ a bootlace. Do it have an empty
resourceless mind?

A grin flung itself to either
side of my head.
In its feathers the smell of
wheat and fogs.

The eagle had become quite
dilapidated under our treatment
Its eyes remained wet though they
had begun to cross. We
Approached it with a want

Inside PA border a Popped raccoon, a
gray bright smudge lit on the
right shoulder

Its shorn plumage a collection
of white crimped straws
the eagle was now
a kind of blunted
muscular porcupine

NIGHT: at night I am very sad. There are
fewer holy forces revealed at night.

The eagle, now a cluster of
white straws, looked at me
sizing me up as if I were
an anonymous dog

"I was always a private man.
It's difficult to realize I was so
discussed." Count Laszlo Almasy

I GAS IN SNOW SHOE, PA
and go to sleep in the lot
of the ratty Amoco

I wake at 5:35 AM CST.

Cloudy morning. Dirty blue to
Gray-Orange clouds

Going out now into the gnawed light (dust)

Shake it shake it shake it
          Snoopy.

Hang on snoopy snoopy
hang on

Why do D and I fight?

Lime Ridge PA Nuclear cooling tower
Go ahead Iraq Make My Day
CAPN JACK'S LOBSTER Restaurant
Susquehanna River
"It's almost the end of grass cutting season,
and you know what that means!"
John LeCarre has warned that "America has
entered one of its periods of historical
madness"

Keep minimum 2 dots apart.
Junction 81 Wilkes-Barre 2 Miles 788 m
uncorrected. I protest the Israeli
occupation of the Palestinian territories.

The west south west looks partly cloudy
7:55 AM The light on 84 this morning
under the shale cliffs reminds me of
the light on the tidal waters of the
Hamma Hamma River

1 millimeter dots of rain 15 second micro-
squall at 7:56 then gone.

"To be irresponsible is to be free.
Make risks. Make risks." Egberto Gismonti

Famous widows: Yoko Ono, Jackies
Kennedy and Onassis.
Famous mental widows: Nancy Reagan,
Eva Braun, the wife of Daffy Duck.

Lords Valley Dingmans Ferry
1 Mile Exit 34
Food Exit 34 McDona...
        Taco B...

The eagle's children are not

my children

yellow leaves clipping & glinting in the

morning light

Port Jervis 8 miles

Why are there so many Danvilles.
Why not Petervilles, Joevilles
Timvilles Tomvilles Bobvilles Robvilles?
Billvilles Jillvilles Willvilles?

Send a dead fly to Scott Simon. He ostensibly
is a Quaker yet he supported the invasion of
Iraq.

Superb swamp Matamoras NY

Stephanievilles!
Belindavilles

Elsavilles? One day I will know an Elsa?

Small porpoise-sized clouds
in a blue sky, green trees
either side road fr. PA on.

No hint of foliage change
in west CT

I enter Rhode Island at Noon

A lead sky dripped
with ingots of gulls:

bullets from the dark of Lapland.

Hopington Westerly RI
1076 M Low Gas icon begins to flash

Salt air.

Pawtuxet River

Mist in the bushes

1103 M Exit 20

1094 M Exit 20 Providence 12:56 PM

arrive 18 BeHappy Street, Providence
9.28.02 Saturday

They are jumping at the windows.

[katabasis]

8:46 AM EST Sunday 9.29.02
Just filled on 6 gallons

"Dad, those poor people are dead." – C___,
re people in an old photograph

Hadn't noticed the great presence of
evergreens in RI before.[7]

---

7 There are seven species of conifers common to Rhode Island: Eastern red cedar *(Juniperus virginiana)*; Tamarack *(Larix laricina)*; Red pine *(Pinus resinosa)*; Pitch pine *(Pinus rigida)*; Eastern white pine *(Pinus strobes)*; Scotch pine *(Pinus sylvestris)*; Eastern hemlock *(Tsuga Canadensis)*; and Tamara herduck *(Booby dendron)*.

It is 38.3 miles from my daughter's house
to the CT border

Crossing Mattabesset River[8] going north
Hwy 9 N 91 S made 100 M 9:20 AM
Cross Mattabesset River again, going
south 101.8 M 9:22 AM 91 S

Poughkeepsie, Peekskill
Turkey vulture over that prison

I have felt a fierce need to
urinate since 8:50 AM—2.25 hrs
of heat under my abdomen

We captured the eagle in an outhouse
Motorcyclists w/ American flag on taillights.
The eagle inserted an American flag in
its behind. It muttered
it was not an Iraqi was
not a comuniss, loved Merica. How
intresting that Merica shd love Merica.
We left the
small flagpole in its anus God Bless Republican
Senator Margaret Chase Smith
of Maine who stood up
against Sen Joseph McCarthy I pass
RED BARON PIZZA Truck 11:22 AM God
bless Joseph Welch, lawyer and Bostonian of

8 The Mattabessett River is polluted and, in its main stem, is about 18 miles long. In that distance
it falls about 460 feet in elevation. Its source is Smith Brothers Pond in Southington. Its mouth is
on the Connecticut River, where it forms the border between Middletown and Cromwell. The
Quinnipiac River and the Mattabesset nearly conjoin at Middletown.

Boston who shouted
"Sir Have you no decency!?"
Thus we interrogated the eagle. Eagle
have you no. It showed proudly the flag in its
fundament Dingmans Ferry Lords Valley
11:30 AM Porters Lake Blooming Grove
11:32 AM Pecks Pond 11:32 Porters
Lake Blooming Grove 1 M 11:33 Let us not
forget Joseph R. McCarthy, it was R wasn't it,
that McCarthy was

an alcoholic, that Bill W, in Alcoholics
Anonymous BIG BOOK writes "Is he not,
even in his best moments, a producer of
confusion rather than harmony? .... [such men
are] politicians and reformers who are sure all
would be Utopia if the rest of the world would
only behave" Rush Limbaugh's
book's called The Way Things Ought to Be.

Wilkes-Barre, I stop and pee in you.
12:33 On rd again got "lost" in Wilkes-Barre.

Post meridian. My cursive
is really
crablike
because
of writing
while
trying
not to drive

off the road. Walter Lippman
held that the presidential press
conference is an organic necessity
of a democracy Our current has had like 2
press conferences in the past 2.5 yrs

427 m Snow Shoe, PA 2:28 PM CST
Rest Area Open 428 M The eagle spoke &
said, "Like Truman living out there quietly…"

Had I barnacles on my wings
in lieu of feathers the world wd call them fins

Leaving Chesapeake Bay
Watershed. Splats small &
numerous. Hazy. "I must say that
the Great Wall is a great wall." Richard
M. Nixon Mercer Westminster College

563.5 m 4:28 PM CST I
pass under a bridge near Mercer PA
on hwy 80, 3 Amish men lean on the bridge rail
their dark horse & darker buggy behind
them, all ½ silhouetted in the low
September sun. They faced the
hwy traffic & as I passed
under one of them waved to me.

Ave speed 65.4 mph through Akron

I seem to be at Meander
Reservoir again.

A slurry of puddles
on the hills of Ohio.
Ohio of Barns. Those pastoral temples.

There is a barn.
Part of: The Hard Barn Collection:
The Connecticut barn, the barn under the
Osprey, a one pasted
in gale blown slush. Troubled barn, one of
brown hill, born with stars in her shingles. An
archipelago of round cold barns across Ohio:
eaves oozing with bees. Barns
with naked men, shining boys. Barns of small
happy women. Barns w cats. Girls running
confused from barns. Barns overstuffed w/
sunflowers in their
boards, but empty of sunflowers on the
outside. One barn
with a man named Andie in it. Hay
gray with rot. A hag on a bicycle smoking in a
cold blue shadow of
a barn. A barn storing melancholic Santas—
another of crippled Witches. And yet another
of wearily burning Hens.

Straight in to cake-yellow pale sun 5:21 PM

though the eagle had no lips and only
a jagged zag of bone where his
beak once had been, it spluttered
proudly Barber Rd next right.

The sun is at one quarter of its way

down my windscreen. This sky resembles
a manila envelope.
3 birds lay—wee popped sausages
in the shoulder. They look like
pillows in the desert. Very hazy
the bug splats collect & remark
upon the butterscotch light
of the sun directly
ahead. The corn stands in lines of
musketeers row upon rank
: It is late corn. It is late.
At 5:47 PM the sun is a
sharper orange, juicier. Then it pales.

What strange fat light is here: as if
a pig is coming out of the sun instead of
sunlight: what white, fat, changing light

Looking above the field of corn I see a mist of
gold bugs catching the sunlight on the little
pea shells of their bodies.

6:09 PM:
sun just down. Up high in the darkening
blue the fuselage
of a jet glints into visibility. It is a
prickly orange fleck.

6:33 PM 700 m approx 50 m N of
Columbus and so we beat the sorrowful eagle

making sure not to burst our knuckles

on the sharpened points of its
shorn pinions

Forty miles North of Columbus a bad traffic
congestion. At 6:45 PM an ambulance
woo-woo's past on rt. shoulder
At 6:47 Police cruisers flicker
silently by on rt shoulder
At 6:50 a Fire truck rumbles &
a harrowing clanging from it ·
passes on rt shoulder

After 20 minutes traffic moves
and I Pass an accident
a terrible spin-out: a Buick CutlassSierra green
fucked sideways at the end of skids
email Maria Sticco re not
mentioning the provenance of
the insult poem in Pitt's

press release

I stop to pee at 7:23 PM

I pass a White Saab:
It is on the opposite side of the hwy
and embroiled in flames spewing from
its engine, engulfing hood.

Rather Clumsy Smalltalk
all my life

At midnight ten miles from Normal

a truck passes me
it reads KRAFT FOR GOOD FOOD

Who would not succumb to melancholia
in such a world?

10.9.02 – 10.11.02

[anabasis]

All my life the intercessors: read this,
fill in this blank, go get this, you need to have this
dinky
slip, find me that bolt, all my life, the
intercessors. I renounce the intercessors.

2:11 PM College & MAIN 10.9.02
Sun on top of bed of high cirrus
DALMATION in back of Dodge
pickup I-74 2:40 PM
Duck standing like a sodomite at
the edge of the highway. He is grateful
b/c each day he wake up in his duckness life,
his shadow is a duck's. 3:09 PM w of
Champaign, The windshield accrues a
Continent-sized bug splat—clear to partly
cloudy bug splat. I have had one foot in life
and one in Knob Creek bourbon for several
years Danville, IL home
of Gene Hackman

The corn is
tall and dry, somewhat gray. Dry Run
Creek Attica Veedersburg IN 98.7 M 4:08 PM
Glad Janis Joplin, in the Golden days, would
kiss the winded girls and sing of praise, and
songs of praise, the sprung in lives.

What the hell is up with country music?
What is the purpose
of this saccharin melodrama?

It is the musical equivalent of crack.

Do "country music performers" ever
affect a suthrun accent?

The southern drawl itself means something.
Its very cadence,
tonal and pronunciative patterns
itself carry a framework of meaning.

When the drawl is conjoined to the watery
emotional pallet, simplistic plot, and
predictable moralism of country music
a profoundly unbearable product called
"country" arises.

And what
Johnny Cash and June Carter geniuses
give to country music
ALL of NASHVILLE & the
"Gran' Ole Oprey" rob. Same goes for
Garth Brooks, that mullet cut hick You want
people in
Indiana to think
the world's on crack?: remove country music
from their air. Boon Co. 130.9 M. Very
little chromatic change in IN I was incredibly
attracted to Blondie when a teenage
boy God Bless Senator Robert Byrd of West

Virginia, 5:18 PM I-70 East 164 M If
we do not clean house often, our socks may
ride away upon the cat

A substantial portion of a cat's energy
goes into the production of fur.

The mentality of the housecat is principally that
of a decentralized bureaucrat, she is a loose soft
clerk who has lost the hot hallways. The groin
is full of leaks.

Vernon Smith father of modern economics
wins Nobel Prize used to teach at Purdue
The chicken will never be let into
the European union because
it is not only impoverished, it is also not a
European country it is a chicken
About 70 F today Dr. Bob Smith
of Akron OH and Carl Jung provided
one of the founding ideas behind AA
Who shall be joyous happy and free who
has an obsession of the mind? Sunset
of a kind 6:20 PM 225.4 M
"That's like I heard a guy said he knew of
a drunk flea that got sober and went
and bought his own dog." Joe McQ,
        5.24.96 Shiller Park, IL
246.4 M IN/OH border 6:40 PM "We can do
nothing about the physical allergy
of Alcoholism. The only hope of our recovery
is dealing w/ the obsession of the mind."

My nerves are a clutch of artillery-disturbed
chickens.

"Thy heart shall utter perverse
things."—King Solomon's warning
about talking while drunk on wine. And then
                              a mouth
bubbled under a wagon of
perversities. Who but the drunk'll
wobble through the brokerage office
broke and drunk on argyle boozes?
I will put & walk
my head in a pot of plaid booze
Then in a pot of polka dot booze
Then I will lay my head in a
pot of pinstripe booze I go through
the shows in the dark
wooden bars, and there are the
muslin boozes, satin drinks, boozes
of terrycloth, the fleece in shots, the
warm dark hats of whiskey.

A chicken is a chain of meat and bone
and a two-watt brain.

Annoying and pompous bombastic
and wrong I wd find the old
Herodotus. What had he but
caked-up wine, a gut made from
fire. His tears a dusted syrup. His eyes
a clamoring pond. He the old man, a head of
History is, ahead of History, not its muse,
whose C___ is

445 M 10 PM
CST 77 E. A belief is a suspicion
Meander Reservoir 505 M
11 PM CST Restless Irritable &
discontent = what self-will
gets you = shame fear guilt
resentment. Stopped sleep at
Travelcenter 693 M—till 4:45 AM CST
Sweetness, I have put away a
kind of mechanical honey booze
for us to drink later—a kind of a

later booze of corduroy w/
cotton ices. A beautiful gray
dirty mist on the road at
dawn 790 M 7:10 AM EST
835.7 M many trees paler new colors
Send dead flies to Dan Keller,
Brandon Chan. The brilliant swamps
of Southern Tier New York.
Only 9 out of 97 laureates had been
women. 9:35 AM EST Welcome
to Connecticut "A nation that
loves itself must be self-critical"—MLK Jr
957 M The hillside trees at River Road
about 10 % paler than last time I drove
here That crazy red yellow alder

To wait with dispassion while I am harboring
                                          angels
They banqueting in me, and roughhousing
                              in wait

These things, the machines that are the angels
to wait among the guffaws, awfuls, the bright
ovens of their faces, the apples
of their throats, the bulbs of light electric in
their elbows—
And while the bridges are heavy
on their eyebrows
and whole civilizations heaving at the bridges
that are festooning their eyeballs

This is patience. The wind is in the ridges.

The strange ridge flexing as a rubberband in
                                    the wind
The dot of the midge in the wind:

All is riding. All rides on the wind.

A young cat enjoys its rubberbands
in patience.
A bird stares at a brick
in patience.
All feeling is gathered in a crowd
In patience
but there are bridges heaped on the angels
like so many guardrails
and I
wait for her
quietly   Hwy 95

          [katabasis]

A crow is a Negro chicken.

8:22 Am Oct 13 02
Depart Prov.
        Delayed 30 min b/c of
OCTOBER FESTIVAL 5K Run in downtown
Providence, me driving everywhere to find an
on-ramp, can't find non-blocked entrance to
highway 95 South 9:58 Exit 16 95 S entering Cranston
A fine mist, rain wipers Janis Joplin is a White
female JAMES BROWN Impersonator
Remains of U.S. sob stories about Firefighters
killed in 9/11: the cultural commodification of
fallen firefighters, the commodification of
"heroism" since 9/11, the sob story, enough
w/ the fallen firefighters 343 Firefighters killed
over & over over mit "Scotland the Brave"
Firefighters tramp the world
en masse to grieve the death of a fallen
comrade I PUKE ON YOUR FALLEN
COMRADE To make Schmaltz of Death what
sin, Autumnal Fire Watch Hill Exit 1 40 yrs
ago: Oct' '62 Cuban Missile Crisis
The disturbing versions of chickens are
roosters 9 N 9:58 AM EST

I want to live sober.
Resentment   Fear Sexual Harm
Harms done to others
Resentment   Fear   Remorse
        Selfishness
Are the grosser handicaps
Most all people use resentments to transfer
blame to other people

Illuminative of every twist of character
Selfish   Dishonest   Frightened
Inconsiderate Try to be the opposite of
whatever character defect you wish to abrogate.
Start trying by ACTING
Gorgeous foliage—dayglo leaves
Escort Area for overweight vehicles Exit 11
Reduced Salt Area Next 10 Miles
Heavy Merge Ahead

"Dr. Bob was a proctologist."—Charlie P.
190 M (in NY) it ceases raining.
Greylags North to South over 84 W
"We MUST lose our fear of creditors."
—Bill W., ALCOHOLICS ANONYMOUS
Insofar as few people love rain (just) as
strongly as they pepper their own dung for
consumption they are
small headed fools
Rain is more glorious than sunshine Dingmans
Ferry Lords Valley 1 ¼ miles
bye bye chlorophyll
Promised Lake State Park
The virginity of the oily duck
A wilderness of sinewy crows
pancreas-colored, sundry villainous axes.
salivating and ugly curs
Look at the ugly chicken—
The small pitchforks of its feet.

severely orange summer lightsoups
are now gone. now come the brown
lightsoups of autumn.

A thicket of icicles
Gray is such a universal color, such a
water and air color, extracted as if
at once from crushed charcoal, wet dishtowel
and from the thousand pound cloud
that we wd not be surprised to learn
that all halos are colored gray
These are the birds the arrogant little
wind-riders. We have Agrarians to blame for
their demise, and the farmer's contumely
toward non-fenced beasts.
SNOW! each flake as thick and wide as a
cracker, the snow fell almost creaking through
the sky, the eagle thundering toward its booze
of lake water, the crow strutting toward
its booze of ditchwater, the heron knee-deep
in its martini.

It was at that time that late youth had
fixed its pus and acne to my skin
in a rich cake—its ache like a bulb of
lumber in my loins—that I fell
in love w/snow.
My rash travels through the hilly
autumnal storms to see a stout housewife for
the good of my pants.

D has beautiful body. And a face akin to
a face, but beyond a face. Extraordinary nose.

In typical comedy, the clown is the flawed
human being, yet he endures. In typical
tragedy the flawed human being is defeated or

killed, by himself or by others. This notebook
and maybe indeed all honest lives are a
Study of Comedy.

Tragedy is thus comfort to the pompous;
Comedy to the humble.

Birds fly from tree to tree, say, yet men
fly from Altar to destruction, and if we
are lucky, back again Imerden Sob? the Chapel
of—? CHPT 2 WUTHERING HEIGHTS
There again another Danville exit 224 80 W PA
I AM SERIOUSLY TIRED OF DANVILLES
bye bye to
All the corn of Pennsylvania
Lewisburg PA 360 M fr. Providence
Mill PA Monegreli then CT
Mistaking the darkened potatoes for
cannonballs PA is large & for
that reason boring. But it is beautiful
except for the people.
Gas 3 PM EST 400 M

I understood then that the swath
of sunlight in the hills
was a copse of silver maples suddenly
come into yellow
The gray & orange of October in
Pennsylvania.
Many deer (upright)—D
says it's rutting season.
Emlenton PA Exit 42 80 W
        539 M 5:09 PM EST

Fr. the bridge just by the sign,one sees
A village mit a steeple church on a
river bend as fr. an airplane in
Switzerland. The eagle, like
J. Robert Oppenheimer, betrayed no
proper emotion
Ohio clear & blue. Sun 2 bright
for driving into it. A gray military jet
rips along on a tin colored strip of thunder

Your eyebrows and mine
like terrible weasels on our foreheads.

Spiders are held together
by very small tendons

the idea of squirting. the fact that in nature
living things are squirted into living things
that the action and the reception of this
occurs at loins

and that bodies come out bodies
bodies coming out of bodies

is so factual and ugly and beautiful

5:49 PM EST PA/OH border
595 M Meander Resv 6:05 PM EST
Alcoholics Anonymous was founded
in Akron OH in 1935
Yet once again I seem to be at
Meander Reservoir 606 M.

DEAR ANIMALS

Many of you do not have breasts. That is
undeniable. I think immediately of amphibia,
the reptilians, birds—none of these possess
breasts nor anything upon which a nipple may
be mounted. I for instance have no fur.

I understand many of you have penises. A great
many animals possess and are fond of their s
exual organs. Some of you however do not
reproduce sexually and are hence devoid of
genitalia. For many of your species, I
understand that in some cases your males may
have penises whereas your females may not
have breasts at all. Futhermore, I completely
realize many of your species do not engage
even in sexual reproduction. Though you and I
have very little in common, and I find your
bodies disturbing, I must say that despite your
biological distance from me, you and I ought
perhaps to have some coffee, should you drink
it—or possess a mouth.

What's more, I know that many of your penises
are odd, your vaginas strange, and your
faces long, flat or otherwise with horns. I
notice none of you wear watches, whereas I
gain distinct pleasure from a new watch at
night when, adrift in blackness, I wake without
temporal reference in the distant AM and press
the "indiglo" button of my wristwatch,
illuminating the tabula rasa of my face and the

hour in a feeble yet crisp "space age" light.
This is a totally human delight. Yet you must
have your own delights, like honking in a pond
or looking at your hooves for hours.

Sincerely,
Gabriel Gudding

And still in the nuts we go chewing
hoisting bright breads and
oranges gone dark w/ night. And
there among the mouses we heard
the unhappy shouts of soldiers.

It is the interior of animals that
baffle us. Their unsnowy insides.
The unsunny inside. The vibrating
and sensing thereness. The donkey Dasein.

            12:05 AM CST 1039 M
    In the US firebombing of Tokyo
in 1945, 83,000 people were
killed. & a million & a ½ people were
left homeless. In Nova Scotia in 1917, 4,000
people were killed in a single blast
when a munitions ship blew up
in the granitic harbor
Walmart: bug tar remover

Right now a great hair on your mother is ugly.

The planet is naked.

Who are these constant men from out of town?

Do you see the rack of jewels toward the top of
my face?

Arrive Normal   1:05 AM exit 135
74 W IL

10.25.02 –10.27.02

[anabasis]

Hair is a kind of laundry.

2:45 PM OCT 25 02 Jct 74 e
Superbly foggy & misty. A cuppedcake
of fog. Ten nights gone now since C___
said to me on the phone, "Dad, I can read."
And D says
she's right in that assessment. D wrote
out "I can dress myself" and C___
read it back Sen. Paul Wellstone has died. In a
plane crash. Flew right into the Bushes:
foggy sad day for
us, charming great man I liked him.
Maria Damon suspects as do many
a assassination Scranton is gorgeous this
morning.

For if, as Aristotle said, that to be fully human
means to engage in the life of the polis,
then what does it mean to have a poet
who embodies the ideologies of
insular emotionalism and
possessive individualism in a public position?
The Greek root for "idiot" meant
a private person.

Can we truly have a public poet if that poet
writes a poetry of the private?

[katabasis]

7:25 am CST Depart Prov.
Going out now into the gnawed light
at Kelly's Gas—
Got 2 old fashions and coffee w/ cream
     fr. DUNKIN
DONUTS
a pack of Parliament Lights
Yesterday in the heroic commando raid
on the hostage/Chechen Moscow theater
the Russian commandos gassed their own
people killing hundreds of
those they wanted to rescue
38.4 m CT border. Dawn light is so gentle.
Now Connecticut has the colors of plaid
   in its fall.

As I pulled out of her drive this
morning, D. did a Celtic
warrior "warp dance."
I fled the fists & flying hair [9]

A pig is essentially a pachydermic dog.
A twig is a bug log. A twig is a log for bugs.

A bee is a kind of duck among insects. Irving
Babbitt: Tradition is "the constant
adjustment of the past to
meet the changing needs of the present"

---

9 Hair is a kind of laundry.

—Eliot was given this idea by Babbitt
Jules LaForgue gave Eliot his "disassociation
of sensibility" by observing that by living one
will slowly differentiate intelligence fr.
sensibility Our lives are marked and
punctuated by defecation
"I wasn't even bothering whether I
understood what I was saying"
—T S Eliot in an interview re writing
the final sections of *THE WASTE LAND*
Poetic value that does not arise from Form
we say stems fr. "inspiration"

Ackroyd notes that where Eliot
wanted to elucidate the poem, Pound
found its very resistance to interpretation
to be "the key to its power."
One final urinic leaf clattered in
the maple. It tattered
on its stem emitting what sounded
like a muffled chuckle
The maple's final leaf was wan-looking
yes, but so yellow that it clung there
resembling a patch of bright urine.
It made a splattering sound as the
wind blew on it. The shadow
of this leaf fell crisply on D's cheek
bounced away, and thudded brick-like
at her feet. "What a heavy shadow,"
D said. She then asked if it left a
mark on her cheek. I said no and
Kissed it. She embraced me and we watched a
small deer

Another burning car—a pickup—
We can afford to be charitable to genuinely
isolated literary figures
Bug splats in PA hwy 80—strange so late
                    in the year
"The whole world is for each peculiar to that
soul."
                    —F. H. Bradley (cf. Dewey)
:personal isolation as a tenet of modernism
C___'s birth cert to HR
Rent to landlords
Eliot powdered his face & wore
lipstick
              Eliot = Alcohol abuser
Who can afford to be chanting
on a mtn. crappy w/ snow
Classical, reactionary, & revolutionary
              as opposed to being
eclectic, Tolerant, & democratic
how TSE described T E Hulme
in a panegyric on Hulme in *THE
CRITERION.*

The october trees shine
              each is a lamp or tropical fish
held up by the cramped octopus of its
              tree limbs

I know today in poetry some real bozos
also buffoons: people out to
make "declamations": cantyonsons, fighters,

"satirists" who set themselves as popinjays.[10]

10 LITERARY NARCISSISM AND THE MANUFACTURE OF SCANDAL

A Literary Narcissist's behavior will not only tolerate but encourage attacks on himself so long as it can translate his own self-fascination into more news of himself.

Just as the Narcissist will use argument, catastrophe, disputation to attract attention, certain people will be willing to dispute the Narcissist in order to participate in the economy of attention. Others will dispute the Narcissist because they are so profoundly appalled by his/her behavior. Either way, the economy of attention is fueled.

The Narcissist needs Catastrophe. The more internal crises of shame the Narcissist endures and fails to heed, the more s/he will need to create external Catastrophes. A chief and signal way a Narcissist might attract attention is to start fights: Narcissists will gravitate toward satire and caricature as a means of creating argument. The Narcissist will attempt to construe strife with health: These arguments need to happen, etc.

The Narcissist IS fascinating—but not for the reasons the Narcissist thinks. S/he is fascinating because the energy s/he will expend in micromanaging the self image is so profoundly exceptional. People just sort of stand there slack-jawed wondering if this person has a life. The Narcissist however will mistranslate the fascination of others as admiration.

Poetry communities will tolerate narcissism so long as it is translated into a Social Energy which others can use to strengthen and promote their projects.

Narcissism and alcoholism. Alcoholism is a systematic way to push down socially regulating emotions like shame, guilt, and embarrassment at one's own self-aggrandizing behavior. The suppression of these emotions is never successful, even in the most energetic of self-aggrandizers, and they will periodically burst upward into brief displays of remorse and convictions to change. These brief spouts of regulatory behavior are sometimes shared publicly and sometimes privately among confidants. These displays however can often easily be re-used by the Narcissist as a way of showing his/her authenticity and emotional fealty to the community.

The Narcissist is aware of the economy of disgust surrounding his/her behavior. S/he becomes more and more sensitive to this and consequently begins to demand private declarations of loyalty from those people whom s/he knows consider themselves friends—even if they have said nothing publicly against the Narcissist.

The Narcissist, aware of this disgust, will create a personal mythos in which s/he will be justified and exonerated by the rewards of literary history. The stronger the disgust of others, the greater the energy used to maintain the mythos of exoneration by history.

Narcissists are only interested in community so long as it pays dividends to their energy: they will support it if it feeds them.

Eliot, like them, was a boor of the abyss.

He was a puppet of his own vanity and a
boor of the abyss.
In fact, vain nihilists, weepy
evangelists, and pop singers are all
boors of the abyss.
"pricks" "fucking" "penis" "bunghole" &
"jewboy" → words found in the later
stanzas of "King Bolo and His Great Black
Queen," which later stanzas were written
after his conversion to Anglicanism in his
later 30s/early 40s—he continued w/ these
stanzas about King Bolo.
· Eliot thought of himself, esp. after
his conversion, as a moralist—when
in fact he was merely a boor of the

The narcissist may outright demand in private that you pay him publicly with praise. Then he or she will publicly repay you with a communal mention.

In their attempt to cause others to adopt their self-fascination, Narcissists will become increasingly paranoiac, constantly searching the environment and community for news of themselves, for fealty or disloyalty.

The Literary Narcissist begins purposefully to conflate *criticism of his social behavior* into an indication of his/her literary worth. That is to say, the Narcissist will try to show that the reason others despise or are disgusted by him is in fact because he or she is a "Rebel," a true Literary Revolutionist—and that the statements of disgust others publicly make at his behavior is merely an indication of (a) their necessary denial of the work because they are threatened by it, or (b) their jealousy of the work.

There comes a point—and the point may come early—where the community thinks to itself teapot and the Narcissist still hears tempest. The truly insular narcissist (aka "the boor") will be met more and more with shunning, ignoring and silence. This will wrest the narcissist from his insularity—such that he will begin another project designed to create Genuine Interest instead of mere scandalous attention. This project, like a new comet's head, will be followed by a long tail of manufactured scandal so as to call attention to its presence in the literary sky.

abyss.
"In any case, let us lament the psychosis
of those who abandon the muses for Moses."
                -E. Pound
Nearly All dark OH/PA border

586 m 5 pm CST OH—Near Youngstown. I
watch a car 100 yards in front drive
into the median & go a ways straight at a
barrier, then, at the last min turn away.
                                horrifying
"Does yr dog do that to frighten me?"
—Vivian Eliot to VA Woolf
Innovation is a label of Capital
What happened to yr breasts—?
Did they fly off into the summer, leaving
two nests of loose skin upon yr chest?

Eliot loved to make pronouncements
yet he cd at times be very diffident
revealing himself sometimes as a
relativist & skeptic in literary matters.
He loved making judgments [illegible]
        yet
Grapes and peaches have about them
an indecent hush. I would have them
speak of their lives as modest bulbs
Fruits such as these are loin-like juice bulbs

and what chronicles and rumors
could they report of colors and juice
and the waters they

are pregnant with. But instead
there is a reticence about fruits
maybe even an arrogance. D's loins
have a shamanic power over me. I
always expect to hear the rustle of

pages when pants come down. It's
the same when I witness a snowstorm: I
expect to hear book sounds, or at least
cold chirps of radio static. Sometimes
I expect to see a fat person, garbled
in a quote of red, stepping loudly
from behind a lip of a white gust
as if the storm were sticking its tongue out
to me: the great fat Santa of the wind, a
metaphysical envoy. Loins are the wind
sticking its tongue out at meat. "I have no
objection to being called
a bigot myself."—T S Eliot

"Indeed his fear of large animals
seems to have been sprung fr. personal
experience."—Peter Ackroy on TSE
C___ counted to a 100 yesterday. It is very dark
now west of Dayton.

How is the young snail riveted together?
Who welds the owls of the north—
                    feather to feather?
What hand had stitched the hornet up
What mouth will blow the darkness down

WRITE LEO DAUGHERTY
Martini, que te quiero martini
Some quarrels come now through lungs
Hair is a kind of laundry.
Do not be the overwhelming vandal
who comes in the yard and pulls
down laundry.

"The killer knew that Jack had some
poop, which wd mean exposure or
worse...."—Mickey Spillane, I, THE JURY
"What I'm after now are the
seemingly unimportant details."
—Mickey Spillane I THE JURY
"Her breasts were laughing things that
were firmly in place."
        —Mickey Spillane I THE JURY

Arrive Normal 2:02 AM CST 1076 M

11.8.02 – 11.10.02

[anabasis]

2:33 PM 11.8.02 FRIDAY
make hwy 74 east super sunny
sun = tang juice very windy
Eric Satie. Lake Erie
far away 84 M IL/IN border.
Omaha Omahara. The cock's lake in
the straw a green Terra Haute Newport
many planes made out of bird bills.
Trees musty brown now. Sunset 4:45 PM
at 145 miles from Normal

"A foreman, wishing him well, announced
to all w/in hearshot
'Harry Truman is an alright fella. He's alright
from the asshole out in every direction.'
                                    It was Harry's
first public commendation."
—David McCollough, *TRUMAN* (a biography)
Telescope for C___.
2:50 Am EST, Lamar PA – sleep
wake at 5:45 AM depart
"Selfish men have always tried to skim
the cream from our natural resources to satisfy
their own greed—
and the instrument in this effort
has always been the Republican Party."
        —Harry S. Truman
"I think the greatest asset the Kremlin has

is Senator McCarthy."—Harry S. Truman
"Congressional opposition never struck him as
subversive. Nor did he regard
his critics as traitors."
MARY MAGRURY IN THE WASH POST

NIGHT TIME - Dan Zanes' music CD
-Get for C___ (Children's CD)

Intricate nest of dogs and heavy cats
on hillside
garnished in a fluttering of Ducks.

The water goes glowing up the Quinnipiac.

In the sun-gilded road winds
the sun-gilded road winds.

Butterflies are the bowties of fairies.

An ambulance siren sounds like seagulls
caught in a pipe organ.

The iron coat will be woven of knuckles and
knobs of iron—and imbedded in it are short
stiff bolts and twigs of bronze.

[katabasis]

11.10.02
Contact Cornell. The taking of PILLS
has been as essential to Atlantic cultures
as the eating of COD

I live in Normal IL founding home
of Republican Party, May 6 1856
at McLean Co Courthouse a mile
distant my one room apartment

1 million alone died
in the Philippines of 1905 or so
And my drives to Providence RI the founding
home of spiritual freedom, 1636 in US,
now a tangle of mafia intrigue and normal
drug neighborhoods remind that good ideas
too die, Poor Noah, eg, ran off, his robe
whacking in the wind, the animals behind him
needing much Alpo. If the world were
suddenly glued together
it would be the noble
albatross that would be glued down last.
May my heart, sewing the wind
behind the ship of my life, be the ranging
and intrepid albatross.

577 M PA/OH border

11.29.02 –12.01.02

[anabasis]

Friday Nov 29, 02 6:55 PM dpt
   Normal
D and I married at 12:15pm, in 134 Francis St.,
Providence RI, Maria D and Henry G
witnesses, after 6 yrs of love flew back Thurs,
yesterday, and now drive again back
then
back and forth then
on the macadam
I am them
Bad pain in my chest. Lyndon Baynes Johnson
had many heartattacks
He had a large heart, big chest, tall guy
Texas heart, sometimes his cardiac muscle
was a twelve pound bag, a werewolf bag

And then there was a horse
There in front by the septic tank
Broad
The scuff of sun in its hair
The noise of river stones in his nose
And in the meat bucket of his heart
A kind of damaged dam

On its groin cockroaches rode[11]

---

11 A THEORY ABOUT COCKROACHES

Bugs are bite-sized. And as such are the living analogs of food.

Black little horses each

Was it a buccaneer's horse?
What horse is this he seems so gay so full
of wind,
a chief of the grass

It is the horse that carried me to

A marriage at last.

In fact
Lyndon Johnson used his history of heartattack
for
                    political gain
I'm learning now as I drive fr. west to
                    east again
It was the interior of his chest that he used.

They naturally proffer themselves as things that could easily fit in our mouths, and that is one of the key reasons certain insects disgust us, most especially the cockroach. The cockroach is bite-sized.

We only become thoroughly disgusted when the insect approaches the size of dung, such as the cockroach. The cockroach is at once dung-sized and bite-sized, making it catastrophically disgusting. Granted the cockroach represents a small dung, but a dung nevertheless.

I have seen dungs of my own that are about the size of a cockroach—while I rarely see dungs of my own that are the size of wasps. It would be a rare dung of mine that is the width of a wasp.

Our feelings for insects are thus delimited by two borders of disgust: that of something we could put inside our mouths and that of something that could come out the other end. We are generally confused on this point. It is only arthropods far too large to be feces—such as crabs, lobsters, and prawns—that we consider edible. What's more, my theory maintains that the prawn, which is dung-sized, is not met with the same disgust as a landbased prawn might be, because the prawn, by dint of its watery habitat, resembles a flushed dung, and is thus scatologically mitigated. A flushed dung is a dung in its appropriate environment, unlike a dung that is crawling across our plate, as an insect might.

Another Texan, Dolly Pardon, used
the exterior of her chest for advancement

My body does not ask me to pay for its use.
  (SNOW 224 m fr Normal—on ground, not
        in AIR) as for the bosom all
the stunning things that are on it
blouses, louses, & small red houses
        of nipples
Co Rd 533 Brookville 268.7 M (ohio)
"What rage for fame attends both
                great & small.
Better be damned that not be named at all."
        —John Wolcott (Peter Pindar)

Slept fr. 1:30-7am CST
85 M S of Cleveland on HWY 71
        400 m fr Normal wake to a
SNOWY DAY—overcast—very cold
The oil in Galicia, on its coast
NO SNOW east of AKRON
        Snow in Wester PA
                636 M—highest pt on 80 east
of MS = 2" snow cover, somewhat misty,
dirty road spray
275 334 72   90.1 FM West PA east NY
                great music
        "hip" music fr. the 50s & 60s
                I've never heard before

[katabasis]

Dec 1, 02 Sunday 25.4 M fr. Prov
       8:50 AM EST bright sun.
88.5 FM—Scranton PA—progressive station
I saw the duck standing, a yellow sock
in the road—a sock so fat
it seemed to hold
a gout foot
The world is really greasy I think
of the greased places on your body. Inside your ear,
the shining nickel-sized mead of slick there.
The rose and umber grease-fields of your v
(and
the mole-geese in that dale). Too,
 the little sheet, as of odd margarine,
which gathers in your instep,
a distillate of hooves.
As well, the
window-scented gel puddling your eyelid
before
you wake. What are the purposes
of these greases?

7:05 pm CST 686.5 m fr. Prov
      traffic jam (2nd today)
7:22 CST 692 m - out of jam
cold wind, The cries
     of turkeys
it is foggy
 the evening light hitting me
     orangely from the left
If I were to die now, who wd care

and who Should? We are empty.
7:19 AM South of Oglesby, IL
Friday Dec 6 02 HWY 39 returning from
Freeport, IL Where I'd read & finally met in
person, after yrs of correspondence, Kent
Johnson—A seemingly decent man, warm, kind
          We talked in *Martinis,* the bar in the
hotel lobby of Freeport hotel, he and his
historian friend, a scholar of the JFK
assassination, they got really drunk
I heard a shot from the pergamon
No it came from the grassy knoll
No it came from the pergamon
No it came from the grassy knoll

Who gives a shit you guys

I remember at my little sister's wedding in
Fargo North Dakota the day of my last
sister's wedding in '99 my biological father rage
eyed and puff chested wobbling at me
puffchest down motel hallway
because he was annoyed
at me over a shirt and I finally saw 30 yrs later
the mindless anger my mom saw when he wd
beat her and I almost struck the mouth
from his face and tipped his anemone
head as a globe backward breaking his throat
and slamming him to the yellow polyurethane
carpet at last for his beating of my mother then
30 years ago, cursing of my sisters via drunk
phone and
attacking me just then with his weird brain

12.7.02 –1.12.03

[anabasis]

12.7.02 Sat. 6:55 AM CST depart
      Normal IL

If there is reason among the birds, if there are
in them dinners and assembly
and cool talk, it is all the better for the trees.
Their family song may be
a carpet of twigs where talk of finches twists
to old tones
that link and climb as a vine of chains, a vine
of thrones. Champaign Urbana, IL 7:30 AM

It is cold.
I have told a peacock it do not have a rectum,
it have a cloaca. 8:58 AM 145 M pass
under bridge of "Jeff Gordon Boulevard"
Illinois McCarty Streets Mercer St.
Lilly Corp bldg 170.4 M 9:20 AM
Downtown Indianapolis Foggy Indy
The Langpo movement was, in many ways, a
filibuster. The reading of the phone book
for 20 years.
      "Hurting? 317-895-PRAY"
on white bus CALVARY TEMPLE Baptist
church downtown Indy. Maxwell Greenfield
Indiana Exit 104 70 east, 193.6 M 9:40 AM
"Nameless Creek" 199 M Overcast since
Indy. Some snow in fields. "Anthony Creek"

201 M

"Six Mile Creek" 202.7 M "Big Blue River"

209 M

9:55 AM

Now much more snow in fields 214.3 M
"Flatrock River" 216.2 M 10:01 AM
1936, 1938, 1944, 1950, 1957—years that
civil rights bills were defeated. "Wilbur Wright
Rd" exit 131 70 east New Lisbon,

IN

"White Water River" 225.9 M exit 137
Hagerstown IN Cambridge City IN 226.4 M
"Greens Fork River" 230.8 M
OHIO STATE LINE 245 M
"Stillwater State Scenic River" 275.1 M
B & O Railroad Bridge 280 M
"Great Miami River" 280.3 M Exit 36
Gray women in an Oldsmobile
"Mad River" 288 M near Air Force Museum
and Wright Bros. Sites
304.6 M huge antiques mall
Desolate "National Golf Links" 309 M
(snow and windy) HOLE FLAGS strain
raggedly. "Little Darby Creek State & National
Scenic River"

327 M

"Little Darby Creek State & National Scenic
River" again

330.7 M

Seventeen geese above the highway
fly directly against the traffic

between the glass corporate bldgs
                  here at
                  clouded Dublin,
OH.

Sign says "MID OHIO NEXT RIGHT"
The partly cloudy cab motors   445 M 76
                                        east
"The death of art is self-consciousness."
              —Marcia Tucker, Art Critic
, it is a Good year
Arlington is snowy, Fulton is beautiful
, the signs say Speed Limit 65, the
                        USA's flag
stretches itself in a continual wind of
                              flatulence
The American flag is trying to follow the
                  condom to the hole.
"Meander Reservoir" 505 M The great fruits in
her hips, are ripe.
In my bed, all I do is praise the Lord. I don't
know about <u>your</u> bed.

The American flag is straining to get in my bed.
Even when my bed is up wind, the American
flag points toward it.
522 M PA border.
2:45 PM CST Sun at "4 O'Clock"—right rear
window—AND LOW.
                  the tenor talk of bees
550 M—halfway point—near Irwin Township
          About 28 Mile fr. border 3 PM CST
"Alleghany River" 565.8 M Emlenton St.

Petersburg

             Foxburg PA

    exit 45

"Clarion River" 582 M

"North Fork Creek" 600 M

River at 641 M before exit 123

Damn dark now 5:25 PM EDT.

I took the pig's shadow and made a

suit of it. The suit smelled of ham

and slop. A suit of ham shadow.

9:05 PM—arrive HWY 84 8 M W of

Port Jervis—after detour

"When I saw a thunderstorm, I got happy,

as though somebody was coming to visit me."

      —Black Elk

869 M NY border

"Wallkill River" 895 M

"How cd men get fat by being bad and

starve by being good?"—Black Elk.

The cold town of the greasy grass.

"Fishkill Creek" 914 M near HWY 9

"Quinnipiac River" 986 M exit 13

             Poughkeepsie

"It is easy on the plains to imagine things

unseen, worlds not known."

      —Larry McMurtry

        CRAZY HORSE

    [katabasis]

Jan 11, 2003 6:05 AM C____

and I depart 6:40 AM. The fireworks

over the city of Providence New Years night
sounded like Teiko drumming. Spent winter
vac on BeHappy St. After terrible fight
with Someone, am taking C___ back to IL while
D & Melpomene go to Ireland to visit family Now 13 M
SOUTH of Providence, Hwy 95 S She's asleep
in the 4-poster bed I've made
for her in the backseat. D
and Melpomene are probably on their way
to Dundalk right now. It's only
11:08 AM in Ireland. Last week C___ said
"Daddy, when I go to heaven I want you
to be the age you are now, that's 36. And,
Mommy, I want you to be the age you are
now and I'll be 5 and a half."

"Exit 7 Coventry West Warwick 1 Mile"
It is depressing the thunder that does
not follow one's book's stroke.
One's book publication makes one ill.
My first book was published a month ago
Dark but deep purple to the east at
6:15 AM Arcadia Beach [illegible]
Wickaboxet Mngmt Area Exeter 1 M
W. Alton Jones Campus 1 M Exit 5B
Deli Store Truck Stop Gas Truck
repair Exeter 102 South Exit 5A

There is no Exit 4. $500 fine for
littering. This is superb coffee I made.
Int'l Scholar-Athlete Hall of Fame Exit 3A
Deep purple to the south now 6:25 AM
One massive nail hole of a star is parked

in the driver side window. Am listening to
Xmas gift from M: Men Are From Mars,
Women from Venus. It's kind of a dumb
good book "Men and women are <u>supposed</u>
to be different" so that we can get along better,
our relationship Connecticut Welcomes You 39
M 6:30 AM Pawcatuck Welcome Center

For xmas D gave me book about
gendered expectations in relationships. Men
want acceptance, acc book. To offer unsolicited
Advice, acc book, to a man is the bedrock of
insult. News to me.
Frankly, what one wants is
not to be yelled at by one's partner. Or if one
has been yelled at andor hit,
one wants at the v least to be apologized to.
Downtown Mystic Exit 90
When in fact many believe insult's bedrock is
the proffer of an unsolicited negative opinion
6:50 AM 62 M fr. Prov. Road lights
just switch off: I have just witnessed
efficiency in Connecticut. Exit 7
GOV JOHN DAVIS LODGE TURNPIKE
ONE MILE I dislikes limousines. "Shrew and
Fishwife are opprobrious terms."

Empathy understanding validation
support is what one shd give, acc book.
Acceptance Old Lyme 1 M Florence Griswold
Museum I think
we forgot TEDDY! [C___'s teddybear] Oh no!
Goodspeed Opera House 81 M fr.

Prov. at East Haddam thin men
on the roadway. Moodus of yr poop
Higganum 1 M everything seems to
be 1 M away CARING
understanding 91 S 100 M fr.
Providence I turn into the sunrise
briefly. Then it hangs on my left
shoulder like a parrot. Cromwell
Berlin. Fly, birdy. Respect.
"Mattabasset River" Sgt Ross Dingwell
Memorial HWY. Validation. Devotion.
Reassurance. 84 W 117 M (5) Wants
(1)   Anger (2) Sadness (3) Fear (4) Regrets
(6) Love "I'm going to make an angry
snowflake." C___ Dec 21 2003

Welcome to New York 156 M
the fire of Alzheimer's Poop. Dutchess
County. 8:30 AM C___ wakes up
5 miles fr. Lime Kiln Rd. We
did not—thankgoodness—forget Teddy.
Nimbus overcast. Salt on the road
like a ground–in dirty white powder.
Old snowmobile trails in the wide
hills. "Wallkill River" 201 M
227 M PA border. BLOOMING GROVE.
Promised Land. Galilee. Heaven.
Bethel. Packs Pond. The Sunny Puppy
of Hawley. The Sunny Puppy of Hawley
Sang. It sang a bark bark.
Good dog. good dog singer! The itchy
angel was annoyed. "GENZYME" on
someone's license plate. Moosic 1 mile.

287 M. shitty smatters of salt

Dogs are furious places. Dogs
are furious mobile places. When a dog
is asleep it is not mobile—unless
it is sleeping in a moving vehicle.

My Polo sunglasses are dirty, scratched.
"Daddy, my bedroom is the angel bedroom
because I have an angel kiss." C___. Now
she is talking about macular entoptic
phenomena (floating white dot-like images
that spot one's field of vision in a dark place)
says when she first saw them thought they were
a "creature in the room"—10:28 AM Wilkes-
Barre campus 295 M, 10:45 AM—growing very
tired. HWY 80 W 315 M. Buckle
up its our law. Snow. Irony =
"Smart" for idiots. We run toward
poop w/ our sack of wombs. "Susquehanna
River" Lime Ridge Berwick 335 M fr
Providence 352 M STOP at McDonalds
(for C___) 11:22 AM. Depart McD's
12:34 PM—C___ having spent 45 M
C___ loved the playground in the
McD—Danville, PA.
"Dad, do angels have brains?"

"Do fairies have bones, Dad?"

C___ keeps asking phenomenological questions:
"How did the universe begin?"

"How do we see through the air?"

"Dad, how do we breathe through the air?"

D said she's going to translate The Inferno for
C___ after Christmas into a child's language.

Massive cliffs 397 M fr.
Providence. "It is my intention to aid,
not to offend." Such appendages are
but oddments. THE GRIPPING:

She is gripping things all over the house
the window now. Now the drapes
got the sash. Now it is the chair
she grips of the hall, wool towel
, grip, does not work well. She is grips her
bottom, now
toilet, putting burning groceries
out house, anything burning
out house, putting Pete
—lascivious carpenter—out house,
will put bad Greek salad out, out
with oleaginous mouth of teen who went
banging and sucking down hall,
it goes, vile mouth goes out house she puts all
out door.
She grips two books, then coffee
grips two chocolates,
a pen, envelope, now a bill. She grips
my nose, my glasses, my
my.

The cosmos is heavy, empty, chaotic. 7
laburnum trees on fire
and a man is punching a ladder under
them→ seen at Rush Township HWY 80 West
436 miles fr. Providence—I saw from the hwy
a man kicking and punching an aluminum
ladder. Then I saw 3 Does the size of German
shepherds but w/ much
longer legs & the color of dried

dutch grass. "1 WAY JESUS" on
white paint on a rock. STICK yr "1 WAY"
up yr ****, Jesus. Christianity is a cult of
Idolatry. Total Jesus, you are at war with
                              Subsistence
You are massah of the plantation of Anger
You are Marlon Brando of the Spirit
You make Holy and sanction the Use of
                              Arbitrary Power
You have long wooden he-model hair
You made July a seawater for nations
You made a covenant with asteroids
          that you would string them together
          as a rocket of beads
You encourage the retroactive headbutting of
          women by religious overweight
          religious southern religious men
You make a sea-hell to come unto beaches You
fish greener eels from dark seabeds
          with your beard hairs
and throw them toward the ancient trees like
          the belts of fat men
Because you are an Idol of Vengeance and not

an Exemplar of Love
Because your followers are makeup wearing
        fatties and fat people of El Gordos

You were once a good kind Rabbi
440 M fr. Providence. High
bridge near Clearfield, PA exit 120
what is that river under it? At 2:24pm I write
that I have seen *NO* roadkill: 2:24 At 2:25pm I
see a Dead hawk or brown buzzard type bird
ripped, pointy and discombobulated upon the
shoulder like a goose sized twisted glue-
spattered shuttlecock
sloping retaining wall under bridge 47 M fr.
Prov. is buckling fr. ice upheaval. Or
was that "hawk" but a collection
of ironic leaves? Welcome
to Ohio 4:05 PM EST 576 M
Brown and gray salt bushes everywhere
5:15 West of Akron 7 miles east of
HWY 71 S Junction and *still bright.*
Entering Wayne County. Roads very bad in
Ohio between Akron and Columbus. C___ *loves*
her arrangement in the backseat.

Jan 12 2003 8:50am Slept in Days INN IN
Ashland OH on HWY 71 About
40 M S of Akron 71 interchange
Woke, gassed in Travelmart & got
DONUTS. Thinking about donuts, I got
on the freeway going North instead
of South. After 6 & a ½ effing miles
of NO exit & finding a u–turn I–turn

Pale blue sky. Sun, being the sun, is
in my driver's window Exit 186:
Ashland Wooster. Great night sleep
Odd old "hexy" big-board mansiony
paint-peely barns of Ofay Ohio
50 muskrats run across the salted hwy
What is this an underground railroad of
muskrats? Mt. Gilead St. Park Exit 151
9 degrees F. Sun colors the snow beige Thick
steady flags of white exhaust in the cold air on
the cruiser & the car on opposite shoulder

Why billboards? These great scar cards of the
landscape. What will their history be? Will there
not be a national felony law against them?
Polaris Parkway. 1876-1960: yrs of
Jack London 270 West Dayton 1 Mile
743 m fr. Prov. "Glen Muir Luxury
Apartments" 750 m—white-sided cookie
cutter "condos" (w/ a fake lake in the middle)
that look brittle and fake in the sunlight
at 10:02 AM EST. Verizon Wireless
blue windowed fortress 270 West & South
exit 17 A   753 M fr. Prov 760 M—
70 W. The tons of pressboard & glue
in the houses of the Midwest since the
1970s have leaked formaldehyde into us for 35
years. In her high voice C___ says "Remember
the 40 thieves. The father was the king of the
40 thieves"—C___ in the back drawing w/ markers.
Under some HWY bridges in Ohio are monstrous
potholes, yellow corn stubble to the right. Grey
corn stubble to the left. 780 M 794

shallow graveyard to the right.
10:30 AM Sun on HWY 70 W east of
Dayton over left shoulder, at
rearest portion of driver's side window

"Mad River" 810 M fr. Prov, Dayton
Next 4 exits. "McMahon's Manufactured
Homes Next Exit." Paul Sherry Vans
& RVs. "Great Miami River" 818 M
"Stillwater St. Scenic River" Meijer
24 Hours. Waffle House Comfort Inn
Holiday Inn Hampton Inn Now Available
Singer Properties Parkville Apts.
Hoke Rd Trotwood Hwy Patrol
Greenville Clayton 2 & a ½ Stop Ahead Stop
Ahead Cavalier Chevrolet Clayton Corp Limit
Brookville Phillipsburg Greenville Clayton
Greenville Clayton North 49 Exit 24
Dead deer broken neck BMX Races
KOA KAMPGROUND "Kamp in This
Woods" Co. Rd 533 Brookville exit 21 FOOD
exit 21 Co. Rd 533 Brookville ½ mile
BP Day's Inn Diesel [illegible]
Co Rd Brookville

U. S. Express Enterprises Caution Meritor
Air-Ride Equipped 833 M Marathon
Petro Pizza Hut Baskin Robbins
Preble Co. emergency Need Help?
Car van-pool Call Rideshare
Lodging Super Inn West Alexandria
End Warranty Pavement Citgo
Sunoco Diesel No Semi's Pilot Dairy

Queen Bob Evans Econo Lodge
County Pride Brazer Eaton Greenville
TA Diesel Marathon BP Road
Condition Hueston Woods State
Park. Eaton Subway Dairy Queen 17
Mile 847 M fr. Prov. Still HWY 70 West a
11:35 AM EST Black beef cows AND
A DONKEY! Cracker Barrel
Lees Inn Richmond Thank You For
Visiting Ohio

Indiana Border 853 M fr. Prov.
Muncie Greenville Indianapolis Tom Raper
Nobody Beats Our Deal Wendys The
Biggest & Best RV Show Grandpa's Farm
Campground Union City Winchester Exit
Smyrna Rd. Wayne Co. Warm Glow
Candle Factory Outlet Stuckeys Super 8
Burger King Chester Blvd. Richmond
Muni. Airport WATCH FOR ICE on
BRIDGES Hardees Eastcase Electric
Love's Travel Stop Walnut Ridge Webb's
Antique Mall D&J Homes Since 1955
Earlham College Tom Raper RV World's
Largest! Tom Raper RV Exit 149A!
Williamsburg Pike Exit 149A Hardee's
Charbroiled Hamburgers Living Faith Church
of God Trucks Over 13 Tons Declared
Gm. Weight. Stucken's Dairy Queen Brazier
BP Dairy Queen Souveniers fr. All 50 States

For Traffic Info Tune Radio to AM 530.
Regular $1.49/gallon "Noland's Fork Creek"

Train Rides White Water Valley Indiana's
Most Scenic Valley Antoine "Tony"
Hulman Memorial Highway Alert When
Flashing Walnut Ridge Family Trailer
Sales & Service Washington Rd "Greens
Fork River" 868 M "Speedco a Faster
Better Truck Oil Change Is On The Way"
Days Inn Exit 123 Free Continental Breakfast
Large Parking. Marathon Taco Bell KFC
Firestone exit 131 Connersville Hagerstown
McDonalds One Stop Truck Plaza
Gasamerica "Free Chicken: 100 Gallon
MINIUM" [sic] Cambridge City Connorsville
Hagerstown New Lisbon Indianapolis
"Whitewater River" Honda CR-V Marathon
Buses Welcome Oil Change Henry Co. Wilbur
Wright Rd. Marathon Diesel

A white wooden cross on roadside bearing in
black stencil the letters "DAD RIP" Meridian
Insurance Auto Home Business Farm
Satellite Radio Be Self Employed! Work from
Home www.knowledge2earn.com Rent 317-
484... WABASH Ford Sterling Trucks
"Flatrock River" Indiana Basketball Hall of
Museum Flying J. Smokes For
Less Cartons Really Cheap! New Castle
Spiceland Spiceland New Castle Harley Truck
Parts "We're Proud of Indiana" Day's Inn
Denny's Teamsters Local Union #135
"See Where It All Started: Hall of Fame
Museum" I LOVE THIS DELL! At Old Spicer
Rd: 887 M fr. Providence. Dollar Inn

Lees Inn U.S. Express Enterprises "Big Blue River"
Greensboro Pike "Anthony Creek" Dried figs
are scrotal, I think that's why
artists've traditionally used a fig leaf—
metonymy covers fr. mommy, metonymy
covers anatomy of tommy from mommy

"Nameless Creek" Wendy's Motorists Service
Information Next Exit Historical Hancock
County. Antiques Malls Restaurants
Chrysler 300 Ponderosa Steakhouse
Arby's Left 1 Minute Steamyburgers White
Castle. C___ wants to write Jane
Goodall a letter on her website
Marion County. German Church Rd.
17 miles from Indianapolis Ruben T.
Glick Memorial HWY First Church
of the Nazarene. 74 West 935 M
fr. Prov. 12:05 PM CST This is
the first time I've driven this stretch
this direction in daylight. Billboards
are the palmtrees of Indiana. 74 W 942 M fr.
Providence. Eagle Creek Reservoir and Dam
945 M fr. Providence. The little river island
going always upstream, and some days,
flying shiningly into sunset "Sugar Cr." 981 M

"Dry Run Cr."
"Graham Cr." 1003 M fr. Providence 1:07 PM
CST Covington Big Boy Restaurant and Market
"Wabash River" Vermilion Co. IN 1008 M.
Statue of Liberty on a sign for fireworks. 2
hawks, one in a tree one on a

fence post 100 yards after, they'll
be gone next we (C___ and I) pass
this way'gin. 1015 M Illinois
border. "Vermilion River" 1019 M
"South Fork Vermilion River" 1024 M
"Middle Fork Vermilion River" 1026 M
The RightWing BurmaShave signs of
Champaign County:
"Roses are Red
My Gun is Blue
I am Safe
How About You—gunssavelife.com"
4 signs at 1035 M fr. Prov., east of
Champaign. Homer Exit 197
Champaign County. St. Joseph one mile

"Salt Fork" 1043
Bears Football Traffic Exit 183
FOURWINDS RV 200 RVS IN STOCK!
Mothereffers.
Origin of KASKASIA River 1059 M
Piatt County 1066 M
"Criminals Menacing?
Lady Alone?
The Situation Requires
Something More Than a Phone—
gunssavelife.com"
"Spread the News
Like Paul Revere
Guns Save Life
All the Year—gunssavelife.com"
What are sand funnels. I will gas
at Farmer City. DeWitt Co.

McLean County 1082 M
Morain View St. Park Clinton Lake
Leroy 2:45 PM arrive Normal
IL 1102 M The mileage reads about 5 miles
over the normal trip length,
wonder if that's due to cold weather
and shrinkage of metal near odometer
sensor.

1.24.03 –1.28.03

[anabasis]

1.24.03 Friday. FROST, dark, not dawn, lay
Goofy, in backseat, cozetted in blankets, frigid air
in car, breath steaming, engine heats 6:20am
<u>very</u> cold. Hard snots of rime mar the
windows. The dark lawn a clutter of crystal
straws 6:40 AM 74 east 5.5 M fr. Normal.
Goofy asleep Driving east into brightening sky,
This book is cold, a 400 Series Strathmore
Sketchpad (11" x 14") because it's been on the
seat all night. I packed the car last night so that
when C___ and I woke we'd just get up and go.
Now we are in Champaign Co. home of IBM,
C___ is asleep and the beginning of dawn:
Light-bearing smoothness into the pillows in
the sky, there are dales and incomparable
hollows in the clouds. I see the Marmalade in
the dawn clouds. The clouds are giant clams.
There is a sun. There is a dawn. The thin tinny
silence of the frosting at sunup. I oppose the
myth of rugged individualism, as it does not exist
is an illusion, the American ideology of
possessive individualism.

When our bodymind is compassionate, it is
boundless—Shunryu Suzuki-roshi wd say. Or
was that Donald Rumsfeld? "The best way
to control people, is to encourage them to
be mischievous…First let them do what they

want, and watch them. This is the best policy.
Ignore them is not good. That is the worst
policy. The 2nd worst is try to control them.
The best one is to watch them. Just watch them,
w/out trying to control them." Shunryu
Suzuki-roshi. There is no problem. "Do not be
too interested in Zen." I think Zen is stupid. It
has been conflated with the teachings of the
Buddha, and they are not the same. The ash
may stick to the ankles of the fire, but it's not
the fire.[12] 9 AM Indianapolis 465-S, 70 east
9:15 AM email Carol Eagan re my strong back
:   Regarding reverence: there is some
self-congratulatory quality to those poets who
speak of reverence and praise.
Reverence is unseemly. It is antithetical to
gratitude. We are but dust and ash blowing on
a road
:   Is there not something democratic
about the earth itself? Are not fertilizer and
manure, for all their dense corruption, at once
nourishing and fertile? Kiss me I'm a poet, eff
you you're a statesman, that's about where
we're
stuck Fuck you Donald
Rumsfeld in your 1960s Astronaut buzzcut.[13]

---

12 There is a bolt that anchors the ash to the heel of the fire.

13 Former U. S. Secretary of Defense. I shot Donald Rumsfeld and captured his ghost in an
antique silver colander. Then I tied his dumb tattered spirit to a string and flew it as a kite into the
eagle neighborhood and into the old brown falcon cities where they clawed it and rent it down
to shade. And then there remained only then the silent plummeting of his kite string—and as it
fell it drew new shapes in the air: it fell through compacted bits of sunlight that so peppered the
winds that one city-sized cumulus was given a fat and flackering hide of light. Then it just landed
in some poop.

IN/OH border
10:20 AM EST

[I switch to a blue gel pen with a small, fine, point:]
:   Does any one of us deny a daily or a near daily intimacy with dung? And do we not carry it into the halls of parliament inside a bag God has slung between our thighs? It is there with us always, yet we practice an apartheid against this substance, an apartheid at once so subtle and demoralizing that great havoc is wreaked in our daily life..
:   The effort we expend in our avoidance of thoughts about dung is incalculable. Many of us refuse to read about it. The moral and linguistic trenches and fretworks arrayed against dung are pervasive and seemingly insuperable. Indeed, the very word "shit" begins with the alveo-palatal voiceless fricative onomatopoeic imperative to be quiet: shh!
:   Many will praise and worship an idealized conception of God, yet the very paste of life cannot go unreviled.
:   Dung[14] and death, procreation and violence: these are the actual signposts and borders of life. Yet rarely do we see them come together except in a battle of sex and shit-throwing in a cemetery.

          :   Shame about dung is a frivolous and

---

14 Following Aristotle's dictum that the Comic mask shows no pain, scatological humor is predicated on the premise that feces is a painless extension of the body.

gratuitous shame, wasted shame, empty shame.
Should not shame serve to correct our action,
steer us from immorality and evil, rather than
provide us merely a feeling of intense and
impending embarrassment about an odorous
paste? I submit that inasmuch as the shame of
dung is the first impractical shame, it is the
beginning of frivolity. What's more, it follows
then that those adult pursuits recognized in
every age for their frivolity (fashion, for one)
are merely embellishments upon, and
excrescences of, dung shame. Vanity itself is
but a false sense of triumph over one's dung.
Shame of dung is therefore improper shame,
insofar as it supplants or is used as a surrogate
for proper, useful, substantive shame. Our
collective cultural feelings (aversive and prissy)
and representations about dung embody, then,
a failure of spirituality.

:   In those people for whom dung is
shameful, the depths of disgust and the heights
of vanity meet midway at a point called
righteousness. And I hate righteousness.
Here's your dung poetry, prissy boy! perfect girl!
:   The fact of the matter is dung has
fought back with great artfulness, vitality, craft
and agility at precisely those moments in
history when proper shame has been
suppressed by not only frivolous shame but the
cultural features that attend shame, such as
violence, officiousness, and the like. This
occlusion of proper shame suppresses

gratitude, pragmatics, use, and decency. And shame of dung is a sign of their absence.

:   It is no mistake that those who are officious, militantly decorous, prissy, priggish, and rule-bound are often called "anal-retentive." These are usually, furthermore, either secretively or openly pompous people; pomposity inheres in them, and this is because they suffer from a frivolous and incorrect shame, a shame that supplants true shame.

:   It could be argued that prissiness is at base a kind of timidity. But dung-based prissiness is a more militant kind of prissiness, insofar as it carries brittle attitudes specifically to procreation and defecation. These attitudes however are typically not obvious or strong enough to express in writing—nor do the prissy wish to see them expressed. It is interesting that the relationship between prissiness and timidity is that prissiness is a timidity of the butt.

When the bomb goes off—and the wind is done—And the stars have stopped their shaking—When will I—think again—

Of your boobies—and our hard loving making?

:   So, prissiness is less an issue of misplaced shame as it is the fear that one's frivolity will be challenged. For who wants to

be considered frivolous? Dung is never
frivolous, and it is therefore suitable that poetry
should be defended by dung. Dung is factual. It
is very real, and the dismissal of dung is
frivolous insofar as it is futile. The official
world is a dungless world

and its dismissal of dung is frivolous.
The official world is a dungless world.

Dung bagel booby mama
Dung bagel booby mama
Dung bagel booby mama
Dung bagel booby mama
Dung bagel booby mama
Dung bagel booby mama
      Wolfowitz Wolfowitz
      Rummy Dick Bush Rice
Dung bagel booby mama
Dung bagel booby mama
Dung bagel booby mama
Dung bagel booby mama
      Wolfowitz Wolfowitz
      Rummy Dick Bush Rice
Write Harvard re Briggs–Copeland

1.25 7 AM on road after "free" continental
breakfast with C___ in Lamar, PA's Comfort
Inn Room 115.
:   "His Buttocks": this poop is not about
me qua individual but about me as a member
of a collective. Therefore the poem "My
Buttocks" is less about those buttocks that

belong to me as an individual than the part of
me by which I am connected to the collective.[15]

15 Jorge Guitart, at SUNY Buffalo has translated my poem "My Buttocks":

"Mi trasero"

> *your buttock*s —Wallace Stevens

Estoy sumamente interesado en mi trasero
por ser la parte de mi cuerpo que casi nunca veo.

Se podría argüir que si estuviera realmente interesado en mi trasero
me valdría de espejos para verlo más a menudo.

Pero rechazo esa teoría.
Simple y llanamente estoy interesado en mi trasero
a la vez que lo miro aproximadamente una vez al año.

Francamente no tengo el menor interés en el trasero de otros.
Si tuviera un solo trasero que mirar, preferiría que fuera el mío.
No se considere eso prueba de que me miro el
                trasero más de una vez al año
puesto que en realidad no es lo que sucede,

Es más, que preferiría que los demás no tuvieran trasero.
Mejor dos ingles que un trasero—una al frente y la otra detrás.
De ese modo existiría la alternativa de mirarse una o la otra.
También existiría la alternativa de preferir una a la otra, ya fuera al hacer el amor
o al ir al retrete. De esa manera bajarían los costos de reparación y mantenimiento
de las ingles (infecciones urinarias, cosas de la próstata, canal de parto en llamas,
cuestiones de hongos): dos ingles y sin trasero. Tal vez un caño de albañal que bajara
a uno de los pies, y al momento de defecar se quitara uno el zapato y le diera un buen
puntapié a la pelota de excremento para que se alejara volando. Los baños
tendrían que tener tableros como los del baloncesto.

Todos los hermafroditas que cagamos por los pies. Hubiéramos desterrado el sexo
anal a los talones. Lo cual me trae a otra inquietud: el nuevo ano que está ahora en
uno de los pies: ¿estaría ese ano cerca de los dedos del pie, cerca del talón o en la
parte superior del pie?

Mi inquietud es la siguiente: si el ano estuviese en el empeine, ¿no dejaría marquitas de
arrugas en nuestras huellas?

:   These are less like cups of coffee than semi-stiff cylindrical bags that collapse when they're picked up.

:   All of which is not to say that there are not honest and legitimate negative reactions to dung. Dung is after all disgusting. But serious grave and moral and national and political and rural issues arise once what is *Physically Disgusting* is not understood as something merely physically disgusting, but is instead confused with the aesthetically, morally, and nationally reprehensible.

:   Prissies believe they are about law and order, when in fact they are merely trying to plant feeble colonies of disgust in inappropriate regions. These prissies are dolts. (That is one class of prissy: the dolt prissy.)

:   But what are these "inappropriate regions"?: Comedy; The North; Decency; Urbanity; Sanity—anything, that is, outside the realm of television. Television *IS* "the South"; television *IS* prissiness. TV is the South inasmuch as "the South" is a collectively prissy response to wilderness (the swamps of MS and LA, eg), the other (the poor, the African-American, the non-Anglo-Saxon, the masculine female, the feminized male), and, well, the facts

---

No, no me gusta el trasero. A pesar que se rumore lo contrario.

Contrario, he ahí una palabra. Me opongo a la palabra contrario.

—Traducción del inglés de Jorge Guitart, first appearing in *Mandorla: Nueva Escritura de las Américas* (reality, eg).

:   Let us be plain: There is something inherently retarded about America. And the reason for this has principally to do with our relationship vis à vis dung.

:   They who feel frivolous disgust and frivolous shame are put off by dung in poetry. As prissiness is a display of frivolous disgust and/or frivolous shame, so also is machismo a display of resistance to disgust and shame. But insofar as machismo is yet another reactionary response to shame and disgust (with a key additional reaction to fear), I must classify it as a type of prissiness.

:   By contrast, there is something very "can do" about dung. Dog-faced and down-at-heel, dung is nothing, yet from it issues life. It is a kind of womb therefore. It is a cross between a paste, on the one hand, and a womb on the other. Indeed, the rectum, whence comes dung, is itself a shadow womb. Metonymically then, a dung is a boy. Or a dung is a girl. Dung are therefore shadow children, adumbrated offspring. The procreative aspects of dung hinge not only upon its biological properties, but its

metaphorical properties. It is a rich and confusing substance. So, out of respect for its complexity, its signification, its use, and our long companionship with it, we ought not either wrinkle or raise our noses at it.

:   A perfect example of denial-of-dung art is Nashville country music. Yet even there we see defecatory qualities: the moaning of the mullet cuts, the tinkling of the steel guitars.

:   Beyond shame, there is a very strong fear associated with dung. Consider that a creature is, when defecating, very vulnerable to attack. To many idiots, then, dung is what one produces when one is weak, it is a product of weakness. But some, I think, feel that a dung is an expulsed wound. That in surviving the act of defecation without being clubbed, the dung represents a wound one had avoided altogether. It is a wound at once avoided and voided.

:   Thus, given his druthers, mankind will choose to dung inside a fortified structure. You might argue that the fact that we chose to situate our dunging machines inside houses is indicative only of a preference to dung in a warm room, outhouses being cold more than half the year in those climes where the flushing dung bowl was devised. I concede this is a strong argument: it does seem axiomatic that one is more likely to freeze to death in an outhouse than be clubbed to death in it. But I refute this theory.

:   If we say, for instance, war is built upon the anus, and that religion is founded upon that muscled ring, the anus then becomes military, poetic,

liturgical, and imperialistic. We may say then
that the anus is the redoubt of comedy, but
who would believe us? Let us instead merely
suggest it is the organ of divestment, and as
such it is the very seat and anchor of
practicality. In the South, the men are smarmy
and the women are prissy. I do
not like the smarminess and the prissiness of
the South. Of course, they do not have anuses
down there. The women do not have anuses in
their buttocks. Southern women do not have
sphincters. They are all vulva. Yet there is a
wasp who guards everyone's anus—especially
in the South. That is to say, each anus has a
wasp that guards it. It is a protective wasp.
When things pass out of it, or when someone's
finger goes in, the wasp is there, taking notes,
watching, ready to Kung Fu to protect the
trade the rectum
makes with the world. The little wasp then
floats behind us

making notes in the steam and gas of us, and
enjoys the sound of our trumpet. For the
trumpet's sound is a cousin to the wasp's
sound.[16] It's an old key feature of menippean
satire: contents of the rectum rocket out in

---

16 The orchards of Norsemen are generally cloudy. The planks of a Norseman's cabin tend to be
long boards of blonde wood. The sun is inclined to shake a salt-light into the ice that hangs in
the bushes of the Norsemen. When a Norseman opens a book, a pebble-smell of a gelid brook is
wafted to the air. Their rivers are filled with gray rocks. The Norseman's geese are dour as black
pumpkins. The spunk of the geese is heavy. A small goose turns into a little girl. The gold in the
Norseman's moneybag has rust on it. It is an orange rust. The dots on the Norsemen's i's smell
of thistles.

their subtitleness, without subtlety, at certain tight and critical moments in history, I imagine, following Bakhtin, mostly at those points when life is ridiculously officious and harmful. The foisting of the anus has then a purpose: It is the ring of shame. It is the ring of shock. It is the ringydingy of fun.

Think of the kingly peacock, how it moons us constantly, showing us its big throbbing anus. Yet do we notice its small dark donut of expulsion? No, we see only its fan. Generally, the anus is a ring too small to be a crown. But if it weren't, our president would wear one: a big ropey sphincter pulsing on his hair like an odorous tonsure! The anus as that which opposes our mouth, the mouth being seat of the "voice," the "voice" being the signature of a poet, the anus being the mouth of the seat, the seat being the proper resting place for a poet (as opposed to the laurels). The anus, which speaks in a syntax of bilabial trills, is the very voice of the applicable, valid world, the spot of spiritual use beyond vain derision. It is a rubbery cross between a lip and an eye, and it speaks more than it sees.

:   "Beauty" is camouflage for the anus. The denied anus is the fount of frivolity, vanity, violence and war.

:   Is not the grotesque, by the very instability with which it skirts revulsion and laughter, an effective way to treat suffering? Does not the grotesque present us with the limits of our taste, our sense of propriety, our very conceptions of what we can endure, and says, "We suffer from the east of us to the west of us; let's come at this a different way: try enduring!" End making an icon of suffering; stop the false solemnity of weeping. The more we look at urine, the less we weep. If as Bakhtin noted the grotesque body is the collective body, what, I say, is the use of the grotesque in poetry?[17]

:   Dung literature appears with the life of officials, with the advent of the officious, when it is impossible to argue or to be kind in a straightforward way. If one cannot anymore be overtly kind, the expression of kindness must become a guerilla affair. The official life, the life of this empire, the life of rules, is a life that does not readily allow the choice to be kind: insurance companies find such choice risky, and corporations find such choice costly. Officiousness is not a thing, but the very action that removes kindness. The purpose of

---

17 To insist along with Patrick Kavanagh that we aren't alone in our loneliness; to second Bill Knott's opinion that a portrait of Marcheta Casati would look beautiful even if hung improbably and inappropriately upon a man's forehead; to write upon my own forehead, as Tully wished citizens might, what I think of the republic; to insist that we are all bookmarks in a holy anthology; that though each of us is a nobody, we are together consequential; that those among us of greater consequence never forget the ache in their forearms; that all anger is unjust; that Jesus and Lenny Bruce spoke the same language; that Janis Joplin could out-sing Maria Callas and Buster Keaton out-talk Christopher Lyden; that buffo, not rage, that laughter, not reason, are the only viable means of wresting dignity from the hands of bureaucrats and professionals; that the ready ease with which an academic will assume someone to be stupid is more repugnant than a barfight; that yodeling at a plate of eggs can satisfy one's curiosity for a better life; that underdogs can be jerks too; and finally to concur loudly, like a car horn with lips, with Henry James when he said that three things in human life are important: being kind, being kind, and being kind.

lampoon is, then in part, to show us that the correct thing is often the improper thing. The purpose of decent dung literature is, in part, to show that the decorous action is often the dangerous action. In
fact, in such an age, in an age of militarism and canned heroism, tragedy is the mere commodification of suffering and the glue of nationalism. A nation does not laugh, it grieves. Yet it is a false grieving; the grief of nationalism is merely a scrim to hide the buttocks of revenge. America

does not know how to suffer because it does not know how to endure. And it does not know how to endure because it cannot laugh. We need dung therefore. Like laughter, the anus is innately disruptive. Dung is laughter. The landbridge of laughter is a preposterous isthmus leading to a seldom visited region of purposeful metaphor, a region where cultural and aesthetic politics matter. And, too, the idea that the comic may be at once oppositional in its uses and concordant in its pleasures is something one may touch upon nicely here. email Burt Kimmelman re Brathwaite article.

[katabasis]

1.27.03 8:42 AM 4.5 M fr. M. HWY 95 S
Johnson-Associated texts seem to be satirical, ironical Mayhem continues everywhere. Will it never stop. Write Mark Weiss Pierre Joris.

Email Melpomene, as to what she did w/ C___'s 1st
tooth. Mozart born today in 1756. Put
poet = rebel thread into "Dung in An Age of
Empire" 12 pence = what? a shilling? Chief UN
weapons inspector Hans Blix delivered his
report today.

       383.7 M 10.372 g = 36.99 mpg
386 m fr. Prov, near Bellefonte PA, 15 turkeys
forage on the right shoulder hill 2:30 pm those
big beautiful cliffs. Down in the valley silos
stand in the snow. A nation of firemen. A
nation of soldiers.
:   Generally it is extremely ignorant
people who are dung denying. The right wing
benefits from anger. 3:45 pm EST near
Pennfield, PA. Shadows fr. the hills
on the left are well over the highway. It is a
beautiful day. I am wearing a red silk scarf fr.
Dublin. And there are many strange hordes on
the earth. Anything Butt. email Lee Brasseur
"We are a special
nation!"gofuckyourselfyourspecialnation… I-
76 west at Youngstown, OH at 5:30 pm EST
Meander Reservoir 590 M Call Victoria Harris
:   of What USE is dung in poetry? Why
can dung too not be put to metaphorical and
substantive use?
       Call Jasper.

2.14.03 – 2.19.03

[anabasis]

Febr 14 It is Valentines Day 7 AM
Cold at curb on Kreitzer Coffee up at Clinton
Gas Station the US is on "orange alert"
4.2 m fr. my apt to HWY 74 Ice Storm
predicted today for the central plains, I will
drive out from under it, Selah, the
cold road is ribbed in frost
under gravels of tin colored cloud the
shorn fields glow dark brown flecked
in remaining straw fr harvest. A
thick and very cold wind collects.

There are Ruths and Pats and Lindas
there are Lisas and Carries all
who must have seen the incorruptible change
of this season turn from cold to colder
and the texture of all things altered,
certainly there is an Athabascan cold here:
tell me we will all walk out
through the canyons holding the crayons we
wrote with as children, and into
the landmarks of change, into the
ostensible unknown where worry rides
the bright and blightening thunder.

We are going to attack Iraq.
8:17 AM CST 68 M fr. Normal
Vermilion River 8:28 AM 81 M

Welcome to Indiana Crossroads
of America Rest Area Welcome Center
One Mile (vending machines available)
84 M 9:30 AM EST. Radio says schools
in western IL, eastern IN
are let out early this morning:

a snow day for states!
What a glory for all: kids love this
The whole atmosphere a movie
Icestorms impending, a ledge of clouds,
a mantelpiece of arctic space tipping down
Think this is easy? Try writing
a book
in your
car. See how well you write trying
not to crash

Most literature is delusional, pretty,
petty and false. 125 m fr. Normal
On this day, Valentine's, Hans
Blix (and I am in Boone County, IN)
makes an interim report.
Distant gray jet wedges above the billboards
to land on Indy airport.
"The 4 thousand 7 hundred and 7th
Security Council meeting is called
to order." I-465 12 M. 145 M. from
BL. "I invite the representative of Iraq
to take a seat at council table."
154 M Eagle Creek Reservoir Dam
196 M; 11:10 AM: I wear on my
car's bumper a 4 x 6" magnetic sign

"NO IRAQ WAR"—and just a mile
before "Nameless Creek"

A silver Ford passes, the
baseball capped driver and woman
inside pause & wave & nod I nod & wave.
"Six Mile Creek"
This is the creek region
of Indiana. They waved in accord
w/ the sticker I wear. We nod
"in total determination" (cf. France
ambassador to the UN during his speech
to the Security Council today)
Schools in Muncie & Marion Indiana
are closing for the coming ice
I am 228 M fr NORMAL, ILLINOIS
245 M: Ohio border—marked by blue
steel arch. And over that a lowering arch
of bright gray clouding.
MASSIVE, nearly ottoman sized hawk
stands in the tan straw of the
                                    median ditch
facing south south east 255 m

At 257 m I see another hawk standing
this one smaller, in the
tan windy median facing
in the gray light, gloriously,
like a gust of gush, the darker
northwest.
                    89.3 FM 91.1 FM
91.7 FM - all channels on which I hear
deliberations at the UN Security

Council. Comedy & its relation to pain
is, I submit, the often only way
to awaken decency at a time
when portrayals of suffering
serve chiefly to aggrandize the heroic
and the emotional needs of state
nationalism. In such a situation, the
suffering of heroes occludes/ the
suffering victims,/ the idea of "heroes"
thus serves the worst in us. "Heroes" as idea
is predicated on a victim mentality.
1:02 PM. Ohio State HWY
Dept truck stuck under a bridge
332 m fr. Normal
20 Geese, again, Near Dublin
fly east, across I-270 N

"We got fabulous men & women in uniform
on the hunt! We got the finest bravest
best smartest soldiers!"
"Liberty is not God's gift to America,
but His gift to each and every..."
Speech on "Terrorist Threat Integration
Network" 1:35 PM—Dictator G W
Bush at FBI Headquarters. I stick a knife
in his jaw and twist, spit in the wound
in his spit box. I shove powdered aluminum
in his jaw. HWY 71 N 355 m
1:40 PM and into his dumb
tooth hole I whisper "terrorist
backlash, Dubya, you dipscum peahead."
Winter Storm Warning for Ohio
late Afternoon near Cincinnati

Then I dropped a new quarter in his wound
and turned his groin like a crank
He shuffled in place w/ his trousers wrinkling
Then peed his pants for the world to see

I put a small umbrella in his rectum
and opened it he said "Mmmff! It's not
raining! it's not misty in the abdomen! stop
it you terrust! I believe in my opinion
of basketball.
         Mmmff!"
2:34 pm I GAS at Exit 187 71 N
at Ashland, OH at 421.8 M
10.118 g   428 M = 42.340 mpg

SNOW predicted tonight in Cleveland.
I am 50 M S of Cleveland, at 3:05 PM
It is slightly sunny &
beautiful—A gelid & generous
but not a harsh light on the snow

505 M 80 east 4:10 EST Sweet warm
white to cliché yellow sepia
evening light behind me slight
vanilla reflections on the steering
                wheel from the rear window

O Shenango River, Robustly bedded
near Gordon Ward I see you
in Dusk Ohio (527 m fr. BL) 4:25 PM

eastern Ohio
There is a cabal

in the White House blah blah
while here
at O D Anderson Interchange
A soft old maculate snow & 7
crow specks hinging in the sky
89.1 FM western Pennsylvania
Mexico has not executed anyone since
                                1937.
"Americans finally had a war
they cd cheer."—Howard Means
in <u>Colin Powell: Soldier Statesman,</u>
<u>Stetson Shoulder</u> in re Persian Gulf War

HIGH HWY bridge over wide snow
covered Clarion River 582 M
the shadows are bluing

Switch headlights on 600 Miles 5:30 PM
near Reynoldsville, PA

Perfume well the sea door,
though boys will ever
school the dark with straining.

The women
carry their hickies
to the campfires

Hickies like the dark on peaches
hickies like
wool

bet Julia Ward Howe wanna write

nuther song fr bush & co, Mine ears
have indeed heard the coming of
democracy: It is pounding at the
edges of the ages where the cantaloupes of leg
meat are jarred; It has loosened
the prophetic bolts of His items, Its
truth is marching ignited. I have seen
in the watch-fires hundreds of fields
that were surrounded by the mothers
of policemen and that they had bolted an altar
into the evening and
that there was this thick orange dew
on their hips; I can read the single
oration, righteous and bilious, by the
ham-colored lamps that indicate by
means of scrotum-sized lightbulbs
that its day is marching ignited. It has
sounded ahead in the sand the looser
tuba which oompas lips and ribbons;
The cult is sifting outside the bakery
the hearts of wives before a
judgment-seat: The old are fast to the
cake, the young are loathe to move,
fat bees float thickly about our feet.
Our ignited God is marching! In the
pulchritude are flecks of corneas,
Mary did not suckle Christ,
her nipples were canoes, Joseph wept as he
tunneled through the sea and
launched swollen jellyfish into small
barrels with a temporary ball of cake
lodged in his chest such that it
transfigures you and not them: And

as he died to bomb the City of
Mosques, let to us die to make certain
men free, whereas the ignited God is
marching.

CHORUS:

When our ankles are ignited
  (like some low and little stumps)
When the angels start their buggery
  (behind the windy shacks)
Who shall cherish those small parts of us
  not yet caught in flames—
These parts may be our groins or eyes
  these parts may be our brains

Our! God! Is! Marchinggg!
Ignited!!!!

Yowza, mine eyes have detected the gore
that was spinning hard from whitey. He
was beating eaglets near the winepress
where the dingleberries of certain Colonels
were warehoused, such that he had
untwisted the prophetic bolts from the
broadsword of horror such that their Truth
is marching ignited! I have seen in the
knocking of the blazes hundreds of meadows
surrounded by many Presbyterian mothers
who had just carted an altar across the
grassland and bolted it into the evening and
that on each of the wildflowers there stuck this

gangling cake of dog-cunt mucus that smelled
of spit and shining rubber, and I can read today
of Any numbers of mothers praising the
soldier-cock, with Pentecostal orators righteous
in the beef-colored gloaming
and that the pastry issuing from duck farms
is indicating by means of energy in the lamps
moreover the day is marching ignited. I have
seen an ardent writing of the Gospel in
my neighbor's elms by the small bosoms of
skunk catchers, such that there is crying in the
shadows found in schools, and the hero takes
the woman and crushes the serpent's head with
Italians, and our ignited God is marching
around. He has surrounded the small men and
exfoliated their date trees because his tuba is
the loud one, my feet are happy that our
Massive Bosoms and not yours are marching
ignited through the forest of crayons (Crayola)
which have drawn the irises of Jesus on even
more bosoms who was himself born through
small wet lips with muffins shoved up his
buttocks, we are marching in the brightness
toward the outside of all of us and he is
wisdom to the powerful, he is succor to the
brave sergeants at the checkpoints so the
world will be his Ottoman and the clock of
time his Negro, our ignited God is marching!

CHORUS:

When our ankles are ignited
  (like some low and little stumps)

When the angels start their buggery
      (behind the windy shacks)
Who shall cherish those small parts of us
      not yet caught in flames—
These parts may be our groins or eyes
      these parts may be our brains

Our! God! Is! Marchinggg!
Ignited!!!!

a car slaps northward along the road
I drive through nighted Pennsylvania
following a string of dimmed orange pearls
like some child mouse-fish
through the bulbous hills
that I see as dark and hulking whales
and the haze of trees flickering
there their spume 7:28 PM 737 miles from
Normal

I seem to have escaped the icestorms of Ohio,
Indiana, & Illinois. I stop at rest
area 740 M Ronnie Reagan lived in Dixon, IL
for 12 yrs.
        Susquehanna River 761.8 M 7:55 PM
An achromatic glint – jet – in sky
gray-silver beacons on its wing

In the dark of Pennsylvania
Out the driver's window, through
the dark, in a scrotum of steam
are two nuclear cooling towers
issuing hot clouds lit by sodium

Nanticoke, PA getting tired been
driving 12 hrs 10 Min.

Gas up 9 pm at Promised Land Fuel Stop
10.347 gallons 419.?? miles
I eat a hotdog & buy a coffee
which I leave on the car roof. Have to
stop to get Another one. This is
annoying.

I stop a few M down 84 E & get
<u>another</u> coffee & a Danish.
I am a hog pig, this Danish
is dusty, dry, so, as is the road is

865.9 Miles fr. Normal, 6
miles west of Matamoras PA

"Remember me as you pass by
For as you are, so once was I
And as I am, you soon will be
So be content—to follow me"
Gravestone Epitaph Reagan noted
in Ireland
        11:30 691 North 981 m
My pragmatic twine, these veins
grown since birth
in muscles torn and caked w/ ache
under days where I carried hours
is, I well know, fraying
        990 M 91 N 11:40 PM
Mattabesset River, then HWY 95 E
11:46 pm 996.1 m the sky beyond

the sodium lights is like
    dusk in a dish of salt

Deep River Town Line 1017 M
1025 M 12:15 pm
Welcome to Rhode Island 1058 m
        12:45 PM

1:17 AM round acute left 1st sight
        of Providence: it's downtown bldg's
                        1093 M
1094 exit 20. Faint sheen of ice on
        Woonasquatucket river
1096.4   Doyle & Hope (left onto Hope)
1096.9 T&S&C Driveway
                18 BeHappy St 1:28 AM

        [katabasis]

2.19.03 Cumberland Farms Gas Station
        Hope St. 6:49 AM Wed.
Traffic Jam in sight of Capitol dome 95 S
WGBH 89.7 Massive blizzard
Mond & Tue. had intended to go to NYC
to read at KGB Bar but it was cancelled
because of 2 ft. snow.
2 spinouts seen this morning
on 95–S, the ice has caused a froth of light
3rd crash on HWY in only 30 miles!
31.7 M fr. Prov 7:22 AM
CT border 7:30 AM

The clouds, a heap of cold clothes

No shoulder in many places—pile up
                    with snow

9:45 Am Stopped to pee. Have
headache. Small semi-clear ice globule
snails across rear window, blown in
a diagonal tack by the fierce slipstream
over my virile Toyota ECHO
trailing a track of delicate wet

Amazing the way the head fits on the
shoulders. Up there cocky as you please.

Pumpkins have migraines. Every
pumpkin is a big fat head of earth
set to explode from ache pain. Pumpkins
hug the loam, fatigued, and want
to be the mommy-vegetable. But no
vegetable has a mommy. Every
vegetable is an orphan. We need
fruits and fungi to minister
to the vegetables. Pumpkins think
they are very mommy-like. The pumpkin
is a bouffant vegetable.

It pleases me when someone badmouths
the terrible corporations.

I did not understand the dog, I think
that is why it bit me. Samantha put
the pizza in her. Then we went. And
stayed. And went. Quonset huts in the
hundreds. Teepees at the dozens. Tents

and yurts—and twinkles to house
ants. A window reflection that housed
a butterfly. Winks housing ostriches. The
horrible lung accident happened on a windy
morning. The lungs burst out of Rory's
throat and began flapping around w/ a
horrifying meat sound, a horrifying
soggy clapping. Dare to move toward
the smelly animal. Without the essay
there would be no autumn.

There was no summer because the memo
ordering it was swallowed by the Gar. Stella
should not have. Who but the fish
can fully know worrisome lilies. Stones w/out
clothes. Tanks, I am inert. We had
been enough. To be then would smother
immensities, just then they thronged
about on the only frog. Lily went along
the long bridge over the frosted steel work
we all went to sleep first, that is because
it was worried—indeed it was worrying—
but we were, neither worried to nor
worrying. And linked around the sun
were many putrid meteors. We detested
those meteors. We told the cherubim
who rode them to quit. Stop all you fat
buttocked cherubim!: you creatures just come
from the puffy bosoms of heaven.

A dog at heart is made of dust
and dust is wind that's mad

In the White House
they cut off
the dogs' fat brown noses
and fried them, and hung
the dogs by the necks from the willow
tree in the Rose Garden, in the Winter
willows are as jumprope afros, they are
as vegetal dreadlocks

Just crossed the Hudson. It is
caked w/ ice floes. Very deep
snow along hwy

A mammoth cloud is strapped to a bee
          who tows it down to make
A slow fog. The meat of
          a bee is weak and tastes of egg.

Meat bees are few in the
winters around Burmingham. Yet
here they fly, like flecks & bolts
of squeaking mutton.
                    Fat Bee: humming
globule of life!, I am 73 Miles

from Scranton! I am maintaining
a speed of 70 Miles An Hr. It is

snowy here but not so Snowy as it
was only 10 Miles Ago. Dear Meat
bee! (Food Exit 2 Dulraney's
Steak House). 222 M   10:27 AM EST
Delaware River, NY/PA border

228 M.

It is a long drive.

There is
very little meat on the human ear. Head
of the beetle will never wear
a helmet. The other day walking
back inside from the rain, the smell of books
was overwhelming. My head was formed
in library, my hope there, and
have always loved meeting lib'arians
may they always be my friends
They are like surrogate aunts. There is
no other job
more marterteral. Today my armpits
smell of chicken soup.
They smell like someone had lifted up my arm
and found a second mouth in my armpit.
At first it appeared a small vulva. But
parting the lips a soon discovered
assembly of teeth, alive tongue, a
second throat descending to torso.
And there, in lippy nest,
was an eruption of pustules and
hay colored cankers: and a large
blond gumboil supporting a flaccid
bleb (bulb, bag) of pus. The whole
arrangement was festooned in crimpled hair.

This relationship feels like
playing racquetball on top of a kite.

Sometimes in our arguments minutes after

minutes kind of wreck themselves against
the clock.

Sometimes I have seen the clouds.
Often some of them wrestle w/
the more awkward Treetops

Ronald Reagan, that thick
                      Melodious Optimist
has given way to a daft
              Malevolent Paranoid.[18]
Susquehanna River 335 M 12:05 PM EST
Reagan had his issues but he loved fountain
pens and used a broad stub nib to write his
speeches even his last ones he preferred
fountain pens

Bees come from a
              land of Clocks

Here Again—at 43600 odo exactly—
Are the great cut-cakes of cliffs
of Pocono sandstone[19]

---

18 "The tyranny of ignoramuses is insurmountable and assured for all time." — Albert Einstein
19 "The Pocono sandstone, X, is more than 600' thick, and forms a bold, straight, forest-covered
ridge of coarse, and often conglomerate white sandstone, covered with bowlders, and keeping a
pretty regular height of 2200' A.T. The Catskill rocks, IX, form a broad, flat terrace in front of
the Allegheny mountain its whole length, which can be well studied in Worth township, where
the old turnpike to Philipsburg runs along it; they are 2600' thick. The Chemung and Hamilton
formations form the foot hills, and the Marcellus dark shales (800') the bottom of the Bald Eagle
valley; in all more than 6000' thick of middle and lower Devonian measures, rising from beneath
the Coal regions at increasing angles from 10° to 60°. The astonishing straightness of the Bald
Eagle valley (N. 450° E.) across the county is explained by the vertical attitude of the rocks of
the Bald Eagle mountain, at the west foot of which runs the low ridge of Oriskany sandstone
VII, and Lower Helderberg limestone VI. At the Clinton county line VII is 130' thick, but thins
southward to nothing a few miles south of Milesburg, and has been seen after that at only one

at 396 M fr. Providence (near
to Lockhaven University) but now
they are wind-smeared w/ a snow
frosting & down in the reflective valley,
    in the fogged-up sun

silos rise like periscopes
from the farmy snow.
The mottled white sea-fields
like paragraphs. A tree
line lies fuzzed & crimped
on hills faintly blued by distance.

I smell the shit of a farm!:
it smells very bad! like human shit!
(not cow dung alloyed w/ the nice
        farmy fume of silage!)
—1:20 pm EST at Bellefonte PA.
It is not a silage fug. What but the stern
irrelevance of the woods
wd cause the cars to steer here
beside the steel grey cold-milky
guard rail, and the continual long trough

---

place; it furnishes inexhaustible quantities of the finest glass sand, is excessively fossiliferous, but seems to offer no iron ore. The limestone VI is finely developed in Centre County, 1020' thick, and has been quarried in the neighborhood of the charcoal iron furnaces. It is both argillaceous and cherty, and, as usual, quite fossiliferous. No. V (Onondaga and Clinton) 1040' thick, makes the west slope of Bald Eagle Mountain, but its fossil ore beds are scarcely recognizable; one thin layer was formerly mined a little at Howard. "Paint Springs" issue from its outcrop. The Bald Eagle mountain rocks stand vertical; the west crest made by Medina white sandstone (938',) the east crest by Oneida white sandstone (710',) and the interval by Medina red rocks (774',) in all 2425 feet thick, containing neither useful minerals nor any fossils, except a few casts of a sea weed called *Arthrophycus harlani.*"—from *A geological hand atlas of the sixty-seven counties of Pennsylvania :embodying the results of the field work of the survey, from 1874 to 1884.* By J. P. Lesley. (Report of progress (Geological Survey of Pennsylvania), v. X) Harrisburg, PA: Board of commissioners for the second geological survey, 1885.

of ditch snow—that is subsiding to tan-green
slush. And the resounding slush
under the tires, a thrumming
in our wheelwells
            What soul had blown
through here/ and left a
clacking bit of heaven.   Out
there I know, beyond the

boxed wind of my car, tree ice falls
cackling/ through the shadowed twigs.

I suspect I just saw rain but
fear they are dot-sized waterballoons.
Thrown by a winter frog presiding
over slush puddle. What a dumb thing to write.
2:50 PM Clarion River—A dark
wispy, lazy snow squall 515 m
My tires lisping in the snow-touch

"Formidable will based on mediocre
understanding of the facts."
                    —Francois Mitterand
on Ronald Reagan. A pall of such
unparalleled politeness has fallen
on the journalists of this nation.

Gudding's Law: The more polite
the journalists become to those who
may lie to them, the less
compassionate the people grow.

Another snow squall gravels into the sky

and grays the square trees.
530 M The sky fades
to a luminous charcoal manila
one flat dirted lemony cloud blankets
        horizon to horizon
Another Squall of Dimness is driven
down by our graylight & drawn down
        to that dopey ditch
that stays beside me
from our Midwest
to rhode island and back
Who isn't sad for his famly?

3:15-3:19 STOP TO PEE 545 M
Z. H. Confair Memorial Highway, O
how boring.

Shenango River 572 M 3:43 EST
Welcome to Ohio   574 M 3:45
Museum of Labor & Industry 582 M 3:50
Meander Reservoir   590 M 4 PM

When we should have hunkered
down in the dark and smoking bushes
of hell, and stared about at
the encroaching river of dung
(which was flashing orange and brown
roiled with half-sunk and blobbing poops)
and noticing the leather covered & juicy fish
that plooped indolently in swirls
we thought of Barbara and Laura Bush
what terrible breasts had they
and what long and daunting

willow trees of hair they wore
above their clapboard faces.

4:40 PM Akron 76 interchange—
traffic jam—delayed only a few
minutes. THE ISRAELI occupation
of Palestine should be shot!
             71 S 650 M 4:58 PM

"The wrong way always seemed more
reasonable." —G Moore

5:22 PM Still bright. A Strange
browny gray lemoned light
here north of Columbus.
Snow in the median looks as
pissed on, rumpled, and soggy
as a soiled diaper. Dimmer now
headlights popping into bright gray
silver dots   against the blue darkling
                              atmosphere
at this end of day. Kucinich→
best anti-war candidate for President.
Let's see if he's eloquent. I hope he
is. I oughta count the number of
American flag decals I see next time
"Americans aren't afraid and we
will be feared!"—Tom Ridge, 1st head
of "Dept of Homeland Security"
Meant to be 24 min's of congestion
          Northeast of Columbus on 1-270.
6:20 PM EST I-270 NE of Columbus
Sun is setting, road is wet w/

melted sleet or just mist. The asphalt
        is a Purple Brown.
The face of the puppy was a
bumpy bacon. Yet we did not
skin the dog for its face. Instead we
sought to catch and flay the meated bee.

The beefy bee was like an large airborne pill
but w/ a coating of meat that made it
        juicy.
772 M   70 West. Partly cloudy Eastern
sky dark w/ clouds and night.
Western sky in front purple as if
        post rainstorm & orange & beige.
BIG FUCKING CHUCKHOLE 775.3 M
        FIX THAT!
Back of "AF" trucking semi: "Never
Underestimate an American" The amount
        of ignorance it takes to write that
on the back of a truck is hemispheric
        406.9 M 9.933 gallons
        Will we distribute spines to
the senators today?
7:10-:35 PM EST ate & peed
                44002 odo 798 M
USA, A Whitey World.
That is to say:
fearful, mendacious, & unaware of its own
violence: that is my definition of "white" as
an adjective

Having eaten two meat bees
for Thanksgiving dinner

we then undertook a feast of
       claws and buttons
Not even eagles wd have sated us
       like these bees and the masala
       of buttons and claws
850 M OH/IN Border 7:35 CST

Cave ab homine unius libri
yo, beware the man of one book.
       —like old suppy—
       whose breath was blown in hay
No! That hickey covered dog
had been beset by women w/ lips
who sucked it as children
suckle. Had they mistaken

the dog for a breast? If so
that is odd b/c the hickey marks
were all over it: they had
kept on sucking w/out finding
       a nipple.
What had they wanted to get
out of it? A milk? What kind of
milk cd be gotten fr. an entire
dog! I can see having suckled its
breasts, but they had suckled its
nape and tail so. Even each
one of its eyeballs had been suckled. They
were American women however so their
ignorance makes sense.

West of Indianapolis 9:45 PM.
Hard to tell in the

dark, but don't see any snow
in the ditches nor on the icky
ditch slopes. "Drinking is the
soldier's pleasure." John Dryden.
This is a medium point Lamy
Vista fountain pen w/ Lamy
blue-black ink. Lamy is a
German family devoted to Bauhaus
simplicity & just prices,
making modest, durable, &
brilliant writers. Alfred North
Whitehead insists the entire
apparatus of western philosophy
is but a series of footnotes
upon Plato. "How quaint the ways of
Paradox. At common sense she
Gaily mocks."—W. S. Gilbert.

Edmund Burke 1729-1797 said
"All govt., indeed every human benefit
and enjoyment, every virtue and every
prudent act, is founded on compromise
and barter." It is interesting that he is
talking about the principle of interconnectivity
but that he casts it in economic terms. I
go hizzing through the weather
        in a car made of rubber
If I do so drive my rubber car
through the winds and plains of night
It is for to hunt the bee
and bring my family food.
Illinois State Line 9:52 PM CST
        1012 M.

But I do so for the sake of Merica,
to quieten its cloying huzzing.

A bee is a pill between wings.

I am like Cordelia who remaineth
quiet. But the bee is not. The
bumblebee reminds America
of the internal combustion engine
—and therefore all bees
must be suppressed:
bee meat is loud.
It is the loudest meat among the plants
            490 M total for 11.9 gallons
                    "Come! Let's away
to prison!"—King Lear
Pax and sex. → Did Lear
say this?
    More snow west of Champaign
but east of Normal Illinois,
I return to Normal.
All the rapacious fishes, the
utility of seashells!
            Your headlights! TOO bright!
Edmund Burke: The sublime is based in
self-preservation & rooted in terror
            vastness, mystery, darkness

10:55 PM Very dark but
many stars. Americans love the Sublime.
But beauty, he said, is
founded in pleasure & our
desire to propagate. Themes

of beauty: "smallness, smoothness,
variety, & shape." delicacy
transparency. Weakness, roundedness.
Stephen Jay Gould wd have noted
Burke's sexism here.
      Bloomington Exit 135 11:07 PM CST
      1096
1100.2 M Arrive lawn of
Apt. One ft. dirty moraine of snow
      cast up by plow & lodged
      on the cold curb

2.26.03 – 3.2.03

[anabasis]

6:54 AM Kreizer Ave. Febr 26, '03 Car
warming up. Grey cloud. Dim dawn. Very cold.
Some snow lapping at curb. Coffee
at Clinton Wareco   Gas   7:01 AM
Set odo. South on Oakland Ave. Delayed
by train at X-ing near Gridley & Lakeland
It is heading north to Chicago, 120 miles NNE:
Urban graffiti on train. 7:05—train passes
7:05 red light Main & Oakland 7:06
South on Center.   South on Main
7:10 AM JCT 74 East trip odo 3.1
regular odo 44640. Turn radio on.
First word I hear is "Regime." 2.26.03
I love Neil Diamond. His song
"Holly Holy" is on. It is from 1969.
The year before the great war criminal
Henry Kissinger came truly to power. At 7:40
I am 36 M from Normal. The
cold origin of the Kaskaskia River.
Today is the anniversary of Sylvia Plath's
passing.

Plath died 40 yrs ago this cold
month. Dizzy stones
of dark ice spin in jerks off trucks like stumps
of penguins, getting rounder as they go
then they shatter in dark
sparks of dirt. Snow in the stubble,

small billboards. I approach Kickapoo
State Park, the beaver-dammed dell
at Middle Fork of Vermilion River
8:10 AM. I cross through
charcoal trees at bridge
height and over Wabash River
94 M 8:30 AM. Now we set out
to find and milk the eagle, she in
her small breast her star-spangled
nipples, her nipples each a milky nickel
flashing garishly as clear puddle.
Snow slightly deeper through Indiana
near Lebanon it's very white

I am this trip haunted by the
face of Nancy Reagan
She hangs there in front of me
I don't know what is more horrifying
Her great swollen head
or her thin withered body.
I imagine her as a lady
who has very prominent nipples
Amazing ones
Each aureole a bailey
Each papilla a bin of grain

Eagle hunting is not for biddies. Something
either is stoutly done or meekly not
but eagle hunting is non-biddy endeavor
Now, Nixon was an eagle hunter. I believe
the hidden eagle is in the national archives.
9:10 AM The snow in Indiana is very

white. 142 M I stop to pee & retrieve
sunglasses fr. trunk. Now NANCY REAGAN
was an eagle. She was an eagle-chickadee
w/ nickel-sized nipples that glinted on her
small bouncing boobies
fr. high above as she gyred in her
prophylaxis over Ronnie. 70 east 10:38 AM
CST. This eagle, Nancy Reagan, had
been beaten soundly & its feathers shorn
by special trauma scissors. Yet now,
years later, they had grown back
and her little nickel nipples did not
flash as much. Indianapolis 10:48 AM
"I've always been a nester."—Nancy
Reagan, My Turn (Random House, 1989)
"And I'd be down in the oval room
wrestling w/ a chair." Nancy Reagan (ibid)

We hunted the eagle again b/c it was
trying to eat our meat bees, preying
on our herd and hive of important
and beefing apians. Awful eagle. 203.7 M
sky almost featureless grey. Anthony Creek
"I was born on July 6th, which makes me
a cancer." Nancy Reagan (actually said this).
"Big Blue River" 212.7 M. Let us burn a
hospital just as an American President might
Let's burn down that nursing home
just as an CEO would. Let's get in the way
of the Antiques & charge a toll at the
entrance to modernity. Whitewater
River 229 M 11:31 AM EST. STOP
TO PEE 11:40-4. Yet all the lakeborn

timid eagles who had loved to build
their nests of wire and pipe and nails
(Welcome to Ohio blue arch 249 M 11:54 AM)
were all we had to hunt the Nancy
eagle with, w/ her chests of nickels,
her shining solid nipples. The
churchyard of Minerva is not where
she sprang from (for that place is
The Origin of Owls), no the Nancy
Reagan Eagle sprang from
the churchyard of manure we

couldn't tell, at first, which of these two the
eagle had camped in. But as the eagle smelled
of poop we suspected the latter. The power
of her pooped youth—no longer smelled
on her, but the smell of the churchyard
of Manure was strong in her feathers,
strong enough to taint most of the weather
in a basswood copse. The Nancy Reagan Eagle
smelled of shining shit: Yes and in that
basswood copse a stampede of bees
that smelled of hamburger in their
meaty beefiness: they! had brought
the odorous eagle there frightening
the bees that slapped like manic dots
the trunks and trees, hizzing from
the eagle glinting in her poopy booby nipples.
JCT 75 N & S 282 M 12:20 PM EST.
I feel tired at 12:30 PM. I feel
like an weakened fish driving his bowl
through the alien air. Over me, in Ohio
sky, the grey—featureless altostratus. It is if

I drive a fishbowl through clear
piggy feet of the sky.

There in that wood were many crows
chickens, turkeys, many
fowl of the air and of the soil, fowls
of the trees and flowing and fellowing water
and there I went in my fishbowl to surveil the
foul poaching of the poopy nickel eagle.
320 M I pass an "oversize load"
cream fiberglass boat, a bulbous
beige shadow slipping over the
snow. The snow in the tan stubble
underscoring the crisp gray cuneiform
tree trunks. Splotches of brown bush
festoon like dun bunting the skirt
of the copse behind which scrim
flickered & pasted (270 N 340 M
1:13 PM) the over-plump shapes of
meat-puffy fowl—and these the
greedy eagle ignored, for she could
hear the crisp small slaps of the meat
bees manic w/ fear. 71 N 358 M
1:30 PM. Flies and speck gnats
toggle about these bees, but the
poop and nickel eagle sees these

as but a jiggling pepper, loose
and flecking clouds of spice food: this eagle
hunts now only the meat bees
(because they're the size of pills,
and Nancy loved pills) 71 N for
some 20 min's now. I seem to be

climbing out of some valley. Stop
to Gas & go Exit 151 71 N 390 M
1:57 PM. Get coffee. 2:07 PM back
on road. Sunny, bright, barking clear
on 71 N in the beautiful, easy breasts
of hills south of Cleveland.

There is a hint of grease & ale here
in these distant foothills of the
Alleghenies. But there/ are no
meat bees here, though I see now
& again against the almost
American-flag blue of the sky the
melancholy smudge of a disconsolate
eagle hunting after the meatbees
over the College of Wooster: I see
Nancy Reagan, her small breasts
flashing, hosing
the very air w/ her sight, seeing

what delicious bees her fearsome gaze/ might
wash out of the gusts.[20] I pass
Galvanized steel grain silos here that shine
silver and apricot in the low sun to the south
behind me—429 M 2:40 PM
"Perpetual, mild reform" was "true
conservatism" according to Teddy
Roosevelt—because mild reform

---

20 "Round she throws her baleful eyes,
That witnessed huge affliction and dismay,
Mixed with obdurate pride and steadfast hate.
At once, as far as angels' ken, she views
The dismal situation waste and wild."
— Milton, Paradise Lost, Book 1.

allows capital to grow w/out
running the risk of revolution.
76 east 448 M   3 PM
The bourgeois society that Teddy
Roosevelt loved was "efficient, loving,
aesthetic, mother controlled," according
to Edmund Morris. Heavy traffic &
many potholes near Akron. Sun in
the right backseat window. Spindly
shadows of the roadside trees crinkle
across the highway—and some of them
leap up & whip silently across my
dark gray dash.

500 M . 3:46 PM   Bridge over wide
long frozen & snow white lake on
which distant shapes sate & walked
ice fishing. Meander Reservoir 508 M
There are 36,000 movie screens
nationwide, 26,000 are in corporate
cineplexes. 523 M OH/PA border?
Shenango River. Less snow here.
538 .7 M HIGH & LONG PILE OF
POTATOES IN MEDIAN, from a truck that
crashed and was towed away leaving the
moraine of its potato cargo, the cardboard
of the potato boxes
resembles half done origami
And here I am again at the O D
Anderson Interchange 543 M
89.7 FM NPR 4:26 PM
88.5 FM NPR 4:38 PM 553 M
89.1 FM 555 M. Scrubgrass Twnshp

Stone Church Rd Bridge   564 M
I blow through the apricot light
of Emlenton, PA   567 M   4:50 PM

Today there is a "virtual march on
Washington" 585 M Majestic bridge across
deep ravine cupping the large
Clarion River diapered in a
surface of snow. In fluorescent
manila sunset flickering through
leather trees & over white snow
I find an oldies station and
Van Morrison's "Brown Eyed Girl"
O How Fleeting are life's perfect
moments: pleasure & insight
combine—and are gone. I flicker
through shadows
and sometimes see on the road
a deeper shadow nestled in
a widening shade.   596.2 M
96.3 FM—oldies station
90.1 NPR 607 M
The Bush Adminstration ships
Patriot Missiles to Iskander, Turkey.
Iskander named
for the conqueror Alexander who stopped
there on his own Anabasis (to India)

643 M I stop to eat—fish sandwich
            6-6:10
104.7 NPR—high channel for NPR
            643 M
6:10 PM Deep twilight. I deploy the

dash cigarette-lighter light
100% cloudcover suffused w/ a faint
tan-gray light   can still see the page by the
ambient light & amn't using cig-lighter
light. This is an Aluminum Al-Star
Lamy w/ I think Parker Quink
(black) and broad stub nib.

The old Nancy Reagan eagle is still
circling high, but circling in a
way we cannot understand: her
gyre pattern is chaotic, the wind
buffles her skirt, she bangs around
the sky a storm tossed cannon
a rusty big-holed skirt-wearing
cannon w/ nickel nipples

and a beak of fury rimmed w/ reddest
lipstick: the lipstick of ire. And around
the great hole of her cannon fundament
are slim and flapping labia. Her labia
are thin as gong metal.
688 M playing tag w/ semi's past
several miles in these PA mountains.
There now off the side of the road
as I approach Bucknell University
there now runs a little possum
which the eagle sees. I see the eagle
dive, its skirt snapping at the air,
the big cannon hole of its fundament
a great rusty zero—the possum,
teeth bared, dives under bush
and the eagle clangs into the pavement.

761 M I see those nuclear cooling
towers at Lime Ridge & Berwick, PA
Susquehanna River 764 M

pulled off to Gas at Mobil in Nuangola PA &
got lost briefly on sideroad—no signs & just
dark woods
801 STOP TO GAS in Wilkes Barre PA
8:30 PM must drive
2.5 m's to station!
412.7 m 10.061 gallons
8:45 back on road
"Youth is a curable disease" T. Roosevelt
826 M 84 east 9:07
"Great corporations exist only b/c they are
created and safeguarded by
our institutions. It is therefore our right & duty
to work in harmony w/ these institutions."
        —T. Roosevelt

"It is a horrible thing to realize
that we have a bully in the White House."
—A former aid to Benjamin Harrison
on Theodore Roosevelt
"Woe to thee, O Land, when thy King is a
child...."
        —Ecclesiastes

Metamoras (PA or NY?) 875 M 9:50 PM

        Welcome to New York 9:51 PM
        876 M

The very act of walking had packed a
grease into our heels' joints, the grease had
slipped & sloughed down fr. the pores of our
bones. That is why Americans stopped walking
in the mid 1980s. The first ones to stop walking
were Southerners: White Male gun-bearing
Southerners, the fat ones, the religious
fat ones. 915 M crossing the Hudson
       at 10:25 PM

The big prison is only a few miles into
New York. 922 M: To the left, on a dark hulk
of air, which I take to be a hill,
a distant colossal cross hangs
bulb-lit in the air. The eagle slammed

into the "Caution Deer X-ing" sign

probably thinking that the black
half-meter diagonally leaping stag
was a thin hesitant jackalope.

What is the history of Stenography?
Who invented stenography?
How does stenography work?

947 M STOP TO PEE AT REST STOP 10:55 pm
       11:03 back on road

Lou Reed—were you an influence
on Rap? ZZ Top is Amazing.

691 east 987 m 11:38 pm

Quinnipiac River 989 M The Doors
996   91 N
Mattabasset River 1001 M   11:51 pm
9 S   1002   11:52 PM
Alongside Mattabasset River 1007
        stoplights   speed limit 45

The Great bruised First Lady eagle
rose up, collected her clanging crapulous cannon,
        her nasty skirt, & her 2 spinning
nickels

and sat down w/ a sob & A
small disconsolate heave of her
wings, her terrible pointed wings.

1064   Welcome to Rhode Island
                        12:50 AM
89.9 FM eastern CT, Western RI NPR station

She hits her head, sputtering. She
is dejected. Brutal luck. Hit
her head. Her eyes cross.

Warwick RI 1089 M   1:13 AM
sad sad warwick. where 97 or so
were burned to death last week
Sad its malls. Sad its men.
        Sad sad its weeping moms.

The eagle shall go to Warwick
and cheer them. That is the
job of the First Lady eagle's responsibility!

Night View of Providence, pinned up w/ light
1099 M   1:23 AM
        1100 M Exit 20

N Main & College, left. 1:25 AM
Long red at Thomas & Main
1103 m   1:30 AM Arrive

    [katabasis]

3.2.03 Sunday Providence Set trip odo
Cumberland Farms Gas Station (Hope &
                    Romchambeau)
7:40 AM EST. Gray wet oily shitty
looking day. It's falling in small dots
as mist or slush. The spray
from the road is only green and oily.
An incomparably grey day. A head
Al Qaeda uncle caught today. Iraq
is destroying its Al Samoud Missiles.
7,000 N of St. Antonio. 8,000 in Houston
gather in Texas to support war.
Wonderful people, Texans. Odo 46541 30m
south of Providence. Rain smattering, wipers
on. Gray, green, white road strips, white
ditch snow, short brown rock cliffs
back the ditches. This is a Lamy
Al Star w/ broad stub.

40 m CT Welcomes Me. Jewish War
Veterans Memorial Highway. I pass
A late model Ford van, blue, w/ "88"
sticker, white male driver. Have

heard this # is meant to signify White
Supremacy, 8 being 8th letter, H, signifying Heil
Hitler. I wish I lean over into my passenger
window and honk, push out my arm, and give
him the finger, moving
my finger, hand, and forearm up
and down ludely while mouthing "Fuck you,
Fuck you." 55 m 8:30 AM Khaled
Sheik Muhammad caught in Pakistan
Switzerland wins America's cup, 1st
European nation to do so.

9 N 73 m 8:47 AM Chester Bowles
Highway. Very wet. CT's very wet,
white. 90.5 FM NPR. Much fog
ragging across the rocksalted
highway. ½ M visibility. Brown
& green and greased and gray. Flash
flood watch for this area.

The Israeli Army is a terrorist organ.
Turkey's parliament rejects
proposal to put US troops on its soil.
Good for them! 691 West 109 m
The chickadee did Kung Fu
        Against the 7 Angels
Fog. The eagle arrested the chickadee.

½ m visibility, light rain as I
approach Waterbury, CT 124 m
9:33 AM God!: St. Mary's Hospital
looks red & warm in its
windbreaker of 19th Cent. brick—o babies

inside, stay warm! I miss someone.
Am sad how I miss her and C___, and Melpomene
No reports today about the NSA
's bugging the offices of UN
Security Council Ambassadors' offices
it was leaked to <u>The Observer</u> yesterday.
158 M Welcome to NY.
Heavy rain, I am hungry.
C___ lost her 2nd tooth in Delaware
on Hwy 95-S 2.26 around 5 PM
eating an apple, #1 lower left incisor
as we drove to Baltimore for the AWP
conference, she and Melpomene and D we all drive in
the tiny car, Toyota Echo, someone fights
in the car again, S and C___ in backseat watch
the fight/s, the song "I really want to be far
away from a Difficult Person, she's
impossible," is heard on radio.
C___ lost the 1st lower incisor
on the rt side of her jaw in Illinois
on I think 1.23.03

Fishkill NY (182 m) you are rainy
but not foggy. Same w/ you, Peekskill.
"Caution Fog on Bridge
REDUCE SPEED"as I approach
Hudson River 187 m 10:30 AM
Some ICE pilling on the Hudson. Seagull 2
o'clock in windshield. Visibility 1 mile
Heavy rain now, 10:35 AM, am
hydroplaning 62 mph Fogs
At tops of hills. Soggy brown deer,
its body twisted as if turned by

a strong wind on rt. shoulder
car pulled rt & lt by streams of
water in road. w/ ethanol fuels
this car gets 10% fewer mpg. Yesterday,
coming up from Baltimore and the AWP
w/ 4 people & luggage in car, I got
44 mpg—using 87 lead & 100% gasoline
Foggy but <u>very</u> bright 202 M

at Wallkill Rier. A light suffusing
the fog, a light at once so apricot
& so cream-white that I
taste cupboard-warm apricots & cool milk.
I pass, in the gray but glowing brightness, a
dayglo orange semi tractor w/out a trailer.
It is brightly spewing a tearing & swirling
plume of oil-gray mist from its wheels.
Rain loud & heavy near Goshen NY
the clean snow here puffy with sog.

I pass a 24' Penske hermit crab
towing a quaint green Citröen. Rifling up
& down the FM band trying to soak
up the last bit of New York, New
England news and progressivism before
I head into Propagandsylvania and
white male "Family" pro-war stations.
And "Pennsylvania Welcomes [Me]"
228 M 11:08 AM.

237 M 11:17 AM ½ tank gone
          39.8 mpg
Promised Land Truckstop 255 m

11:30 Exit 26, PA, heavy fog
        255 m
3,000 American soldiers left last week
for the Philippines. 102 yrs ago
Henry Cabot Lodge rose on the Senate
floor to report Atrocities committed
there by American soldiers comm'd by
A General Smith who told his men to torture
and kill Philippine guerillas, &
they did: disembowlings, beheadings,
castrations (then the gagging the guerillas
w/ their own testicles.) I heard a report
at the AWP on Friday, relayed by
James Cervantes, that an American soldier
in the Gulf War had a photo album of
himself in the acts of
disemboweling & beheading young
Iraqi soldiers (one a young boy). Rain stopped
11:45 Some fog remains on hilltops

380 N 275 M 11:50 AM.
81 S 281 M 11:56 AM
Teddy Roosevelt studied jujitsu
"You have slain uncounted thousands of the
people you have desired to benefit."
        —Senator Hoar to Teddy Roosevelt
Can see cloudy sky 1st time since RI:
has been fog since then, am in Scranton PA
at noon, passing Scranton airport 12:05.
        Some of these browns here in the
ditch
near Scranton Are so wet and dark
they are Almost Blue.

Grasses hold these browns, & some rock
and bark (though I see some
birch trees too). FOG: NEAR
NUANGOLA. Visibility 1/10th M.
Now 100 feet! And KABOOM! the
hill slopes & out of milk we
whang—about 4 cars in my pack
into washing sunlight weakened
by very high clouds.

315 M here 81 S rides precipitously
Above the tiny broad valley.
80 W 317 M
The old head of the eagle, like a gourd
    too heavy for the wind, decided
that it wd keep its body there on
the road in the loose wind slung
by the whooshing fret of the traffic

until she'd affixed the asphalt-nicked nickels
back on her tender breast cones.
"My body and head struck that sign
so hard my nipples jumped ship off
the light frigates of my chest.
I do not like to see my nipples peregrined
among the loose gulls, my nipples cannot
swim!"
            expansive snow in the valley
to the south—much melted in its
height but not in acreage
            365 m cross wide
Susquehanna 1:10 PM EST

Lockhaven about 30 miles from
Susquehanna River warm today 30+
391 m 9.775g 1:30 PM

      Ingram's   Market
     Loganton, PA   40 mpg
395 m outside Loganton, where
I see 2 horsebuggies—one going
uphill past Ingram's Market gasstation
and one downhill—while my tank
was filling. The horse going uphill
was walking, the horse going
down was racking. The people,
I assume, were sitting.

Now here in mid-afternoon near Bellefonte
80 skirts the south rim of a white valley
and, to the right, through picketing trees,
a mile off I spot a crisply white SUV
hurtling parallel me, at speed: a fleet
shadow. It is the government CIA my shadow
hater of poets administration God Bless the
Patriot Act and John Ashcroft, perfect
candidate for a cross-dresser every
generation needs
its J Edgar Hoover.

2:05-2:19 Stop at McDonald's for
Fish Sandwich & coffee I have 2
fish fillets. Passing through the brown & white
Alleghenies, whizzing along many
cliffs, speckles of rain perch out of
the Air & dry on my windscreen.

Wind is gaining, buffeting my slight & efficient
Toyota God Bless the Japanese
I set the 3 vent dials on my dash
to the right titration in flow & temp
and wait for my coffee to cool
This Automobile is tight humming pod
under zooming crows, cackling
as an arrow past the tan &
blurry deer. 2:45 PM EST Passed by silver
Stratus w/ US Govt Plates, 2 passengers
driver wearing phone mouth mic
big man, baseball hat 75 mph

457 M, passing through a rill of
runoff traversing hwy near bridge
car slows markedly & I hypothesize
the 40 mpg this morning due in
some part to the earlier rain & hydroplaning
            465 M Highest Pt on 80 east of Miss.
            3 pm EST.
Teddy Roosevelt was, yes, anti-trust
and pro-regulation. And based on
his concerns re the coal crisis in
his 1st term, I can't help but think
he wd have found the current administration's
deregulation and fiscal policies irresponsible.
This is now a Lamy Vista w/ broad italic.
Gorgeously composed farm—its bldg's
hill, cattle, & bales—the snow
there—487 m, near Reynoldsville, PA
2 M's before its exit—lying to the
right, the sky so gray & uniform, the wind
puckering in my windows, that

the tans & browns are
richer than a rainbow.

North Fork Creek 496 M 3:25 EST
Dennis Lloyd told me yesterday my book's
sold a thousand copies. Said it's not selling
like a first book. Snow
prickling against windshield.
Separated by 1/10th of mile are 2
packets of flesh on the white dashes mid-road:
Packet 1, a collected gobbet of tan-brown fur
& Purple intestines; Packet 2, 6 inches of
a raccoon's tail. Nothing else
Allegheny River 531 M 3:55 pm
            am passed by blue Chrysler van
w/ sticker declaring "I believe in
angels" snow fluffy now, not
specky & hard
All Around me the hue of dishwater
all day—and tan brown bottoming it
550 m—halfway pt. 4:10 PM EST
6 miles before I-79 snow
the size of teeth, I have
            to defecate.

O D Anderson Interchange, Now I-79.
Dusk-like brown light at Shenango
River 572 M 4:30 PM
"Welcome to Ohio" 575 m Snow
Flurries, high winds, but warm: snow
teeth turn to waters on the windscreen.
Light brighter now, more like dishwater now
Must so often reach in and pull my scrotum

forward & up for the pain that I may
consider driving w/ my pants & sport briefs
around my knees. Museum of Labor &
Industry Akron Hello Meander Reservoir!
Hello 4 ducks! Through the shitty plume of grit
in its wake I approach & pass an
aluminum semi-trailer w/ a filthy, sodden
American flag twitching shyly on its stern.

It is at once fearsome & delightful
that Nationalism is the retreat
        of the tacky & the stupid.

607 M Stop to Defecate 5:01-07 PM EST
        Upon exiting restroom car & vicinity
        Covered completely in snow specks.
Slush on road. Snow larger now: its cold
cloakbuttons fall on the road.

Dried leaf (oak) falls to rd & rises
        like struck & desperate bird.
The wind sounds desolate

Kent State University next right.
Squall is, apparently, full-on storm.
Am approaching snow plow
71 S 652 M 5:52 pm EST
655 m Here's that stupid
flag-ass truck

"As civilization grows, warfare
becomes less and less the normal condition
of formal relations." Theodore Roosevelt

6:08 pm EST light fading snow still
falling.Visibility one mile
windshield fluid low, A dash
            light tells me.

Jetta stuck in median after
slipping there
"If a man continually blusters, if he lacks
civility, a big stick will not save
him from trouble; neither will speaking softly
avail if back of the softness there
does not lie strength, power."TR re Pres 43?
            Light purple dusk
6:30 PM 694 m
Damn dark now 719 m 6:55 pm EST
720 m I stop to fill up
wiper reservoir & get tacos
at Taco Bell. 7:15 pm back on
is G. Bellicose Bush an
simian blowhard?

road slick with snow, on rightwing AM radio
I hear callers encouraging
the US to leave the UN. China rumored
planning Taiwan invasion for "Bush
Doctrine" pre-emptive reasons.
I dislike pulling over to eat,
pee, defecate, and gas, and wd
prefer to cross this nation musing
in this almost bodiless way: but isn't that
just very American of me: I believe in Angels
too! And wanna be one! Let's incite
Armageddon

Jesus Loves me this I know
for Jerry Falwell told me so
8:10 PM EST 782 m 4 Car
Accident in right ditch—spinouts
wide & far into ditch, police not
yet arrived.
10.179 g 393.9 M
Gas at South Vienna, OH 18:15-22
     & Pee

Very icy. Must not jerk wheel.

840 m no longer icy. Black Women
were first entertained in the White
House by Theodore Roosevelt.

Can't see a damn thing out there,
Ohio reduced to the hwy, the
headlight cone, high   sodium
lights, wild ices have perched on
the armor of the road

Thank You for Visiting Ohio
     850.0 M 9:24 PM EST
What is the deal w/ Indiana and
billboards? Again the tugging
of the scrotum: it is a delicate
skin. Thank you, God, for pens.
This is a Rotring Core med or
     broad nib.
AWP in Baltimore was interesting.

Very good to hang w/ Pierre Joris

We talked of fountain pens &
to Watch D take
two panels through its presenters.
Meet Kazim Ali, Anastasios
Kozaitis, Patrick Herron, Diane
Boller, Josh Corey, Jane Sprague,
Rebecca Wolff, Lynn Emanuel,
Forrest Gander, Terrence Hayes, Natasha
Trethaway & see Jim Bertolino,
Crystal Williams again,
I saw thistles jiggling, saw
tumbleweeds hunched pensively
in some Alcoves & Corners of the
Renaissance Harbor Hotel waiting
their turn at the elevators. At one point
a guy asked a question at the panel,
I walked up to him afterward and shook
hand and asked name, he said
"I'm just a student." and I wanted to
say "Jesus Christ, man, get a grip" and
give him a hug
898 10:05 pm EST STOP to pee in
        Rest Stop. Near Indianapolis
124 m at ¼ tank consumed. I pass
smoking pickup, as I pass, I hear
it rattling. Outskirts of Indy
        9:30 PM CST.

In Indy now: the hilly Lilly building
hunkers imperiously on the right at 926 M,
under large orange lights that
spell "Lilly" in Cursive—each side
beaming the name toward the 4

cardinal directions of the planar Universe,
and above the Quartet of Lillys
an huge AMERICAN FLAG shakes rigidly
In a Southeast Wind, the flag is
very anxious-looking: looking in need
of PROZAC. How perfect the company of
Prozac and Forced Sleep has given Parisi's
POETRY MAGAZINE a 100 million dollars.
74 W 940 M 9:51 pm CST
"My United States of Whatever"—#1 song
on MTV in Germany

Dark and quiet west of Indianapolis.
Few cards on road now except this one,
Jack of Spades. I miss, in this dark
driving and its hard pinpricks of lamps
the early day and its boiling teeth of snow,
greasy mist, random almost whale-breath-
smelling fogs, the luminous dishwater sky
the wet-brightened tans, blaring
charcoals of the damp trees (at times
their barks almost blue) and the sogged snow
clumped and frumpy as damp table salt.
Now it's just a steady reeling into
blackness.
            10:20 PM 975 m Providential break
in clouds affords me stellar view
of most of Orion in my driver's window
I count 12 towers blinking now Across
            140 degrees of horizon fr. a slight

promontory near HWY 231 interchange
before Sugar Creek 978 m, all

blinking red, the singular color
of information's pointillism
10:35 PM CST STOP TO PEE 990 M
          Waynetown IN 10:37 back on
74 West. Graffito as I peed: "Top
needs bottom 1/3" This is A
Waterman Phileas, medium nib.
"There is nothing more practical
in the end, then the preservation of
beauty." Teddy Roosevelt, at Stanford
University. Molar-sized snow briefly
near Shale Pitt Rd. 998 m
          What Teddy Roosevelt shouted
when naturalist John Muir burned a
dead tree for him:
          "THIS IS BULLY!"

1012 m "Illinois Welcomes [Me]" too
          10:58 pm
I am very tired and approaching
Champaign/Urbana 1040 m 11:22 pm
Gnats of snow streak in my
headlights "Bloomington 33" 1066 m 11:45
Tired. Worried about there being a
post-it note on my door when I
get home, by my landlord, the
policeman Rick Davis, for rent.

Nancy Reagan lay at the roadside
all day, frightened by the gloomy
passing horses, until she remembered
she was an eagle—and she rose up,
finally, into the cold cloak buttons of

the snow, hauling the great
cannon of her torso and
            its rusted orifice

into the ranch of the air's ceiling,
the throw pillows up there,
the cool afghan of the jet stream.
1090 m A glow Above My rt side
of windshield: Bloomington

glow is sodium colored, electric,
in low cloud, electrical gray yellow haze

exit 135 12:13 AM 1096 one
last tug at scrotum, then off hwy.

            12:20—at yard.

THE BRIDGE

There was enough of me, everyone said, and I should leave. But I could not leave, and I said so, I could not leave. But they said I should leave and I could not leave and I said I could not. They insisted I leave. I explained I could not. Leave, they said. No, I said. Goddamnit no, I said. Leave you simple Mudderclipper!, they said. No I said. No I said. Look I said. Goddamnit they said. Goddamnit I said. We stood there saying no and goddamnit.

So I left.

In the consequent explosion were several leaves, some last coins, the components of a chicken, some blue in the form of paint that had been torn from a plow at the beginning of the explosion, a plow, the farmer's boot and feet, the pulped hooves of his ox, the completely "intimidated" sound waves of the ox that had been lowing.

So I left. And the hound and the men with drinks welcomed me among them who were especially pleased with the comfort given by the hound's considerate mitigation of its own annoyances.

I told them in the coming prohibitions we will go behind bushes and stow our bottles in the warm grottos of our animals' buttocks. We will insert our beer bottles in our dogs and work our wine well into the cows. Cats will take the tiny airplane bottles of liquor. Yes, we will put bottles in the buttocks of our cats.

[Silence. A pause.]

So I said to them again, "I have funded the flight of weird owls. And still the chickens creak under their melancholia." They told me get the eff out. We are Germans, they said, und du bist ein widerlich Geier.

I said that they would eat the ant's venison, a beef of the dragonfly, a paté of tawny moths. You'll do all this. What's more, that chancre looks like someone clipped a pepper to your lip. The world is but a quilt of inadequacy. You sicker effer??!, they said.

I said I saw a bull in a lily. It was a big lily, a small bull. Leave they said you are an abuser of corn.

And peacocks are steeds for eyes, I tried. That a toothfairy convention would be loud because of the tickling.

So I said: Indeed, consider the booming made from a fox's butt when it is placed beneath a tractor.

Go, they said.

No, I said. Go you simple Mudderclipper, they said.

Oh, I see, I see, Fine. I see. I get it. Fine. Very very fine. You would make me to walk out into the field on my horse whose bones are, though not as delicate as eyelashes, weak?

Yes they said. Yes finally, they said.

["Then a victim due for sacrifice (when the construction of the winter camp was complete) escaped outside the rampart before the work was done. Moreover, some soldiers' javelins caught fire—a particularly significant portent since the Parthenian enemy."]

3.7.03 – 3.17.03

[anabasis]

Friday, at curb, 3.7.03 6:27 AM set odo
At Kurb on Kreitzer cold
120.5m 3.719 g 6:40 get gas
and top off Air in tires
I-74 east 6:58 pm. Have headache
Have stuffed nose. The back of mouth
and throat crusted with mucoidal stucco
& gypsum. Am however wearing
soft brown corduroys.
I I-74 east into morning light.
Blobby sun (not crisp) 10 degrees off horizon
in left side of windshield.
It is a cream a milk sun
made so by faint blue cloud
that stretch wisped
North to South up to about 15 degrees above
horizon. Grain elevators and
islands of farm copses sit hazy
in blue post-dawn silhouette
all over the east.
Le Roy, Illinois 1 Mile 70 mph.
"Military forces are merely responding
to Saddam Hussein's hostile aggression."
—Kuwait Central Command US Spokesman

After Iraq, why not invade Israel, why the
eff not. Apparently
Resident Bush last night on White House

TV said Hussein has "surrounded himself
w/ Killers"—7:23 AM As the sun climbs,
creaming, it pulls a shelf of milk clouds with
it, so the origin of the morning light stays
creamy "origin of Kaskaskia River" 45 M,
After which fields give way to a
statistical woodedness. Morning traffic
in Urbana Champaign. east of it
a land of silhouettes in smoke blue
trees, still blinking towers, early bridges,
power lines, moving patches of billboards,
all's hued a child's powder blue.
Road bears a faint damp shine.
7:50 AM 74 M Ignorant Indiana
approaches, I pray for fog &
lightning storms to cross & lid the state

that I may not see it or hear there
77 M Middle Fork Vermilion River—
A great dell here w/ large sloughy
beaver-dammed area. "It's a humbling
experience for me to know that
thousands of people have lifted me
and my family up in prayer."
—G W Bush, last night in press conference
I wonder if next time they lift him
we could Give him a little shove into the
Potomac (Welcome to Indiana, Crossroads
of America—8:02 AM 88 M)
No fog or lighting storms.
But if we cd get his whole family
lifted on a prayer vapor
we cd drop them from A great

height by suddenly turning off
the Vapor Prayer beam.

Laura Bush wd survive because her
skirt wd Act as a Parachute
we wd see her attractive groin region
as she fell, the tasteful Amount of fat
on her thighs / rippling Rigorously
in her grief plummet.
As She lands next to the bloody bone pools
of her husband (next to the fur stubble
and purple gut ropes of the family dog) she
sees that atop the splat of mush that was once
the 43rd President, the only intact relic
recognizable, like the Wicked Witch
of the West's black cone of hat Atop
the Melted witch, is the hawky pointy
flared nose of Bush's not-too-bright
face today Hans Blix will make an interim
report to the UN Security Council
Sugar Creek, God Bless you: I lift
you up on a crowd of prayers, 123 M
from Normal, Illinois.

Last night in A speech,
before the ill-informed gullible country-music-
listening pious sanctimonious violent nation
Resident Bush said
he does not need UN Security Council
permission to wage war & we wonder
why he asked for it / in the effing 1st place.
This reminds me why I take such great
pleasure in disobedient youths & why

I am annoyed by obedient students
who ask, slavish, obsequious, what I
want: people like them become cops, hold
guns, cruel managers, glaring bureaucrats.
8:55 AM 74 east still not broadcast
—like that of Febr 14th—of Blix
and Al Baradei's interim
reports—can't help but think this is
b/c the last one was so embarrassing
to Bush & this one is expected to be too.

9:20 AM—152 m AM NPR station—
about to "go over to" Blix's report!
"From NPR News in Washington, this is
a Special Report."

Eagle Creek Reservoir: its big gray
dam, snow-streaked. I feel very friendly
toward that reservoir. 70 E 167 M
"the delegates are beginning to fill the
chamber." Am blowing on the elevated
highway through clouded Indy. Now
I am passing out of Indy. The sky gray
with snow gristle. 9:25 Am CST Assoc. Press
reports 2 small sons of Bin Laden's lieutenant
have been "captured." We are a nation who
captures children. I pass A white semitrailer
pulled by matching tractor, on
the trailer's back & side a "Map" of
US & superimposed on it A cartoon
cheesy "scroll" & over it
the word "Covenant" & under it "Transport."
Christianity is a cartoon religion.

A gavel slaps 4 times 194 m 9:35 AM
"The 4 thousandth seven hundredth &
14th Security Council is brought to order."

"I invite the representative of Iraq
to take a seat at the council table."
"I invite Dr. Blix to take a seat at the
council table." "I invite Dr. Al Baradei
to take a seat at the council table."
"Nameless Creek." 203 M 9:45 AM CST.
east of Indianapolis, new snow, lately fallen
"Six Mile Creek" "Anthony Creek" 206
Switch to 92.1 FM NPR 210 M. The garish
double-decker billboards begin
219 FM east central Indiana: the
trees here, leafless & dark, are taller
than in areas to the west, impressive,
at times in these small-chested hills
the road flies through copses, which
are by nature thin and shallow, making the
road at times seem shallowly & briefly
forested. Wilbur Wright Rd,
228 M 91.1 FM. Uniform
luminous gray above "White Water
River" near the "Amish Cheese Shop"

Grackles burst & whirr fr. Rt shoulder
as I pass. I do not see them Again
in my mirrors, perhaps they are flying
above my car a raincloud of guano-bearers
After half mile without seeing them
in my mirrors, I unroll driver's side
window and look up, glasses almost blow

off face, but I don't see the flock.
10:12—10:17 AM CST STOP TO PEE
at 235 M rest stop in Indiana.
Warm out, upper 40s. Ohio State Line
250 M—that blue steel arch
is still there! God Bless the Ambassador
from Syria—I say this from the
depths of A hothead nation, 4
miles into Ohio on 74 east, to
my rt. & lt. A freaky flicker
of maple copses—for mentioning
the recent worldwide protests against
the Bush Administration—and
for saying he doesn't understand why
the US seems to think War is
"the best—and not the last—option"
God Bless the Goddamned Ambassador!
I can just hear 43 saying to
hisseff "Goddamb that Jewboy Arab"

"An Act of Robbery"—that's the
phrase the Syrian Ambassador
did USE: yeah eat it, Rumsfeld
Faraq Al Sharah is his name.
Change stations: 91.7 FM, 264 M
Some warm bouncy sunlight
boo-bah-loos here under blue
mackerel jet-streaked sky
have not seen a sky so jet-streaked
it is the evil jets of the Military
State Scenic River is brown & bouncy
flickery on its surface but
branchy & muddy on its banks

The Great Miami River is high & brown
Clouds are clearing sun is very
bright but slightly cloud-dimmed &
tinged w/ cloud manila. At Mad River
near Air Force Museum 292 M,
cumulus like slow-moving yellow-green
sheep-birds converge. F-16 passes over
HWY on its way to land.

300 M 11:10 AM Another MASSIVE hawk,
—powerful body, compact,
like an Aerial bomb
that eats & poops bunnies—hangs or
rather perches in small twiggy tree
staring south south east, its tan
brownly speckled wings folded as flat
pistols on the holster of its body. It does
not have boobies.
                    It is an <u>American</u>
hawk.
            11:26 AM CST
thoroughly cloudy again. Same blue
mist hazing distant tree. The pain
in my throat has lessened.
Little Darby Creek State & National
Scenic River 331 M, am making massive,
snapping sneezes—clear flopping mucus
sparkles on my right hand. I wipe it
reluctantly on my brown corduroys

I-270 N 342 M 12:50 PM EST
sun out Wham! As I bounce over
the Olentangy State Scenic River

356 m fr. BL & Northwest of Columbus
2 Canada Geese traverse hwy
50 ft Above car. They do not honk.
It occurs to me I should have
honked at them
On rt, in bright sun N of Columbus,
375 m fr. BL, I see, in a muddy,
furry oval of hay, a press of
horned Kine in tumid Anoraks
feeding & lazing in sun booms:
I notice in shock they are bison.
Small hawk kites over median,
southward, yawing
     STOP TO EAT, GAS, PEE 1:30 exit
151 10.1122 g 390 m = 38.57 mpg very low
mpg 1:40 A fish sandwich
at McDonalds. My sinuses ache me.

1:52 pm EST back on road
and so Laura Bush picked up her
husband's hawky-pointy flared nostril
nose, smelled it, sniffed hard at it,
cried about it and put it safely
in her bosom brassiere. There in
turn it sniffed and snuffed in
little booms her bosom smells
76 east 2:44 pm 450.7 m fr BL.
Long steep downward slope near
Wadsworth OH, never noticed before
Traveling perpendicular to me on
an underpass beneath
the freeway, I spy a large clear white
Ford pickup w/ an immense American flag

on a 6 ft pole flickering Above its
hitch-bulb and I am once again shocked
at the ghastly, kitschy, tacky, tasteless
and disturbingly hick-like & white
non-urban, gun-bearing & ignorant

nationalism, which is. Nationalism is.
490 M 3:20 pm near Mt. Union
College, am very tired.
3:33 PM I sneeze explosively.
And, simultaneously, the loosened nose
of G W Bush sneezes between
Laura Bush's easy breasts w/ a puffy bang
rocketing the wedge of flesh
up the Valley of her cleavage
slopping her firmly under the chin
and slipping back w/ a snotty swash into
her silk and smelly valley.
Meander Reservoir 510 M 3:39 pm
80 e 3:41 pm 513 m
"For the first time in my life I have
had to confess I am ashamed of my
country."—Richard Olney, 1903, re:
Roosevelt's seizing of the Panama Canal
Pennsylvania Welcomes You 527 M
STOP TO PEE 3:53—3:57

In Western Pennsylvania near
Clintonville, A bright but long-
shadowed March afternoon as the Alleghanies
begin, smattering of snows remain in
the woods and the large
meadows/small fields, but in

median, a shallow-v in cross-section
the tan dead grass slicked-down by
snow melt.
Am very achey.
  Behind U. S. Mail truck 5303
speed 75 mph. Sun directly behind
me, I pass the mail truck on a hill
The slant-lit plate of clouds
behind me filters sunlight to an
at times green-apricot wash that
warms & cools to my right rear, trees
& hills interlarding fat & slim shadows
into which I agreeably dip or
invite to whisker through my car
in flickers.

600 m 5 PM, 500 left to go.
7.5 hrs remaining at 67 mph ave.
Must Urinate Again.

Items aching: Teeth
                  neck muscles
                  knuckles of hands
                  (all 26)
                  wrist joints
                  lower back
                  rear of pelvis
                  right & lt. knees
                  joint of lt. big toe

Bladder has orange pain in it, like
     a little bun of sunlight

—a coin of heat in my urine bag. At 613
miles
 5:10 pm Rest Area
on rd Again 5:14

Items aching after rest stop:
                    Both ears
                    Forehead Above eyeballs
                    Throat
5:16 pm Take 2 Advils

5:38 Pm Most Aches have been
suppressed by Advil. Ears however
are popping more as I ride the Alleghanies
than before. Before my body
was, well, warring part against part, an bellum
omnium contra omnes, but I have
taken the UN Peacekeepers of the Advil
and now my neck is the only
pain in the neck, it is the
Mothereffy USA of my body.

Sun a dark bobbing tangerine or
red clown nose direct behind me
honking in the back of my hair
& damming a puddle of flaring orange
in my rearview—its light is
punching my eye pupils.
5:55 PM 661 M Switch on
headlights.
          280 M since fill, & ½ tank gone
          6:06 PM 47 mpg

Now 80 e here rides high in
Alleghenies at twilight, sun down,
deer glimpsed opposite hill (676m),
very snow, foraging. I light an
American Spirit (light) and pass
Bald Eagle State Park near Altoona
feeling both more & less American
than America itself yes that's it. 683 m
the light is such it looks like
my headlights aren't on though they
are, a semi tractor jackknifed
against its trailer in expansive right ditch.
            Odd bluing butch-cut
dromedary hills to the left
"Be Kind   on
Be Careful   back of
Be Your Self   semi-trailer
Be Your Best Self—
            Kane is Able!"

700 M 6:30 PM. Those great
cliffs that so make me feel
like I'm driving a toy on a
counter past half a cut cake.

705 M
"The neutral tinted individual
is very apt to win against the man
of pronounced views & active life."
            TR to George Otto Trevalian

776 m 737 feel terrible, tired,
have sneezed, just a minute ago,

messily (3/4 tank gone 388 m)
(81 N 783 M 7:44 pm)

And so the president's nose fell safely
back into the warm breast valley, from which
only a moment before it had launched
itself by expulsing w/ force 2 twines
of clear snot roping after

into which post-twine snot puddle
it flopped & settled w/ nearly
post-coital relief.
807.6 m STOP to Gas 416.1 m trip
                        9.310 g
                        44.7 mpg
829 pm back on rd.
8:44 84 e 825.2 m
GW Bush wanted to play the holy
warrior but thankgoodness all
that's left is his nose
welcome to New York 876 m
                        9:28 pM

88.5 FM Cool Radio Station NPR—
        type station
900 damn blessed miles Good God
        9:48 Pm
Cross the fat windy Hudson

This song as I cross the bridge
10:02 pm 926 m
makes me think of twirling
crazily in the wind

¼ tank gone 110 m
"East Branch Croton River" 942 m
never noticed this river before
CT border 945 m 10:28 pM

STOP FOR URINATION 946 m

975 84 e CT small snow—
it is fruit fly sized. It makes
me hear cellos.

691 e 985 m 11:10 PM exit 27?

She patted her bosom nose mouse
her George nasals safe in her bosoms
her fleshy double rocket wedge
995 m 91 N
I feel very friendly toward trucks
1001 m 9 S 11:25—100 M fr. Prov.
Snow. My car protects my scrotum
        fr. the snow.

You've got to be healthy in body to
Appreciate punk. I'm little under
not well.   Must …. drive. Must …. drive
M….
Each night she beds it down
in (95 N 1030 m 11:51 pm) A
box of Kleenex, the snuffling
blind nose
New London, CT home of bubble
Machines: USS Nautilus & Sub
Museum (closed Tuesdays)

A tall corpsman is crossing
my damp road. He is carrying a
Kleenex box, the wind is puffing
on his small delicate hat
96.7 FM East Hampton
        "progressive Radio"

God bless Aristophanes
Welcome to Rhode Island The Ocean
State, Jeepers it's dark here
I am in "the Zone" I feel like
that skipper in The Perfect Storm
of the "Andrea Gail," strapped to
the wheeling and sneezing
        I am wearing a Salmon Patagonia
jacket
People Are praying for Pres. Bush's
nose, which is once again nestled
in Laura Bush's breast bosom valley
of her booby cones like
A 3rd, a smaller breast
Approaching Providence "Historical Providence"
John Cougar Mellencamp 93.3 FM
        Hard Left

Bldgs & Steam of Providence
wind SW 8 mph 26 degrees F
Exit 20 1099 m 12:53 am
1100 m Exit 1
Woonasquatucket River on rt. water high
        Mirrory
Lt on Main. Restaurants still open
    people on street.

Chuckholes! A damn moonscape
this town
lt. at Doyle & Hope 1101.6
Rt on Cypress 1102.0 m
    Rt on BeHappy St, unplowed 1102.1 m
1:01 AM in driveway
    humming in my head really
    loud.

        [katabasis]

10:21am 3.16.03 1.3 m
fr. B & S & C Approaching
city ctr. Providence, sunny day
warm 55° N. Main & Steeple
bells ringin 10:25 AM. Rt.
onto Memorial. Nuggety reflections
of morning sun crinkle onto car. 95s 10:26
AM Someone, D, told me to get out of the house
this morning, to leave, go, this morning, this
Sunday that maybe divorce wd suit us,
Someone said this at About
9:45am. And frankly it wd. Packed. Said
goodbye to C___. This is a Pilot EastTouch
Broad w/ blue ink, ballpoint. Turn thought
toward the bearable: There is
something warlike about poetry
itself. Why have there been
so few peace poems?

Even the peace poems of Julia
Ward Howe are Absence of War

poems, bearing still militaristic
metaphors. Truck Lane
500 feet. CT Welcomes me
38 M 10:58am EST. New
London CT 56m   11:15 A
sandwich of blue, blue water
under the massive hwy bridge
blue sky over & then I drive
into brown prickle trees. Send dead flies to
Gerry LaFemina email Holli Bundy re
next yr's class. Have seen 2 maybe
3 hawks thus far

Hwy 9 N 71m 11:27am
AT 80m, near East Haddam on
Hwy9, passing Nathan Hale
Schoolhouse, I remove my wedding
ring—and I place it in a Small
white cardboard box I keep in
the dashboard, the box already
contains a blue glass Sperm Whale
purchased for me in the New
Bedford Whaling Museum
by D. in the Autumn.
Crow. Aircraft Rd one mile
88m fr. Providence. Am
incredibly sad. blue steel
double-arch "dromedary" bridge
over Quinnipiac River 95m
small bridge over Mattabasset
River as it confludes w Quinnipiac

91 S 100 m 11:53 AM

691 w 107 m Noon
Am incredibly depressed. I
gave it my best shot.
Quinnipiac River 113 m
I tried my damndest 84 w 114. 7
very warm, window open no
snow on shoulders now in median
but there it is in the hills
and the white opaque icefalls
on all the cliffs along the Danbury hwy
O Danbury, CT, I come again.
St. Mary's Hospital, I bless yr babies
as I zoom on
from you
very sadly.

Six inches of window roar
in my left ear, window roar &
tire treble. Beautiful day
it reminds me of youthful moments
driving in the West. The Housatonic
River is brown & crinkly w/ light
it is free of ice, I bounce off
the bridge & despite my sadness
for C___ today I feel again
A large bee zooming low &
steadily through grand things
Dead doe on her rt side
partially sunk into the soft mud
under the dead grass of the Median
It is morning and glorious!
Welcome to New York 155 m I
love going over the Hudson River

It's coming up soon
Crows worming at the edge of
some snow in the median
Croton River. Truck with an hundred
of orange bird cages stopped on
shoulder God I'm sad. Something
dangling from that SUV, A
light on a wire. The cliff
banked roads of Southern NY
Are bright in my sunglasses
A 23 yr old American woman
lay in front of an Israeli
bulldozer today as its operator
went to demolish
a Palestinian household. She
was crushed. [21]

      I turn fr ridiculous
NPR There is a "special"

Report" Don Gonye is in
the Azores. It is 1:05 PM
the US is calling this a
"Quadlateral" meeting wow
that's an idiotic Ari-Fleischer
backflip—quadlateral, not uni-
& not multi-, quad-
Hudson River 185m No ice
under the great "Hamilton Fish"
bridge—just a fleckish string or
two glued against the western shore

---

21 Rachel Corrie, alumna of The Evergreen State College.

9.792g 192m STOP TO GASS
& pee. "We conclude that
tomorrow is a moment of truth
for the world."—G W Bush
at "Azores Summit."

Who was it who said
"A good man should and must/
Sit rather down with loss, than rise unjust."
—Is that Ben Jonson or
Samuel Johnson?

WALLKILL River 200 M
1:35 pm Where O Where
is the IRAQIKILL River?
Where is the Rubiconkill?
Apparently it's right here.
"And that wealth will remain
theirs—[beat]—administered
by the UN."—Tony Blair,
british puppet and evildoer.
The swamps here in the Western
part of Southern New York
Completely covered in ice,
looks thin though
Pennsylvania Welcomes me
I drive through the turkey woods
far away sadly to my home. One
of my left upper molars is
bleeding

Brown, then white maculate snow
rt. & lt. road, a few dead

deer last few miles, fur matted
dark tan, damp. Near
Dingmans Ferry Lords Valley
see buzzards.
Stop to Defecate 254.6 m 2:20-29 pm
Eat 2 iburprofens due to molar ache.
The degree to which great works
of literature contain improper
things—or if not "containing"
improper things, is in itself,
its form improper—look up guy
at Duke Patrick Herron suggested.
Bad Traffic stall 276 m at
84—380 interchange 2:49 pm

Jam clear 3 pm 278 m
81   S 3 pm . Last night,
in her great pine bed, C___
and I had a jam session,
she on the ukulele, I on the
tin whistle.[22] Expansive brown
Nuangola Valley into which I
roll listening to Fleetwood Mac
Go Yr Own Way! I climb
out of yon Nuangola valley
w/ yr puffball making
chimney there on the north
hillwall listening to CCR
You are a beautiful valley
80 West 3:35 pm 316 M
Dog size retreads 3 times this

22 This was the last time C___ and I would hang out and play in her great pine bed, which I put
together and made.

afternoon

Maybe the warmth weather
will rise my mood
Mighty Susquehanna river
near Lime Ridge. Sun throwing down
late afternoon saffron from
behind a scrim of alto-cirrus
I find late afternoon light very
sad, I am very sad today
that crow looks crazy happy
Lightstreet Bloomsburg
Bloomsburg University. I hope
there are no sad people there.
I hope I am the only sad person
in the world. I am a Hope that C___ is not
sad. I hope she can be a happy
little person all her childhood
all her days. I will help her
all I can Buckhorn 2 miles

Farm, of Pennsylvania, Farm Pond,
Farm Pond ducks, trees trees
trees trees trees-trees trees
I love you C___ "I love you
Daddy" I love you C___ "I
love you Daddy" I love you C___
"I love you Daddy" I love you
C___. I love you I love you.
Here is that crazy Susquehanna again
below 4 pigeons & above
2 crows zuzzing and looping
over bridge. 4 wild turkeys

heads down in the
tan dead grass.
Switch 89.5 FM → 91.5 FM 385 m

Think I see bugsplats. Cant be
sure. Strange to see March
bugsmears. This land's cape is stiff
2 feeding deer. O hard Silos in
distant farm valley, I just
passed those mountainous
cut cake cliffs, I love you
little Valley. The fields of
Lamar PA at 4:45 today
are empty of snow, corn stubble
in mess of matted grass &
dead leaves in rt. ditch I see
a mat of oak leaves, there,
there, below, an Amish buggy
it is black its horse is brown
it is somewhat hearselike

The name of the
American student protester
killed by the
Israeli Army
was Rachel Corrie
from Olympia, Washington, my
old home town God Bless
Her God Bless her family
& God Bless the ignorant soldier
who killed her.[23]

---

23 There are Hezbollah signs in southern Lebanon in an old Israeli torture prison in Kfar Kila:

            Shadows long. Sun now ¼
of the way down windshield
yes, 2 definitive bug splats lower
left-hand quadrant, small
opaque grey, dipteric
Highest pt on 80 east of Miss'ippi 462 m

Tug at subjugated scrotum 5:45 pm
At 5:47 I drive straight into sunset—
or low dim saffron ball, and into
a glare washing the road & matted
grasses in the medium, about
20 translucent plastic objects of trash
in the median catch the light just so
& each clear piece of trash holds
its glint like a flower, each is a
little cheap beacon and then
the road turns
and each trash piece drops
its glint blossom
485 m stop to pee 6-6:05 pm
Retread debris. Sunball fulgent orange
like lambent chili grease
6:17 pm switch on headlights
Sun under hills now near
Strattonville 6:20 503 m

"A Room for Investigation and Torturing by Electricity"

"A Room for the Boss of Whippers"

"A Room for Investigation with the Help of Traitors"

"The Hall of Torturing-Burying-Kicking-Beating-Apply Electricity-Pouring Hot Water-Placing Dog Beside"

I miss C___ terribly.
Clarion River covered w/ snow
or ice but its surface is somewhat dark
as if the ice is thin—512 M Twilight
am thinking of drinking
email Verse Daily & change bio.

At Alleghany River
there is a little light
squeezing about the sky
ETA Normal 3:30 AM CST
Rachel Corrie was A student
At The Evergreen State College
my alma mater
551 m 1/2 way 7:03 pm
Dark in car but   sky

damp w/ light
      572 m Welcome to Ohio
   7:20 pm EST   ¾ tank gone
took me   380 m
Have eaten nuts & dried fruit
all day.   Meander Reservoir
I am very sad. Do you
drink, Meander Reservoir?
89.7 FM 593 m eastern Ohio
   PRI station   76 west
Very dark & lovely, I love
   you C___
Fill up   7:50-8:01
      9.561 g 418.5 m
43.8 mpg
8:10 pm it is dark again on rd 76 w

And after sustenance & coffee gotten
I am again very sad.
71 S 650 M 8:50 Pm EST
This road sucks! Some
cook who needs holes
for his pots cd come here

There are places in the night
one can only drive to
with a bosom car
that really big place under all
that is a bean field of pain

Stop to pee 729 m
    10 pm

Is music not Akin to sorcery
and what is night? There we go
crying again. But you
are a lovely River, Olentangy
State Scenic River and
though I cannot see you
at all tonight—just yr happy
roadside name tag reminds me
how you look in the day
1/4 tank gone 140 m = 47 mpg
I make 70 W just west of Columbus
Ohio 10:24 pm eastern time
at 10:55 it is 59 dgrs Fahrenheit 777 m
The whole night this nation,
fr AM to FM, from the hymn of Ode Island
to here in Ohio, the her of Ohio,
the whole cold nation

is loving the war
through my cold of sneezes and
my head ached
and wrecked w/ dusty asbestos
snot, mucus katabasis: snapping head
katabasis, wiping small snot-
sheets katabasis, snatters solid
and cold as snails snapped
from my nose & slapped
against the windshield
though that cold in my nose is gone
the disembodied flaring member
of George W Bush, his nose,
a little 2-holed cunt

is still wet. It was a lonely nose,
lonely for its face, lonely
for its clothes, lonely for
its dumb hair and head
Thank you for visiting Ohio.
11:45 pm EST Steady 70 mph
I STOP PEE 858 m 11:55 pm EST

43 m east of Indianapolis, at
12:19 AM eastern on this day
March 16th, 9 month & about I
or 2 weeks since I bought the car,
I have driven 50,000 M
I spend the miles going 70 mph

    270 m for 1/2 tank
   45.4 mpg
I am smelling skunk 30 m

east of Indianapolis.
I pass the house that Prozac
    built[24] 12:55 AM Eastern Time
I pass the waters of the Eagle Creek Reservoir Dam
floodlit, sharp
pointy waters
spumante Bye Dam Waters Legs
aching something woeful. I-74 West
must email Peg Steffanson
Bright night—just
noticed the almost full moon
Directly above car full moon.
I'm an ApeMan. I'm an ape
ape man. I am an ape man.
Ape

2:05 AM Eastern Western Indiana
Covington IN 1000 miles
8.924 g 393.1 m
44 mpg
Illinois State Line 1009 Miles
Fog moonlight
flat expanse, circle of
lights

This moonlight will be the
same moonlight illuminating
Iraq.

Champaign/Urbana 2:56 AM eastern

---

24 This is the Eli Lilly Building in Indianapolis. It is readily seen from I-70 and markedly lit by floodlights and topped with a mammoth American flag. I-70 passes on stilts right through downtown Indy.

Origin of Kaskaskia River
I love you O loneliness
I love you Kaskaskia River
your "heart of gold" prairie glory
more than 30 million men
suffer fr. a large prostate
Fog in great grandmother shawls
blowing & tumbling across
    road.

1070 m Fog Very thick
visibility 200 feet.
Sometimes when I press the
light button on my Timex
wristwatch I pinch some Arm
hairs in there and pull them
this wakes me up when I tire
when I am alert this annoys
me. Big fat new deer dead &
bright, eyes reflecting, in
in left lane, that cd have
really damaged me

1093 m 2:40 AM Central Standard Time
3:40 eastern
off hwy 74 W
enter Normal 64,000 miles on odo
road wet & w/ fog
email Kazim Ali
email all friends a
hello, reach out[25]

25 "I have noticed that the experience of suffering makes us kind and indulgent toward others
because it is suffering that draws us near to God." — my old friend Thérèse of Liseaux

4.10.03 – 4.14.03

[anabasis]

Separated after
only 4 months marriage.
Met Maria 3 days after Someone
mentioned Divorce—on the day
the US invaded Iraq

I dreamt last night
of Dawson Lake
It rose up on round wedges
of water and carried itself
as a large coffee table of green glass
above the fields
The fish in it falling out in the corn
A windmill tickling its underside, a green
mist spraying. And there by my side
Was Maria Helena Schmeeckle[26]

She is so kind. Feels like years
since someone was so kind.

April 10 2003 just now finished
teaching nightclass Grad Poetry Seminar
Gas Virginia & Clinton set ODO 9:07pm
17 miles from Bloomington
The sky is purple dark, clear:
Star-pocked ceiling. Lucia Getsi
is beautiful (but disturbed). Lori Propheter

---

26 Schmeeckle: pronounced "Shmeckly"

is very beautiful. Maria Helena
Schmeeckle is very beautiful.
Maria Helena Schmeeckle let
me kiss her neck. She would not
let me kiss her mouth. I am so
happy someone is kind. She let
me touch her back, her bare back
I touched her left hip. I rolled
up her shirt sleeve on her
left arm and touched it. The tips

of her fingers are thin and small
Her nails are striated and round.
She keeps them short. Her moles
are light brown & broad, her skin
very white, her hair is dark dark
chestnut. Her eyes are large and
beveled and brown
and green, and she says there is
blue in there too but I have not
seen it 10:20pm Middle Fork
Vermilion River. Did I say
I touched her left hip. It was
round, and very nice.
She was wearing black pleated
pants when I touched it.
Her waist is small.

That was a destructed Coyote
twisted fat fur neck
thrown back. It is unlike
Maria Schmeeckle's neck. At
115 miles, 10:58pm, I see streaking

4 inches of my windscreen a gold
meteor. Curiosita—
curiosity. Demonstrazione—
experimentalism. Sensazione—
cultivation of sense as a means
of enlivening experience. Fumate—
spuming, smoking, a willingness to
embrace paradox, mystery, ambiguity
and uncertainty, arte-scienza—
balance between science & art
Corporalita—cultivation of grace
fitness dexterity poise. Connessione—
an appreciation

of the interconnectedness of all
things. "Confusion endurance is
the most distinctive trait of
highly creative people."
Leonardo Da Vinci sd
"I do not depart from my furrow"
I feel that way: First this hwy
is a furrow, I just swerved into
the left lane, Old Spiceland Road
am very tired; Second, I feel
confused & naked near Maria
Schmeeckle. I do not know if I kissed
Maria Schmeeckle's cheek. I think
I did. Yes, her left cheek,
near her mouth. Her mouth
is beautiful, and sometimes it is
not beautiful. Sometimes I see her
thinking when she's talking
and her mouth falls a bit

and it is not beautiful
but it is touching. And I think
it is tender.

226 miles. Western Indiana. High winds.
Her teeth are very beautiful.
They are very even, and they point
slightly inward, like the best of
teeth. Her cheekbones are
prominent. Her voice is somewhat
deep. It is authoritative. I think
she is kind. I do not think she
is above teasing me. She seems to
have demonstrated that she likes
to do that. I like to tease
Maria Schmeeckle myself. She
smells good. Her hair is very
soft. She does not wear
perfume. I think she has
ducks on her shower curtains.

When I am around her, I am
bashful, & I think that I look
funny. I do not think that I
look funny around other people.
Her shoulders seem broad. She has
nice clavicles, I have seen them.
She practices Tae Kwon Do. I think
she has nice legs, though I have
never seen them. I like her feet.
Centerville, ½ mile: Maria
Schmeeckle has 2 distinct & fleet
darkbrown eyebrows, they are

crisp, above either side of her face,[27]
and they remind me of birds,
and above them is her
exquisite forehead
It is round & high
It is white & smooth

and it is very smart. Ohio
State Line 252 miles. 1 AM.
Her mind is quick. She
reads Rilke, she knows the poem
that I have always known &
she likes it, too, the one
begins "Ich lebe mein Leben
in wachsende Ringen"
I live my life in widening circles
She is a sociologist
She reads spiritual books, she
wants to understand the world,
all of it, she is very controlled
around me, I don't mind, she
wants to alleviate social problems
anyone would say she is nice
Dayton 31 miles

308 miles. Very tired. 1:52 AM
362 miles a few miles north of Columbus
about to pass out: w/ fatigue.
2:45 AM: I pull over.
Sleep at Exxon Quickmart
5:35AM—back on hwy

---

27 Intentional use of redundancy: figure known as Pleonasm.

w/ coffee. Very cold. My sleep
was broken due to cold.
Dawn 5:40am. Very good coffee
at BP there at 362 miles.
385 miles 7am Mid Ohio hwy 71 N
I am thinking of Maria Schmeeckle
again, about her eyes especially
about how sometimes I think I see
something scared in her eyes.
I think she's scared of being hurt
I want to tell Maria Schmeeckle

that I will not hurt her. A
small flock of starlings, perhaps
30 birds in toto crashes
east to west across the sky
The sky is both pink & blue
at once. It is dawn. I am
thinking of Maria Schmeeckle.
I am maintaining a speed of 72 mph.
There is fog in the air now.
There is also frost in the fields
as if the bottom of the fog
had been painting. I can smell
woodsmoke. It smells citrus.
There are hills here now, near
Mansfield Ohio, for the 1st time
in 400 miles.

The diesel trucks smell good through
the morning. They smell citrus too.
I wonder if Maria smells citrus
in the morning. I want to kiss

her mouth. PA border 9:05am
EST. Overcast. Slight green in
median among tan. The cold
gray cardboard of the trees now
bears buds. Duffles of low cloud
at 9:43am Duffles of rain. I
estimate after one minute of
rain there are 4 thousand
rain specks on windscreen.
9:45 The rain stopped & w/in 45 secs
every dot has evaporated, &
where each water fleck was
there is now a little round patina of
translucent dust. I should not say

dust as it is too fine to be
dust. I should call it a film
Heavy rain now, wipers on
½ tank gone 245 miles traveled
on 5.95 gallons
Rest Stop 10:16am 614 miles
Her nose is small and fine. It is
quite possible that when I return
to Normal Maria may
not care to see me again.
If it is in the cards I would like
to show her how well she cd
be treated. Pick up CD of
Nusrat Fatah Ali Khan
676 miles near Boggs Township
I notice loose patches of snow
a large, strong, hard rain
extending 5, 6, 7, 8 miles now

Very very hard erection last
10 miles. Through the road mist
I see clusters of tall stiff silos
in the valley. I am exhausted.
I think I am having flashes of
micro-sleep. The massive shale
cliffs are shining w/ rain. The erection
is back. I unbuckle my jeans
Rest Area 720 miles. Had
one glaze donut & 2 bananas
for breakfast.

1 pm back on rd after gassing
and food. Susquehanna River
1:10pm, 770 miles. I am
driving through the Alleghanies
The hills themselves are greasy
w/ bitumin coal, but now the
air too is heavy in mist. Mist
is a gray grease. Have 20 oz.
of "Columbia Supremo" from
gas station. It is nesting in the
cup holder at my rt hip. I
remember again touching the left
hip of Maria Schmeeckle the
night of April 9th, Wednesday, 2003
Her hips are beautiful. I don't
think I should be thinking about
her hips. But they are very
beautiful. I've watched

her walk form the back. I was
walking w/ Carrol behind Maria

Schmeeckle, who was walking w/
Heather from the Math Dept, and
Carrol was talking to me I was
grateful he wasn't looking at me
because I was looking at Maria
Schmeeckle's hips. I was looking at
her hips intently. I did not look
at Heather's hips, I looked at
Maria's hips, I looked at how
her hips blended into
her thighs. And how her thighs in
turn turned into the backs of
her knees, and how her knee
backs crinkled her pants
and I looked at her small waist
and her shoulders, and her back
and her neck and her jaw
as she talked and smiled

And all I could think of as Carrol
talked to me was that I had
touched the left hip, Maria
Schmeeckle's left hip, the one
nearest to Heather, the night
before, April 9th, Wednesday
while I kissed her left ear
as we sat on her couch, she
did not, and maybe she never
will, let me kiss her mouth
Prior at dinner we had talked
about our families & past over
eggplant stuffed w/shrimp, Pho Ga
and some kind of additional

vegetable plate.

2:30pm 849 miles pull off
at rest stop sleep for 35 minutes
in a whitewash of encompassing mist
that leaves a bright prismatic glaze
on the windows. The wind buffles
the car. A fantastic sleep.

3:08pm back on road. Wet
spray, a hard fine
rain. Its sound on the windshield
is not like a normal rain's
thrumming, this is more like a
swishing.

New York State line 877 miles
3:31 PM Mist everywhere
I want to ask Maria why she's
afraid of intimacy. Was she
once hurt by a lover, was it because
her mother died when she was 9
Does she dislike the feeling of not
being in control. 903 miles
Just saw in the mist an
emu-sized wild turkey
on the rt shoulder   a 100 yards N
of the WALLKILL RIVER.

I cross the great Hudson and
always feel ecstatic when I cross
the Hudson. It is mighty. It is
mighty American water.

The phrase just heard on NPR
is catachretic; to whit:
"mopping up pockets of resistance."
Connecticut Welcomes Me 947 miles
Rest Stop 997 m 91N 5:32pm
How does one mop a pocket.
More effective to vacuum it.
Welcome to Rhode Island
Ambiguity reigns in my life:
w/ Maria Schmeeckle.
I feel this ambiguity
at my wrists

at my eyes, in the loins, and
in each big toe.
Does Maria become anxious about
relationships w/out knowing it
and then does she engage avoidance
procedures that curtail relationship? Wd
like to ask this, am curious about.
Motel 6 near exit 15 Jefferson Blvd
Historic Providence 1099 miles

[katabasis]

4.13.03 Sunny. Gas at Cumberland Farms on
Rochembeau & Hope 3:59pm EST
S on Hope E on Cypress
down the hill. Afternoon sun.
bright sky. Red light at N. Main
Providence Fire Dept red brick & bright.

On 95 S 4:04pm. Almost
had accident crossing N. Main
as I pass Filenes. Bright Day bright
day. I pass flames. I pass sunlight.
I pass buds on the tree. The day
is large. The grass is green. There
is sand in the median. What a
stupid looking car. I believe
I have said that the Ford Expedition
is an abomination.

After her birthday party yesterday
which was in the house w/ D
I took C___ to room 206 of the
Motel 6 on Jefferson Avenue
She watched Cartoon Channel
(Tom & Jerry) until she got hungry
when we went to a theme restaurant
next door called the Bugaboo Den
that being full we went to Bickfords
a smoky greasy spoon next door
(some intervening blacktop notwithstanding)
after that we returned to motel room
which was very large, w/ 2 beds
& a high slanting ceiling

and C___ drew while I read Martial,
Seneca, Wyatt, and Robert Creeley
She drew in *this* book. Then we took
a bath together and upon getting out
I chased her around the room w/
the small remote controlled car I
got her for her birthday. The sound

of C___'s giggling could cure
kings. At 7:48pm I thunder across
the Delaware and enter Pennsylvania.
At 7:52pm it is thoroughly twilit.
The trees, the road, the ditch, it
all is like a dark room
lit by a light down a hallway.

At 7:54pm I tug my
scrotum. I find it
interesting Maria Helena
was a mime in college. I am
thinking of her superb eyes
and where Thoreau writes in *Walden*
"Could a greater miracle take place
but to look through each other's
eyes…. I know of no reading
so startling and informing as
this would be." And I think
of how many men & women
how many of her students
her colleagues, must look at her
eyes and think how beautiful
they are. But I wonder what
it must be like to look out
from them. So, she looks out
them, and the others look at them,
and fewer are able to look in them.
The other night at dinner which cost
22.50 for which she paid & to which

she wore a black trench coat
lined w/ faux fur, I had

the scary good fortune, scary
because she is so shockingly
beautiful, to look in her eyes
for 1.75 hours, fr 7:30pm
to 9:15.

10:45pm–10:55pm Gas at
SNOW SHOE, PA—Not reason
I stopped, bc I have plenty of
gas, having only traveled 225.3 miles
since last fueling, stopped to
call Maria Schmeeckle & wish
happy birthday, which I did.
One think I wanted to say to
Maria Schmeeckle but I never did

is that I did not intend for that
one email to imply that if we
did not become lovers we would
go our separate ways. Am thinking
here of the one email where I
said that if "this did not happen
I wd wish [her] all the best that
Providence could provide" or something
like that.

I cross the CLARION RIVER
Dark 513 miles at 12:30 AM
12:50 to 12:56 AM Urinate & purchase
coffee via vending machine at
Venango PA rest stop 543 miles
Collect coupon booklet for PA motels
for June 20th trip w/ C___.

I am listening to a violin duet.
The violins are echoey

like they are playing inside
the groin of a giantess

Gordon Ward Interchange 1:20am
Not tired. The duet of violins
is now a trio of violin &
violin & static as I cross
Shenango River, which is
a very beautiful river if
seen in the daylight, if
seen at night it is a
very dark river. Venus
hangs 2" from the top of
the windscreen. Welcome
to Ohio. Hubbard Twp Limit.

Transripe, Mobile Ripening Systems.
This is a Danish Recorder
concerto composed 1974 those
blue & silver sounding bloops
are a xylophone on a wooden
"melanoma" (I think the radio
announcer meant to say a "marimba")

Death hath come to *that* coyote.

Kent State University next rt.
Come on and twist a little closer.
"Rubber Bowl Exit 26"

There is something Norwegian
About Rock & Roll Music

The butterfly is a spirit being.

By extension, then, so is the moth.

I think "And the rest is history"
is perhaps the stupidest
phrase in the English language.

2:50am Stop to Urinate my Pee

Ask Dad what Mileage Fed Govt
allows for travel—or find out myself

70 W 4:40am bright ¾ moon
due west—One inch from
top of windscreen—stone blue silver light

Thank you for Visiting Ohio 5:48 am
Still very dark
Moon now outsized bloated
and sandstone colored
Now piss yellow & snagging
in the bare spring trees

Every now and then it crashes
into a hill.
And drags along the earthlit floor
like an anchor
catching in brambles and at bridges.

Heck w/ that looting in Baghdad
Just glanced over rt. shoulder
after noticing purple in the
west in front of me and I
notice a blue a pink, pinked blue
back yonder aft me.
No sun yet but it's a pinker
puck of light coming up behind soon

like an unlocked flame
from a barn

6:42 am EST getting very tired.
As dawn comes to Indy I turn
on Air high—to stay awake

7:05 am on west side of Indy & sun not
yet up but very bright.

Several erections since Youngstown.

I pass Eagle Creek Reservoir

w/ an unrelenting erection
I am plagued by erections
on these trips, this one
especially. Sun up now

I am told that redwing blackbirds
are the most reliable
harbingers of spring. I have
seen 7 to 10 of them since our
sun came up.

7:45am Flashes of micro-sleep

We tacked yr rock-n-roll hair
to the housecat

WABASH RIVER
Danville National Cemetery
20 miles left. Sunny windy
getting warm rest stop 1070

Commander!   Commander!:
The tractors've tipped
in the wind, the dogs're rigid

w/ swans—our uncles
are perched on the signs

Great creatures of paper
blow in the field—and Commander

My semen is full of pepper
For god sake it's all full of pepper

Let us take seriously the
memories along the
road—but not so
as a warning to drive
more carefully, but as a
call to the road as a
place of grief, and frankly of death,
and as its own thin and long locale
where all the lovers go.

8:28 am 1094 miles
birds on trees, pink blossoms
white blossoms. Kreitzer & Grove
8:38 am 1098 miles

5.11.03 - 5.14.03

[anabasis]

May 11, 2003 1:57 pm CST curb
at Kreitzer. Set odo. Miles on car:
53,713. Overcast. High wind advisory
Illinois. I am traveling to Providence
to read at Rhode Island School of
Design. The great
blue dome of Illinois
is today tossing & fretting &
Gray God bless Abraham
Lincoln. West on Grove. Twigs
& leaf bundles & 4 foot branches
drag on the crowned road
A neighbor's America FLAG raging
& hopefully ripping. The dark
violet mulberries are limber
Oakland & Clinton 2:02 pm the oaks
jostling. Strong West Wind I rise
onto Highway 74 east at 2:10 pm
fulgent tail wind, the wind is
clear wild goat hair: cheese sandwich &
pickle. Little black cows to the
right near Le Roy Illinois
You are getting fat under the
galloping sky

Cow stench. One would think
cow stench too heavy even for
wind this stiff. Why is not their butt

stench dissipated by the stirred air?
I should imagine some other
smells get snagged in the ditches.
Cow smell is that of its derriere—
dairy air indeed.
Origin of the Kaskaskia River 44.6 m
Ditch grass hairy and grass and
waving flax blue & flex–ible & brilliant &
a ditch under A bridge near
Champaign is shiftingly green Traffic
brilliant & Dutch
Those gray green Russian olive bushes
look underwater in the wind.

After our days of fighting I take down
and look at photographs
from the wall. I see you smiling. I see C___
and Melpomene laughing.

And I am now eleven hundred miles away
in a sad little town,
and I am very, very down.[28]

---

28 GERARD MANLEY HOUSES

 GLORY be to Houses for wetted lawns—
For doors couples colour, sunlight laundered low;
  For rose-moms knelt to weed, their backsides helloing Jim;
 Fishfire-camps ardent-pins; fitting things;
  Padlocks pitted and picked—fat, tallow, and dough;
And áll tiffs, their fear and cackle, their grim.

 All counters gummed, Reginald punched, laughter strained;
  Someone pickled, wrecked (who loves now?)
With sweeping slow; sweat sour; dazed and dim—
 They bicker-forth on credit loath to change:
      Save them.

Salt Fork.Vermilion County Illinois: 66 m
from Normal! Middle Fork Vermilion River
77 m and 3 Canada Geese in dell water near
Kenekuk Co. Park Salt Fork Vermilion River
Indiana State Line 88 m from Normal
Wabash River 95 m on a pole a 10 foot by 15
foot American flag rippling stiffly, then stops,
rises up like a
horse on its back legs and comes
down in another direction and
gallops its ripples to the southeast
Aubergine colored Ford
pickup truck passes me, Indiana
plates, its windows tinted, in
white big letters on back window

A 2' x 2' window decal
that says " 'NUKE' FRANCE"
and I become depressed. Are
people—yes—that
ragingly slackjawed stupid? 120 m: wind more
from the south now vast brown and
sometimes gray silver puddles from rains on
the fields 158 m East Creek Reservoir DAM
flumes are open, to release the pent up rain
water 160 M ¼ tank gone. 70 e 167 m 4:35
pm I now begin the traverse of Indianapolis
on the elevated highways of it I-465 to I-70
At 4:37 pm while on the stilts of Hwy 70 I
see the city ctr oz-like under blue dome—
gray bumps of girder buildings.Those Oz-like
gritty crumbs the buildings of Indy are tall

crumbs I pass beyond the city of
Indiana the city of depressing Indiana

Indiana land of modern day KKK. Indiana
land of the Flatrock river which is 220m from
Normal lllinois Indiana of Tan plowed fields
Indiana of slight green fuzz in some and
brown water in others Whitewater River of
Indiana, 230miles, is brown tumid mud banks
cut w/ flood cuts fat w/ mud, three cows
next to a sign that reads Dayton 62 m Oh,
Ohio! I'm coming! at 242 M from Normal I
begin to see
the poisonous signs of eastern Indiana the
TOM RAPER RV signs. At 248 M "SAVE
TODAY TOM RAPER'S WAY." O, Hio
State Line (250 m from Normal) I love seeing
your great cervical arch cloaking our woods
and hexing the personnel of Indiana
5:48 pm. Wind direct behind me since
leaving Normal I cross the Great Miami River, Swollen,
        bosom-like 284 m. The rains have
swollen
all the rivers: the day is the color of a can.

The Mad River at 292 M is not shabby
The birch trees and cottonwoods
near it
Are red in their green, a smock green,
Kelly green, a bottle green.
Wind now from WNW 38m w
of Columbus.
6:49 pm CST I switch on

lights. Just finished listening to
The Reader by Bernard Schlink, trans-
lated by Carol Brown Janeway
Rain specks 325 m for ½ tank gone
54.62 mpg—13 mpg over hwy
average: 54 miles per gallon is
unprecendented! due to tailwind!
270 N 342 m 8:10 pm EST
          Getting dark

8:15 pm STOP for food & coffee
          360 m 71 N

Your oddball cherry-cobbler neck
O Nancy Reagan, does not
disturb nor bother me this slackjaw nation
even though you are still skinny, O
head of Alien on boney shouldered woman

Your ruined forehead, you ruined and ruled
this nation
with your bobble headed husband

erection north of Columbus. I always
seem to be visited by an erection
north of Columbus Ohio. WHY?

Rain begins, erection leaves

Cold today: 40s & 50s F
I make I-76 east 450miles fr Normal at
10:10pm

Driving in the nightlight:
Get camping stuff, get movies,
        Get ink.
You know, when you get a lot of
flies in A room   & they're big
& clumsy, like fatted
buttons, they sound
somewhat electrical.
        Meander Reservoir 510.5 M
STOP TO GAS in Niles, Ohio 512.9 M
I drove 512 miles on one tank of gas
514.8 m 9.995g = 51.51 mpg

Pennsylvania Welcomes You 527 m
O Shenango River, How many
FBI Agents have driven over you today
Fitty witnesses run across the
road. runnin at duh judge
saying I saw him, I saw the bad
praysident run dissa way
I have issues w/ ill-bred women
Highest Pt on 80 east of MS 637 m
My rt ear pops.   1:12 AM
I hear
that from the burlap of myth
a swale of words comes out
of a verbal ditch

At 1:20am in the dark mts of
velvet Pennsylvania I am again
accosted by the floating head
of Nancy Reagan: her great ringed eyes
her raccoon-like anger. AHHHH:

What kind of mad Kabuki are
you into now, Lady! That
disturbing
      thing you're wearing
      that stuff you're shouting
671 m REST STOP PEE. NEED REST.
      1:46 am BACK ON ROAD
ANYWAY
3:10am 766m Susquehanna River
81 N 784m 3:28am
½ tank Gone 287m
FOG hwy 84east near Forks Bridge Rd.

4:35am a luminous purple to the
North—dawn at Dingman Township
856m It is Monday efffing morning I
have driven all night I
am tired. I am bones. More fog again
Welcome to New York 873.8 miles
After & over some bridge. Port Jervis.

Dawny Dawn Dawn. 5:10 AM

FOG—mild, diluted—visibility
150 yards Must get coffee
feel strapped to wheel
Heavy traffic since 4:30

5:30 AM Fill on Exxon 47.55 mpg

2 coffees & "gourmet" pound cake
& pack of "Starburst" "fruit chews"
pain in left knee

Hudson River, fog occluding
the hills

691 e 984 m 6:50AM
91 N 992 m   7 AM

Rest Area 994

Depart Rest Area 11 AM

Mattabassett River 998 M

Exit 22-S Hwy 95

999.6—1000.1 m 11:03 AM
Chester Bowles Hwy
Foliage near Beaver Meadow Rd
near Haddam drier
pricklier, sparer, trees thin
& yellow green, almost autumnal,
lots of rocks
          Casserina & Martin
          Moving & Storage
          860 347 8888

partly sunny

Anguilla Rd near No. Stonington CT
          Pawcatuck
      Mashuntucket Reservation
Welcome to Rhode Island
I believe I just saw A pig

dead rt shoulder 150 M
Exit 20, exit 1

At 1098 mile from Normal 12:32pm
I drive up hills into Providence up
up above the Woonasquatucket River up
into the bricky air,
into the ginkgo, the footpaths of shale, the
slate roofs of Brown, the dollhouse center
of Providence, a scent of
the Wanasquatucket like a rose above into leaden
waterish windows and long legs of
the walkers and into the little
hostel house where D got me
a room.

    [katabasis]

7:28am May 14 Eastern Standard Time I sit
in my ECHO above the Wanasquatucket
and Set odometer at Prospect & Angell.
Make 95-S 7:33am Bright sun east to left
A Wednesday morning—gave reading
last night in Barr House to crowd of Brown
RISD teachers students. 89.7FM NPR President
Putin Powell in Russia. Wind in an
American flag shows a wind fr. West

Do not come at me w/ yr hurry or
                    hurt hair,
nor come with yr hair out windy, yr eyes
backpacking lids, not pouty lips of worry

Blue sky, w/ high & pink cloud
32.5m I stop in W. Greenwich
for Dunkin Donuts X-Large
coffee w/ cream 2 old fashions
CT welcomes me with its signs
Park clouds. Up down. Hike!
hike! Bye Bye Ford. Rode & Red
SUV. St. Mary's Hospital our bodies are
"Vanity that we parade around,
then bury."—Chris Whitcomb
Such are our bodies.
Housatonic River 139.4m
84 W still Connecticut

Amen, Amen, Maria Helena Schmeeckle
Glorious her moving piano hands
Glorious her sense of wonder
Glory : her home
Goodness : her house
Smiling : her ease
Amen for Maria Helena Schmeeckle
Amen to parked clouds
Amen to "I do not think clouds ever
park." 10:04am EST 158m
NY Border then east branch
of Croton River. A river is
not illegal I hope the head of Nancy
Reagan does not haunt me this drive:
        Fishkill Creek 183.5m
Hudson River   Goddamnit
I repeat these clouds
seem parked to me.

Wallkill River 202.3m
10:44am EST Wind WNW

[DID VORCE, TO A PERSON
FOND OF CONTENTION]

Now you came out of the puffing wood
with a
pen on a string, and wood on
an axe head and glued to the pen
were, like, eggs. And Samantha
too was running out
and a gold dot on her
pen, polka dots on her pen and seashell
swirling pasted on her pen

Now you came out of the snow dirted and
spotted sick in vegetations, strung bark
crossed your scars and flecks from logs
on your teeth glowed out brownly as if
thin paths and your hair-do
bore the weight of the
cold air and you are yelling at me, you fresh
from the snow woman kind of yelling at me

Now you come out of an underwood
with a pond sloshing on the small spoon
of your tongue, and of a sudden I do not like
you
nor trust
nor want you
and as if you knew this you
start to let out some words

blah blah, blah blah blah
and I am sorry for all the want
I ever
ever brought you

Have felt my own *ife was a bully
PA border 228m Matamoras PA
STOP Milford, PA 11:15am
236.3m fr Prov 437.2m in tank
10.074g = 43.40 mpg
Depart 11:24am—w/out peeing—
got eyeful of old man fr. New Jersey
on toilet in gas station, grossed me out,
why old man leave door unlocked?
His thighs pale muscled, his face-skin
liver spotted and loosened from his head
bones, the cheap baseball cap framing his
shocked look
I SAW HIS *THIGHS*

It must be a fine thing
to be a radio: giving and giving
racking up great blessing
for constancy and generosity
What a fine job, a radio in a car,
little box of good
in greater mobile box of curiosity
Sunny wind but gray dull clouds
Western Pennsylvania in the afternoon
has a light conducive to inducing headaches
I have noticed this
Rest area 257m 11:43am
on road 11:46am

Rain dottles 12:01pm 273.8m
Near 81-S interchange lots
of construction, sun comes out
briefly, goes away
big deer dead under bridge
"Keep right on going, and
nothing will happen."—Richard Feynman

large dog or small deer
80W 318m 12:43pm
Big deer 327m
           After seeing this deer I
wonder if it wd be possible to kill
A deer using only a thumbtack.
How many times wd I have to
stab the deer w/ the thumbtack in
order to kill it.
           Susquehanna River 336m
I believe that big deer was
fr the shining of the Housatonic

O look, some
birds, starlings maybe, poking
the beaks into tilled dark garden
on rt in a home above the ditch
Susquehanna River 366.3m
1:25 pm. Seem like very little
wind.
           ¼ tank gone 145m = 48.5mpg
Sun out but very cloudy
1:41pm EST
leaves here small, immature 386.7m
Here are the big flat cliffs of tall

height and fat and wide cliffs like
the kind you would see at the sea! 395.5m

Having got 54mpg on the march
up country a few days ago, it occurs to
me that wind's more a factor than
previous estimated. DUH. 2:31pm Sunny partly clouds
witness crow walking to the
rt of a torn up much decayed
deer carcass on rt shoulder 441.1m
with the intention of Eating its face parts?
2:42pm very tired. Must get coffee
2:48pm am at McDonald's Exit 120 Hwy 84

In my trunk are a dozen
or so National Geographics
dated 1940s. They were in the hostel
at RISD on Prospect Street just
being mounted by dust: much on war, much
anti-Japanese racism, many fountain pen
ads, Norwegian soldiers shown. 3:19 I stop
to pee, reststop on rd again 3:23pm. Bright
sun now. Ragged-topped cumulonimbi
Wind at 500m looks
to be from North 3-5mph
Sun very bright now
No A/C but vent ran on
high. 3 or 4 vents of my Toyota Echo open
all directed at my face. Sometimes
the coming heat of spring is
depressing to me

½ tank gone 273m

45.88 mpg
Clarion River 515.3m
4:46pm I finish my coffee.
282m in tank I turn on
A/C this is a Rotring Core fountain pen
Crane dismantling a bridge
over hwy 80 west 525m
          Allegheny River 531.5m
          3:59pm EST
Shenango River 573m 4:35pm
575.6m Ohio border 4:37pm
Meander Reservoir 591.7m 4:52pm
5:05pm 607m Rest Stop pee
5:11pm on HWY

8.925   43.47 mpg—¾ tank
  gone
71 S   652 m   5:49pm
Cappy   cappy.
  675.4m Exit   186   71 S

STOP   TO   GAS
          439 m in tank
6:12 pm
          439.2m 9.553   45.98 mpg
             6:17 on rd.
6:51 pm Frothy charcoal
clouds. Getting raincloud
darker 717m
lights on   7:09 PM

RAIN SPLATS 7–8 mm diameter
  About 10–15/second at first.

Then about 20/second & 12-15mm
    I don't use my wipes.
270 W 742m glorious
 White pale yellow slantlights
similar to diluted milk
759m 70W 7:32 pm
Why do some people talk
about their teeth?
This road is not a bunch of
crappy shit.

Mad River 808.5m
Shirt sleeve weather
What if instead of one shorter distance
between things, there were two
shortest distances between things?
We wd have our choice of economies—
what a thought
Great Miami River
Powerful rain 8:30pm EST
Still light out and ¼ tank gone
143m traveled—rain—
gray-blue road, ungrabbable clouds

8:50pm EST Darker yet—
& hazing low after A certain
time in the day it gets
darker real fast
850m IN border 8:52pm
small drops of rain
Big Blue River 887.5 m
dark dark dark
        9:35 EST

Far faint flashes of lightning
        high in windshield above car
mirror as I approach Indianapolis 912m frequent
(1 per second)
but very high. Dark dark

10:10 EST At edge of Indianapolis
Approaching A Massive horseshoe
shaped lightning storm

am going into middle of horseshoe
with great blue-yellow and green
lightning veins to my right and left
treetrunks of light
slapped out of heaven then gone

941m 74W
9:37 CST

horizon-breaking lightning stroke

270   ½ tank   45.38 mpg
9:50 CST out of T-storm
and west of Indy 956.9

10:10 Getting somewhat tired.
450m ¾ tank gone
                44.82mpg
I notice a Bright nearly full tin-colored moon
top part of driver's side window
which I watch crost the cornstream of Illinois
so tired
I in danger. Last night had chat with

Mike Magee, runner of Combo Press
11:53pm Exit HWY 74 at exit 135
traveled 1,097 miles, tired tired in the dark

6.17.03 – 6.20.03

[anabasis]

2:16pm June 17, 03, On
pavement at Toyota Quik Lube
mit just had oil change. Bright
sun—mesocumuli hung on
the watery horizon of the blue ceiling
Morrisey & Veterans Pkwy 2:19pm
Main & Veterans 2:20
I rise on 74 east 2:23pm bright sun & set
odometer pavement a flat porridge-colored
mash of grey & tan (thus beige)
cut like a line of Hopkins instress
beneath the robin's egg frosting
of the inverted cupcake of the firmament
and past the jiggling green
I am bound for Nova Anglia

I yacht thru vegetal Illinois
past Le Roy now
at 2:34, past clot on rt
of black & brown sunglistened
cows ears out to cool themselves
past silos & small Norman
grain bins (too silver
in the sun). Radio towers I
am doing 72.
                    The small corn's
three octaves darker
than the waving wheat-green fescues

of the ditches, Piatt County 24 miles.

The way the houses rise here without trees
on these undulant soils
are as frigates of faucets and shelves
they have gone on the sea of towns
I drive for C____
to bring her back here
the summer

Saffron sun. The corporate corn.
Vegetal seaplain
a wind feels straight
of Tunis but w/out the dust
And humid. Salt
Fork River 55m 3:12pm
Specks of gritty flowers near the
                                    bridges
Vermilion County 61m The Mandan
Around Fort Clark North Dakota
traded for a yellow paint called "Vermillion"
The MANDAN NATION was exterminated
by small pox around 1839

Their Chief MATÒ-TOPE
was painted by Carl Bodmer
in 1833. He had reputedly killed
several white men by the time
he stood for Bodmer's portrait
which took 4 days to paint
This Continent was "settled" by
Europeans via a Campaign of
biological Warfare—whose fruits

we now see in the vermillion ears
of the good Corn
        Kickapoo State Park 69m
In the Middle Fork Vermilion River 72m
I saw greasy man-length green threads of water moss
smeared under the water shine
Salt Fork Vermilion River 74m

Reality can be felt deeply
in 2 ways:
rightly & wrongly. When rightly
our welling response is love
and curiosity. When wrongly we react w/
pride and fear. Awe
is the blend of both fear
& curiosity—and is as close as Americans
come to curiosity. Indiana border—
80-odd miles.
        Wabash River Fountain
County 90 m 3:44pm
        The state of Motels is
indicative of the Health of the Polity
        Graham Creek how you sun 93m
        Dry Run Creek 98.3m
        Slightly rolling shallow
        be-treed hills here

Stratocumuli dimmer, bigger
"the enormous aggregate that is
our war on all the lands
and seas of the globe"
        —Ernie Pyle, apologist
        for death makers

"Everything of this world
had stopped, except war."
—Ernie Pyle
Sugar Creek 118 miles from Normal

HER LOVELY VULVA:

The cold came and the chickens
cramped up in the straw. The limping dog
was bright as marmalade as it crossed the
                                        farm

We had seen the cormorant
singing to the spattered dove, had hitched
the anxious breakers to the gale

But what had clapped the coat of light
upon the chickadee
and blown the brownnesses

into the shadows of the sails

The nipple-sized toggles of the bees
ran heaving into the gusts
from the green shins of the corn

The air in that cloud seemed woven
of rust; every long rain drop was cold
every thin one hot

I called to my body, Come Back
But it was bold
And it did not

All of it, the sky, measled w/ cloud
that massive tundra of Air
the russian olive trees shaped
          like cumuli here
I see many old framed telephone poles
grey crisp wood bleached stiff
as cocks bent by the curves
the catenary weight of the wire
curved like woman
What an idyll is my yachtcar
in Boone County I dash
          in an lidyll car

Did the Mortar shell make A
terrific quacking sound
An instant duck come to life
and then gone in a quack
          packed with shrapnel
I believe it was that which
burst my yacht
near Advance, Indiana at 135m
I see dill patching the rt ditch
its dull yellow almost
a digestive stomach-lining yellow
the cat tails then, huge & reedy
holding their small poops vertical.

Redwinged blackbirds sit at their desks
on top of them.
Are there no gentle
          men in America?
It's my doubt these Indiana pickups
hold Any. No in this

                              Jesus country.
Eagle Creek Reservoir 154m
                              4:40pm
70east Indy 4:49 162m
Here in Indy
the cat tail spoor have burst.

I see the Indy City Center
hazed blue, blue itself its buildings
At 170m in Indy I see
                    there
the Awful Ziggurat of Lilly
        Ziggurat of Morphia
Ziggurat of boring verse
Ruth E Lilly who bequeathed a million
to Poetry Magazine. Eli Lilly who made
a billion on Prozac, Lily Poppy,
Morphia done
in the land of the dead Indians
            70 east closed must take 74east
Heard this BS lie on NPR: "US forces
continue to mix humanitarian aid w/
Military muscle."—at 5:10pm

70east 5:10pm CST
2 days Ago in New Harmony, Indiana
I heard "Ellen Bryant Voigt" "read"
her poetry, she
        ah she
kept repeating
the 20 yr old Yeats' pronouncement
that poetry's about passion but I think she has
confused Passion with

Melodrama, strange
she should be so prim her poetry
limp, the melodrama inside it
her poetry prim wordy
sounded
like cats effing
Nameless Creek 203 m

Anthony Creek. There
are the Goofy Hoosiers in
in the distant field
w/ shorts on, Stadium Empty,
huddling at some game in the sunlight
Montgomery Creek
There Are the Hoosiers in tractors,
men & women west
of Big Blue River cutting
thick median grass
and the grasses of the ditches
That odd butterfly
        seemed so happy
the light in the east lighting her

Optimistic little things
though I know sometimes melancholy
Generally a butterfly is
guileless, a wisp on a hinge
only slightly tougher than the wind itself
Whitewater River there are no
large bugsplats yet
Moving by me are blossoming dill
5:56pm 237m rest stop
6:01 back on 70e the sun is

237

nested in a sick haze
behind me.

In my mind, since the separation,
all the units of thought are pain huts. The
egg of hope is rippled with imaginable grief.
The average American woman has
19 square feet of skin. Good lord.

I wasn't pushing you away I was
feeling your chest.

And we in all these births, now in a sea, now
a wood
or before the marked hieroglyphs of storms

Sun: what do you know
about a
little girl
trans-historical dandelion

bladder of halos. bubble of heat. blubber of light

I arose my mother arose my daughter arose
the lily arose, the river arose, the tulip arose,
old ankles arose, Warren Williams arose

and there were theaters in the toys
because of you

you hang, an indigenous
dandelion of dust

Lucretius says
that you are the size
that you appear to be. Which still begs the question
of what size

you appear to be.

Do I perceive you as big
          because I was told you were big? What
          the hell

You fitted these bodies with vents
you mantled us in sphincters
swathed us with blisters
pasted us to chancres
you strung us with nerves
what the hell

That you tear

and fold the gingham of fogs. That you come
through the Canada of space. That you signal green
from the crush of destruction. That you blow a tangle

of crumpled shade from a copse of oak. That you
anchor
such dejection
to me
          thank you. That

those eating millet seed, Those eating potato chip,
Those unscrewing hooves, Those discussing a goose,
Those who know Jim Berhle, Those eating the leg

muscles of rabbits, Those eating a firebug, Those in the
house of sorrow, Those in the ringing valley, Those
using a haircomb, Those who hit their dogs, Those
farting in front of children, Those eating kale, Those
smelling of lake water, Those delighting in mildness,
Those delighting in goodness, Those cutting the little
creatures, Those liking the cheese, Those liking the corn,
Those liking the other yellow foods, Those
crushing a boy's kite, Those who walk on the air, Those
who lost it, Those who puked on a plaque, Those who
lie with dwarves, Those who lust for horses, Those who
collect excrement and sell it, Those who collect
excrement, Those that are busiest at dawn, Those beset
by pains, Those who camp with joy

cannot be but a companion of you! Those oak trees
cannot decline you

That you are here above the mommy world
in this parliament of Natashas
this clattering of knees

blonde sun, pulsing rice grain, fulgent rice boulder
basically spewing bright wedding rice
into the boards of the world, thank you
for hinging the moments together

the clouds, those great condiments of foam
roam the sky basically like weird
puffy pilgrims
pilgrim-condiments
foaming the upper balconies of the earth
blowing without their buckle hats

, yes the cloud, sun, these odd amorphous kites
happen because of you, thanks

we are down here under you, a bunch of meat

We are basically a great family of meat
made by you, hung here by you, made fuzzy by you
—we are real—
there could be nothing, thank you

Sun, thank you for coffee
Sun, thank you for Toyota
Sun, thank you for C____

Sun, thank you for C____
Sun, thank you for C____
that you made this an Iliad
I really really thank you

"The point was that we on the
shore knew we cd substitute
machines for lives."
        Ernie Pyle
Ohio State Line 250m
    (Shelton Fireworks on
Indiana side—stop there on
way back)—250m ½ tank gone.
Long constellation in median
of blue & white wildflowers
—superb—always happy
to leave Indiana. I wish I had more
compassion in me, I wish I had
less judgment head

Let us build A creek over it
and wash Away republicans

"We had eleven Negro boys aboard,
All in the stewards Department"—
        Ernie Pyle, <u>BRAVE MEN</u>
"They were all quiet nice boys
and A credit to the ship."—Ernie Pyle
        "They all had Music in their
souls. I had to laugh when the ward room
radio was playing a hot tune, I'd
notice them grinning to themselves &
dancing ever so slightly as they went
About their serving."—Ernie Pyle
        "One of the boys was George Edward
Mallory of Orange, Virginia. He was
32...."—Ernie Pyle
The Hoosier Ernie Pyle

6:28 CST 269m
Weighty sky
        orange-blue clouds roll
encompassing & burly
from the North   I must take off
sunglasses, I stop @ Brookville OH
& consume 2 fish sandwiches.

I see grass islands in
Stillwater State Scenic River

bugsplat, almost blue, near
Great Miami River   I believe
it had been a beetle

        Brandt Pike Huber Heights
Carriage Hll
  Mad River 293m

Talk to Colleagues, faculty About
Charlie's line re someone pub-
oriented, po-mo lit & willing to take
over UNIT for Contemporary Lit.

Ulysses S. Grant was from,
I think, Point Pleasant
Ohio   I have no idea if
that town
is anywhere near Springfield
Ohio where I currently Am
7:28pm at dim apricot evening
an hr before an Ohio
        sunset
When he was a boy
Ulysses Grant
swung from horses' tails

Fewer pickups in Ohio, not
As hot—Massive junkyard of
farm equipment 330m
Ulysses S. Grant stood 5 feet 1 inch
I see Llamas there
        Ho Ho Yamas!

270-N 7:48 CST
        Acteon had seen the goddess bathing
seen her breasts & hips
had seen the light blowing beneath

                                                       her arms
her hair like bright vegetables
her hips a platoon from her
                              vulva
Northwest Columbus wall to wall
          gray clouds mollify
      orange dusk All our lights
Are on. Where are the geese.
Has Achilles Ate them? His
Whiskeys Are orbiting. He
cannot get to them.
          Achilles has ate the ducks.

Achilles has Ate the llamas.
    fewer US flags this
  trip than any other trip.
Achilles has Ate the brandy,
          the quinine
        the geese he ate
The horses & mud he
jawed them. 360 m 71 N
A terrible footbridge over the
    HWY at 362m is festooned w/
U.S. flags
The gelatinous sausage meat
    was made of a were-stag, a deer-man
formerly Acteon. I see
a skulk of foxes in the rt ditch
          near Sunbury OHIO
Large field of white wildflower
constellated on rt, each white
clump approx. 3x4 feet, maybe
400 clumps strewn upon 5

Acres seen despite a settling
mist & impending dusk

Greasy flank of dark cloud
on right tree line   ½ mile off.

Andrew Jackson, the Mothereffer,
killed the Choctaws & Cherokees
What A Great Idea!
And After, for Jackson, the voices and the
laughter—the glasses and orchestras
strewn thru spring
        Mansfield OH 409m
            darkness
Fill on Ashland / Wooster OH
        Exit 186
          426 m 9:04 CST
     37.6m (since fill) 9.845g
      44.45 mpg
I set these matters down not
to instruct others, but to
inform myself—or so said
John Steinbeck.

"We find after years of struggle
that we do not take a trip—
a trip takes us."—John
Steinbeck, Travels w/ Charlie

"Thus I discovered that I did not
know my own country."—JSteinbeck

When I stop in them gas station

And see
ignorant peoples
I wonder
Why they ignorant
Why they gullible

Where they should have had passion
              and Love
they have fear and pride
How they can be so proud
              and so simultaneous dumb
IS THIS CAR NOT MY
              ROSANANTE?

76e 451m 9:41 CST
10:44pm Eastern time I burst
through A castle of paper
that has appeared on the
road ONWARD ROSANANTE
Confetti blizzards behind me
It may have been a nunnery of paper
Have I burst many nuns
There is a slightly naughty
quality of fire to breaklights
The Amber kindles gripped
by the asses of cars
As if each trailed 2 bundles
              of burning broom straw

But we do not speak of it on
    the road. Our cars, our
yachts, our turtles, our steeds
our hermit homes—look forward,

pioneers, O conestogas—forward
  and have no traveling end
We are Stern and bow
      have no aft or end
They before me are not Americans
  for Americans have no Asses
    We Are All Assays
  Meander Reservoir 511m
lit w/ sheen of orange sodium
lights luminousing in low clouds
      beyond trees are dark.

80 east 515m 11:41 eastern
Pennsylvania Welcomes me w/ a
      blue sign.
Shenango River: gray
  half-dollar flick of wings
            My windshield missed
a moth. I have often wondered
if the slapping swirl of air from A
passing car would cripple a
Moth or hobble
    A butterfly.

Fine grain of mist past 10 miles
  wipers can't quite take it off
they smear it into a thin condiment
  made of bug meat and cloud water

It clings there w/ an almost static charge
  to the clear silicate toast of
    my windscreen
138 m ¼ tank gone.

Now A crackling rain 8 miles
        West of CLARION   1245am ESt
Shippenville 2 miles
The rises drops & turns of this
        stretch cause the dinosaur sized
Median trees to drop rise &
        sway their leaves strain
and sift the lights of the
oncoming traffic which are not
yellow. Or beige nor tan. But a
kind of off white, a sallow white,
        though some of the newer cars have
                blue

And in this raining night
their reflections glister like
those prism blobs & corpuscles of light
one sees on the eyelashes
in a rain or if one has cried
and tried to see. Punxsatauwney,
North Fork Creek
There is a mist whose rate of
deposit on the windscreen falls
slightly below the first indexed
wiping speed, which causes a slight
annoyance in the driving
1:15—1:19am Stop to Defecate 619m
Chesapeake Bay Watershed
Dense fog aluminum colored
        in the lights.
Descending the fog elevates
I drop to Curwensville Lake.
I ascend out of whatever

valley I was in, and on the rise
A happy rain giving a sound
of crinkling small candy wrappers.
ONWARD ROSANANTE
I believe I am hydroplaning
Lightning flash (blue-white)
2:10am I am being
followed by someone who insists
on staying behind me—and recall
that this Doppelgänger always
        appears

On this lonely Allegheny stretch
No matter if I reduce my
speed to 40 or bolt away
at 80 it follows. Back
there 3 or so miles it
got right on me & I coasted
to 40 mph. It did not pass!
but decelerated as well.
        Dense fog & thorough thick rain.
Rain rain Rain rain Rain
        Lamar Lamar
            699m
2:37am EST
Stop to Sleep at Lamar, PA
        Travel Ctr (TA)

Wake to heavy rain from an
        Aluminum sky 7:28am. Fill on
    6.377 gallons—at 42.53 mpg
back on hwy 80east 7:45am
The Mighty Susquehanna here

near Milton I squeak over
the tin brown water. Its
width here is similar to
the Wabash at New Harmony, IN.

I cross the Susquehanna again
at 768m. Sky lightening
but still low, mist stopping
dragging gray rags part way
up mountains on rt, tops
occluded, road drying Wedn
the 18th of June TODAY I see C___!

81 N 785m N to
Wilkes-Barre Mist again
on 84.   Black twisted hanks
of tires, retreads delaminated,
lay at the rt shoulder
            like exhausted black muskellunge
Smaller fragments rest curved
            resembling fingernails
or charred forearms cragged w/ bones
stiffened w/ their radial steel wires
rest stop urination   846 m
            9:56 AM
The Sway and Swish of traffic
through eastern Pennsylvania

is balletic and calm
near Lords Valley Dingmans
Ferry. The dense thin trunked
oaks and birch rise in a great
green poof mattress on

close grassed hills either side
of tin-skied 84. Metamorphic
and shaley Rocks knuckle out the grass
    easily here

At NY border high shale
cliff brow above trees
and bear square bold numerals
in whitewash: 91   1999
    2000

Near Port Jervis A petulant
red early 90s Chrysler
convertible, beige canvas top
down, flings itself past me.
A stiff cheap plastic
    American flag on its aerial.
The flag, raging like A
multicolored choked pigeon[29]
bursts free of the Aerial
and falls grateful & exhausted
 to the road. I am
careful to run it
over.   Fog.   I am at
        dewpoint

and the road rises & pulls
me up & into it, only to pull me out

---

29 Pigeons. I submit that pigeons are the bird who arose on the earth because of the Crucifixion. Mary Magdelen took a bird egg and squished it into the hole in Jesus's side at some point in the afternoon on Good Friday, into the wound made by the Centurion. Round midday on Sunday just before Jesus died the first large pink pigeon fell like a pus-bleb out of Jesus's side and wormed into the air. That was a pigeon. Now it is a mini-flag that I just ran over.

when lowered.
Wallkill River 900 m
Now here again under low
        tin roiling clouds
over the wide Hudson I travel
the Hamilton Fish bridge & steam
into a delta of cars backed
at the tollgates. Blonde
makeupped sweetfaced toll lady
"Thank you Have a good day" A
smile, she takes my dollar bill

then a half mile of willows
on my left
Fishkill Creek near Poughkeepsie
& Peekskill the clouds Are
an Alloy of milk & glowing lead
A faded blue bumpersticker on A Ford:
UNITED IN PRAYER
URINATE IN EAST FISHKILL NY
930 m 11:15-19 am
942m EAST BRANCH CROTON RIVER
CONNECTICUT BORDER
946 m 11:33pm 55 speed limit

691e 985m 12:10
Must meet C___ & D.
at Martin Luther King Elementary
School
        Quinnipiac River
in silver mist
        91 North 994 m
        9 S heavy mist low

252

featureless sky dull of color
but bright
       Mattabesset River
               traffic
heavy Mist deluging spray
Are we driving through
      clam juice?

95 N 1030 m 12:50pm
Approaching Rhode Island
No mist, sky gone up its
ladder
New macadam the odd burnt butter
smell of tar
         1063 m R I border 1:19pm
Down a wet straight aisle in the
   mirroring macadam new clouds are
framed, scudding kinds, south
  to North.
Arrive Motel 6 Warwick 1:48 pm EST
  will Bathe now and then to C___'s school
where soon she's getting out,
   then to summer with me

      [katabasis]

4:29 AM EST June 19 Southbound
Hwy 95 2.1 m fr. hotel
After Dunkin Donuts, o j
for C___, Large creamed coffee, me,
4 old fashioneds (plain)
Sky faintly glow purple
Glory Glory Glory it

is morning
And what a Grand Girl
My daughter is
Connecticut A pink blue scene

Dark seagulls right to left
at New London. Across the
Massive high arching bridge
I see the sub base docks
the purple water smeared
            yellow
w/ the greased shine
   of sodium lights
Delicate fog, coffee good
Fog & Empty road on 9
North to to Mattabesset River
Fog lifts at Middletown
C___ asleep at 10 to 6.
691 west 100.3m
Sodium lights at Watertown still &
                        mist gray

6 AM C___ snoring
Descend hill to Quinnipiac River
Am near Milldale, Cheshire
Waterbury   Danbury
Cheshire   Prospect
Hello St Mary's, the hospital
in yr foggy brick.
Southford, Southbury
Newtown brighter now
Sandyhook   wind
   sodium lights off

Brookfield Connecticut
morning traffic
Bethel
I am leaving Nova Anglia

84 W 145 m
New York State, North Salem
      Brewster Fishkill
Poughkeepsie Peekskill
Newburgh Beacon
Wappinger Falls
The Hudson River whited
w/ a Milk Fog opposite hills
faint green—green milk hills
Highland New Paltz
West Point Walden
Montgomery Newburgh
enough w/ the Newburgh
Middletown Port Jervis

Maybrook
      No fog, just haze
in the middle trees
Willows 8 foot swamp grass
   Akin to Wheat
Binghamton Goshen
Greenville Oh
      What a superb swamp
      rt. side cum duck grass
      elevation now 1254 ft. at top
      of colossal hill
dead possum—small rt shoulder
Sussex Port Jervis

Delaware River
Pennsylvania border
                Matamoras

4 small birds in flight
Scree at base of cliffs
            cool day
Milford óne bǐrd
Dingmans Ferry   Lords Valley
Porters Lake   Blooming Grove
Pecks Pond   Lake Wallenpaupack
Porter's Lake   Blooming Grove
Taftan   Gray   Gray
Palmyra Gray   Gray
Grentown   Gray
Newfoundland   Hamlin

Mt Cobb   sumac
            water greased cliffs
cold milk haze   cold milk sky
Dunmore Throop
            Carbon Dale
Wilkes-Barre   Scranton
Avoca   Dupont   Pittston
Bear Creek   Nanticoke
Nuangola   First sun
            Strained thru gray
                cloud milk
& chopping trees
cut cakes of cliffs

Conyngham   Nescopeck
urinic sun   dishwater sky

Mifflin township
Goofy reading
          Madeline's Rescue
in back   9:15am
Mainville   Mifflinville
pale yellow, pale blue, & hard pink
          wildflowers all over
ditches—also egg white
Susquehanna River
Lime Ridge   Berwick
Bloomsburg   Buckhorn

Danville   Limestoneville
repaving 80 Westbound near
I-180 junction
Susquehanna River
Lewisburg   Williamsport
Few   US   Flags   now
Under A bridge where some itiod
had painted "Trust Jesus"
someone else painted out the
"Jesus" and painted "Yourself"
in its place.
Mile Run   Tractor-trailer
are Annoying how they
speed up down hills   or

to pass & then block
traffic slowing on an
  incline

Many dinky dirty yellow
          flowers

FOG Densing near
          Loganton
ghosting grey-beige soughs shoulder
through the trees
Lockhaven
C____ re panorama of the forests
near Lockhaven: "It looks
like broccoli!"

Porter Township   Lamar
"I'm learning to read! Madeline
books are my favorite now.
They're special. Aren't they Daddy!"
Marion Township
Bellefonte
Dead body of Chihuahua sized
   chocolate colored piglet
   rt shoulder
   stiff w/ sunbloat
Milesburg
"Daddy we're right near the
mountain.   It's just like driving
on a nice river."
SNOW SHOE 10:45 AM

"Dad, were you ever a cowboy?"

"Dad, you can be one and block
cows. And I can be your partner."

Philipsburg   Kylertown

"I see a horse[30] in the sky. It's made
out of clouds."

Woodland   Shawville
Curwensville Lake
West branch of Susquehanna
    near Clearfield at Exit 120
Penfield
        Dubois   Brockway
Hazen   Brookville

Sigel   Punxsatawney
North Fork Creek
Union Township   Corsica
Clarion Township   496m
Strattanville
New Bethlehem   Clarion
    500 m
Monroe Township   Shippenville

---

30 GERARD MANLEY HORSES

GLORY be to Horses for dappled manes—
  For eyes of couple-colour as a brinded cow;
For rose-mares all in stipple upon fetlocks that
        swim;
Fresh-firecoal chestnut-tails; haunches' wings;
Paddock plotted and pieced—foal, fallow, and
        plough;
And áll studs, their gear and tackle and trim.

All geldings counter, original, spare, strange;
  Whatever is fickle, freckled (who knows how?)
    With swift, slow; sweet, sour; adazzle, dim;
  They nicker-forth whose beauty is past change:
        Praise them.

Clarion River
              Beaver Township
Knox
              St. Petersburg   Emlenton
Foxburg   Allegheny River
Butler County   Clintonville

Barkeyville   Franklin   Oil City Area
Slipperyrock University   Butler
Dottles of rain   at Grove City
Windy flags   at Grove City
Grove City   Shady Lake   Mercer
Lackawanna
New Castle   Sharon-Hermitage
        Shenango River
Ohio Border 566m
Trumbull Co line
Hubbard

Youngstown   Girard
Canfield   Niles
Rain spats 1x2 cm 1:38pm
Meander Reservoir

King Lear sky 76w
Rain SPATS AGAIN 5x1cm 1:40pm
1:47pm I ask C___ to draw
our car. She says, "I'm
on the case, Daddy." and
begins to draw.
Berlin Lake   Newton Falls
  Lake Milton.

FLAG ON A CONSTRUCTION CRANE: WILL
we ever be rid of the
FLAG PLAGUE?
Alliance, Ohio
Rootstown   Ravenna
epiphytic growth vines on tree
Kent State   610m fr. Providence
Akron dim sun the
             full sun semi-heavy
traffic
Canton   Barberton   Lodi

Massillon   Norton
Wadsworth   Ohio
Rittman   Medina
Seville   Lodi
Finlay   Ohio
71S   2:50pm
They fixed the evil problematic
    macadam on the
exit ramp
College of Wooster   Wooster
Massive HWY construction N of
    Ashland
Congress   West Salem

The US flag has become
the pin of half wits
666m Stop at Days
INN at Exit 186
Ashland OH exit
6:10 AM on HWY
C___'s developed an eye

bother, maybe pink eye
Sun direct behind me
C___ asleep in back
Sunbury   Mt. Gilead

Delaware. Sun low in the
left door   Ohio Wesleyan
Worthington   I-270 west
Columbus's ring road heavy
traffic   Marysville
Dublin   Muirfield
Upper Arlington
        Hilliard Ohio
I-70 West 7:24 am
Dead Kitty w/ collar
     Calico, pretty, on its left side, rt shoulder
w/ its back to road
Plain City

London   Summerford

Land flattening now—
yet slightly rolling—land in
view of the road varying
between 20'-30' in heights.
Springfield
Ask D. if she
wrote to my parents again
Cedarville 801m Sun
bright & to the right—
right rear
        Xenia   Urbana
Enon   Donnelsville

Mad River 813 m
Huber Heights   Brandt Pike
the Great Miami River, 821m,
looks beautiful, brown, &
intimate
In effect, the ubiquitous display
of the flag is akin to
Hussein's—or any dictator's—
use of portraiture
Eaton Greenville
    Rest stop   852m 8:45am EST
Indiana Border

The billboards. The hell
of billboards—And
so commence
the billboards
of the Hoosiers

Greens Fork River
Cambridge City
Connersville   Hagerstown

Fr. the backseat: 888m 9:15am:
"Daddy, What is the soul?"

        [explanation]

"So, Angels are souls! Cool!"

New Castle   Spiceland 890m
Big Blue River 892m

Montgomery Creek
Six Mile Creek
Why do they name the rivers—
    They don't need to
Anthony Creek
Nameless Creek
Stop rest stop 905m
(rest stop mileage is 9 miles over
the mileage tablet in the cubbyhole
that I made up to measure all the reststops
between providence and normal)
GreenfieldMaxwell
Bright blue crisp sky No clouds
Moon ½ stage
Mount Comfort

New Palestine. And so we go
on, all of us, finding dentists
465 ring road around Indy
—detour for repairs on 70—
miss ogling Lilly Billyding

Bush sticker—1st & only one
 I've seen this trip.
"Lick Creek"
White River West Fork—

    Directly south of Indy
½ tank gone   270m
45.378 mpg

I-74 949m 10:18 AM EST
10:20 AM Pass Eagle

Creek Reservoir—its shining
green grass embankments
newly cut—can see
the straight parallel marks of the mowers
on the dike grass
inexplicably (for it is steep)
pinstriping its flanks

Take C___ to Lake Evergreen
   to show her the dam.
She's asking what a dam is.

"Is it like a hurricane?"
she asks

Pittsboro
  Lizton
          Lebanon

"It sounds like 'sons' are
the sun in the air.
But they're not. They're
   little kids."

A mile of dill on the rt. ditch.

Jamestown	Advance
Crawfordsville	Wabash College
Sugar Creek	Linden
Waynetown	Wingate

"I wish you were famous & rich."
"Why?"

"Because you're such a good daddy.
Daffy Duck used to be rich.
Because remember how he made
the dog laugh. On the news they
said 'Someone must make this sick
dog laugh & get one hundred million dollars.'
And soon he was down to his
last million. And he looked &
saw a sign that said, 'You lost,
Daffy!' And he looked and it
was right."

Veedersburg   Attica
Covington   Graham Creek

Newport   Terre Haute
    Illinois border
Prison mile on the rt.
White towers at its corners—
looks square or pentagonal, rarely
come through here in the daytime
Still no clouds
Danville   Potash Center
        Massive barnlike
structure filled w/ potash.
  Traintracks come to deposit
or retrieve the potash
   wind shifted to my stern.
18-23 mph Vermilion River

Salt Fork Vermilion River
Stopped pee & play at idyllic
rest area west of Danville—

shady, has pond w/ aerating fountain, big trees,
clear slides etc. C___ played
w/ her new blue ball. When we
got out of vehicle, saw that
A sparrow had become lodged
in rt. side grillwork. Pulled its still
pliable body out, head
remained in & fell to
depths of engine compartment.
11:51 CST depart rest area
C___ bubbling ball in back
Am bearing 3 heads to Normal:
2 human heads and one sparrow

Fithian   Rankin
"Roses are Red
My Gun is Blue
I am Safe
How About You?
Gunssavelife.com"
—Nazi Burma Shave
Signs near Homer Illinois
The American concern for Safety
Cleanliness and the Freedom
to be Selfish, Greedy, and to Retain
the Right to bomb other countries
to dependency

8.29.03 – 9.2.03

[anabasis]

8.29.03 I depart for C___ late, night,
but stop first at McDonald's drive thru Hwy
51 on south side Normal
purpose to eat fish sandwich
9:45pm I set odo 66907m
I rise on JCT 74-east 9:48pm
and 70mph through dark car-coal again, tire
tone, no stars, it rained today
Must Apologize to F. for
making crack about Saturday
and his traveling to meet a mistress
DeWitt County
And that was a strange bldg

And I then saw my daughter, how
low and wonderfully other. I know
there is a far place
that she has been to and I have not:
I failed her, and tried not to, and failed her
trying not to

Will we live responsive to facts
or reactive to feelings?
Sure I'd drunk wines, merlot, chablis
Sure I had and bourbon, scotch, and single
malt, double dank gin, tequila, ouzo, rums,
amaretto, absinthe, Becks
beers whiskys blended, champagne

Courvoisier, Corona, crèmes, Drambui in
Seattle, the fog I walked in, sherry to write,
the Grappa first in Philly in '89 (first canola
then too first
cheesesteak yeah) Jaegermeister you
tenebreous drink, brandy,
rye whiskey, sake, vermouth and port, and had
hid
medicinal-grade vodka above the spare tire
of the blue Ford Escort station wagon in
Mississippi hell state 2001 and that
was all about feelings I say truly, chained
was I to feeling.

And I had gone to schools, had the
mommy headed teachers, the box hearted
male math teachers,
and that was supposed to be facts, facted—
supposed but they are inert things if not
taught in the shade of the wings of Peace
Dead if each of us is not treated as a child of
genius Dead if not rippling and licked in a
thrum of airlife
between people do you
   know what I am saying! I am
saying I dropped out of school
and did not return until I was 26, all
because I hung my thoughts on feelings
so seriously as I was
taught as all Americans to feel feelings as
Oprah does mostly because Feelings

and most especially Desires and Wish hold

our wingbones in transGlobal economies of
Late Capitalism: is in the interest of
corporations to keep "us" reactive, to take our
feelings personally so that we will desire, feel
deficient, need and ultimately buy
—This is the principle reason Americans are
so reactive, reactive in both their foreign
policy and in their own
privatized individualistic lives:
Reaction benefits Capital.

Ughg.
"My daughter, my daughter, what can I say
of living?"—George Oppen

NO, POPSICKLE!

No, popsickle: stay.
Don't be eaten. Remain in the freezer, the
super market, lodge in the long
far-traveling fridge truck—Be convoyed,
                                    indeed
be conveyed—for a Dakota
a Missouri—but when the truck arrive
at its depository
—or store—at the end of what hot bridge in
                          the dim forenoon,
stay, little bulb of colored cold,
far in your cozy no-no.
I say chill, be a child, popsickle, refuse.[31]
I been to the Supermarket

31 Passage about popsickle dedicated to Kerry Mahan Griner

they are very organized in the supermarket
Lot of thought goes into the supermarket
Much more thought into supermarket than
airport or lib'ary Indiana State Line70 east
164.6m 12:13am
171m the Lilly Bldg

Dream of Fatherly Ineptitude: I am
on my bicycle
and am towing thru the desert
for my daughter's birthday
a cartload of bubbles.

The chocolate-colored steel of a freight train
bears itself a boa over
overpass rt to lt.
STOP to PEE 12:45-49 198m
Ohio border 247.5m small rain

Thru the mind of rain
          thru the fog
I smelled a flower

that was a long way away
and between the flower and me
were birds—& farms w/ dog
there was a family
there were hills & river elms
there were valleys
and there were shadows of cow

I began to run toward the flower
smelling for it

it was a flower surrounded by fogs for miles
and turtles in the miles
                              and mites on the
turtles
and I related to the weather above the turtles
I related to weather and to
turtles that were not hot
          or cold but just right
and all around was present and rested &
content: the clouds in their rugosity
          it was beautiful and it
supported the flower
STOP SLEEP REST STOP 319m 2:50am in
a lovely covering rain, warm and gritty
I rest in a high gray bed of dreams good
enough for older bodies

Wake at 7:35am in my car turtle. Depart
reststop Grey Overcast
I am coming, C____

7:57 270 N to Cleveland
          354.1m Exit 10 270N
          Stop to Gas Columbus OH
          67251 odo, 40.34 mpg
71N 8:37am CST 362m

I seen an Amish buggy

76east Lodi Akron 10:58am EST
450.4m fr Normal
On bridge: "follow condom to want"
Meander Reservoir 511m fr Normal

is an manmade widening of Meander Creek
over which a low pontoon bridge is sentried
on the rails by dark double-crested cormorants
who are fishing
these are rare birds these parts
Pennsylvania border 528 miles

Shenango River, I am Sad. My Life
is falling apart: it is embrangled.
Gordon Ward Interchange, Why
is there weather?
                              There are holes
in
my hair. The river
                    goes by the
oak,
now there is a sunflower on the road—
alone, which I think thinks. It is a tall
sunflower, has a Fibonaccic head
Its seeds like little bird beaks
Trees now are in the clouds.
Rest area 3 ¼ mile. Fog low
MUST GO SEE WALLY. [32]
Stop to Gas in Clearfield PA
2pm Eastern to 2:05pm
Taco Bell 4 hard Taco Supremes
2:05 to 2:20pm
I listen to bluebrass as I eat. Overcast

It is summer but my life feels
crushed. Am I sadder than I have been in

---

32 A previously violent man related to me.

years. Thoughts of my daughter on the
                                            road.

Then a river and a clipped vision of brown
mergansers: I am Adamic briefly, a crispness
smeared thru
a blurred road where signs are bolted
to sunbeams. I am fairly certain
we were all once children.[33]

Still reconstructing bridge at 665 miles
resentment: not being able
to choose to go read alone
or eat/go dinner alone for 7 years
while with someone who hits one or
seems constant angry with one—cd make
one resentful. Rest area 744m 3:45pm PEE

I am not the only one
going through a divorce, separated
from a daughter, son, loved one, life

4pm dark sky ahead, stone house

pain meandering my life 81 N 4:32pm

6:10pm EST Stopped At
reststop to call C___. BUSY.

---

33 Children and their icecreams, the sun swollen on their knuckles, the wind moving the dog fur,
the dog moving the dog fur, a wind sneezing up the smell of puddles and mingling it in the scents
of sandwiches. There may not be any sleeping horses in the regions under the puddles, there may
only be rotifers, paramecia, and nematoda. But so what. All the children smell and are in favor of
the puddles—puddles are the butter of sunlight. Puddles are the humors of winds, the sinuses of
wind. And children know this.

Left message.
Cross Hudson late after
noon thru a balmy blue sky
Breeze south down river
CT Welcome Ctr 945m
        7pm
Geese greylag going south west
sun low marmalade pink in
altostratus to west
Never been in Waterbury at
dusk before, Milky.

I remember the smell
in C___'s blankets,
her good dozing. How all
about her
was a little cheer, and the
 methods of winsome sounds
she practiced. I departed. May she
not grow to think me
hard hearted.

Children Children: and harbors are filled
with children. In their glinting boats.
And there they went with cupcakes
to kaleidoscopes. We watch them in love
from love, with all possible things. All the
world was warm once. There were many
days. There were things that seemed
not to allow joy. But
there were odds, eventually, and
oddities those odds would warm. And we
grew each into such

little fragments of flux and
color. And under us always the worms
change, they bend and wind
waiting for all of us, the flapping wing
the happy kid, to be brought down
out of the wind. Keep dancing, kids,
long as you can, in your bones.

[katabasis]

9.2.03 12:51pm EST Providence RI
Cumberland Farms Rochambeau & Hope
3.505 gallons
$1.82/gallon
Down Cypress Seattle grey
day—Dropped C___ to School
this morning at MLK jr Elementary
& then to D's house at
9:10—just left, we talked of possibilities
Probably the last time
I'll ever see C___'s bed, which I made.
12:56pm At corner of Cypress & N. Main 95s
12:58pm I drive away from Drama CT
1:33pm 40m from Cumberland Farms Gas
station now

Approaching Waterbury on 691w
The gray sky is a drab dull cold furnace of
            cloud
and I, under, in my little clear bun of a car. I
make 84 west and spy a
SHOCKING TURKEY on rt shoulder.
Traffic

heavy now.
Leaves dark and
bright green. The North American turkey
can fly at a top speed of 55mph.
Passing Hawleyville
Welcome to New York and Putnam County
Hudson River, my man! 3:50pm: you are an
melancholic and drained looking behemoth of
water today:
You make me want to pee, I stop to pee at
Rest Stop
near Wallkill River, 2 urinals for thousands of
men 204 miles

236 miles I clack into a luminous looming
bank of fog
& late afternoon darkness: a MIST pends
COLD too on my chest a
gray wool sweater amber
lights ruffle from the backs of cars, my own
lights
are tossed in wrinkles
on an aluminum sided truck
as it passes
There are things I have been
And know I have been
Too I know
There are things I was and am
That nothing in me knows
And that nothing in me can know
Somehow
                    there is nothing
                    I have well been

There is a beautiful light near Dorrance
on the high nodge of hills
at the Bloomsburg junction
A wide mist presses down
from the whale-colored shelf of clouds at
dewpoint

Stop at 321m 5:48pm
near Conyngham, PA & gas
at Subway
          A brown corn stands
like a fluffy species
                                        of grass
This world is gray
and dotted with bottle-brown deer
Laura Kipnis—*Against Love*

From now again A mist
   and fog, the gloaming
Wipers. 7pm
        Rain crinking, peanut-sized splats
Sky a luminous pie of plumbate glaze
road glazed
WRITE D. ABOUT
BOOSTER SEAT
9:44pm EST I have decided!—-
and it is exciting!—to travel
80 to 55 rather than to 76, 71, 270, 70, 465, &
74! arriving Normal from the North, not the
West!

10:02 pm take ticket onto 80 turnpike near
Youngstown

11:35pm Stop to eat fish san. at Burker Ging
& get coffee—air temp noticeably warmer
I saw the fishes in the sea
The fishes saw me
I let them be
As they did me
Bye Bye fishes of sea
The night air near Toledo
Smells of egg and rusted paperweights.
The sniffy manufactories
let slip smokestuff to the stippled air.

807m 1:39 AM small thin
Tollbooth at the End
of Ohio Turnpike, housing a nickel-thin Clerk
$8.35 to cross the State
809.5m from Providence the Indiana border
"Amvets Memorial Highway"
FOG & chill in Indiana near Howe
875.7m Stop in Indiana somewhere
to get Dunkin Donuts (rare these parts) Large
Coffee & 2 Boston Creams 2:40-45AM
Eastern

What then should I have been
that even the wind should stay in my hair
if I close a door
or climb a stair?

Truck with "Molten Sulphur" passes

I am passing now New Lennox, IL
4:30am Eastern, 3:30 Central

on HWY 80 987 miles fr Providence

Fog thick as a muffin. I do not slow
fear deer
I-55 Junction 996m
Now South Away fr. Lake
Fog gone. Immediately
Des Plaines River
Kankakee River 1006m
Fog again 55 miles N of Normal
Mackinaw River Porcelain Fog
Money Creek 1079m
Fog hegemony, visibility 1/4m
BLOOMINGTON NORMAL EXIT 2 MILES
4:52am
OFF 55 HWY 1079.5m from Providence
4:55am
Rt on Washington Ave 1083m
Lt on Mercer; Rt on Grove
5 blocks Rt on Kreitzer
Park 1084.7m
5:04 AM
CRICKETS

10.30.03 – 11.4.03

[anabasis]

It is Halloween-Eve and the Wind is
Heavy. It is a verminous stage curtain
9:20pm Normal
outside apartment Corner of Kreitzer &
Grove
I travel to see C___ for Halloween and to
be Divorced by someone on Nov. third
in a court of Providence
The trees in my landlord's yard
are still caped in leaves
caliginous apricot colored leaves
and from out a common vein of sorrow
A wind of the dark is blustered in
the dark 70,499 on Odometer I
am in a college town, hear my condition:
South on Washington To stygian WalMart
get batteries AA in WalMart's bright box of
storelight
for old Minolta
Fill 8.3 gallons of 87 octane 9:40pm at the
WalMart Gas
Out of Walmart
Now McDonalds—fish sandwich & chicken
coke large coffee HWY 74 junction east
Dark Wind reset trip odo at 51 & 74 east
                      junction
just leaving Normal Passing
Rantoul 10:25pm Smell of Cow dung

STARS Warm 64° Heavy Southerly gusts
DRY piss Yellow Maple leaves caught
under wipers LEAVES ON THE ROAD
The leaves seem to have small minds
like they can't decide where to go The wind is
                                    stirring
everything as in a pan of cold, even the city
of Champagne is jostled
and Homer too, Homer IL Clouds
hung there now bathed by
sodium haze of some little distant city or corn
                                    town

leaves frog on the road, frog-sized
snapping and bounding
          wind frogs
          slow and small the large
          leaves seed the gasses. Now
          now birdwise in swirls
the dam of Indianapolis
at Eagle Creek Reservoir: the large curl of the
water in the spillway, profluent now, and the
dark trees bordering the
spillway in sodium fuzz silhouette
so "Baptizing in the profluent stream, the
sign Of washing them from guilt of sin to
life." No, John Milton, no one dips in that
stream or any other, much, in America, Pair
of Dice Lost, today:
from your Book 12 of 1665 to this of 2003
70 east 164m 12:45am Central
Chemical smell from Aluminum
manufactory approaching

city center Indianapolis
"Really Free Checking" on billboard
173m City Ctr the Indy City ctr Sky scrapers
are wickered in sharp blue & white light
& proud bright signs

All the hwy through the city
lit dim saffron of the tall bent
lamps, from each one hangs a shining cone
"Nameless Creek" There is a typing school
near here where "the girls"
learn the typing there are birds
and leaves, my sister Theresa Syverson, now
Hoffman, now an evangelist christian who
homeschools and voted her for George W
Bush, he of the Anger,
went to typing school in the early 70s I think
"Oppression
and no food," According to
Martin Scorsese, was what was
in Sicily, much like my childhood
It is dark here
no farm lights east of Indianapolis
1:35AM Central Standard Time I
Am driving to Providence Rhode
Island to get divorced on
Monday November 3, 2003 at 9AM
at One Dorrance Plaza, Family Court

In 1900 76 million people
lived in the United States
most on farms
for light gas lights for

power horses
        Rest Stop   234 miles from Normal
1:50am 2 cups of Strong Coffee from
green Automatic coffee & hot chocolate
dispenser
w/ "whitener": the code for these cups of
coffee
was (on the electric touch screen vending
selection pad)
A – 7 - *H –
Not seen on cars an American flag decal yet—
this is a substantial
change from previous trips—the political
mood is shifted
now that we're 6 months into Iraqi civilian
murder
Great blue Fingernail–Clipping Arch
at Ohio Border: 247 m 2:10 am
Teddy Roosevelt, as a young idiot,
wrote "WAR IS ONE OF THE HIGHEST
FORMS OF HUMAN ENDEAVOR"

The Spanish Colonies of Cuba,
Puerto Rico, Guam & the
Philippines are what TR's
delusion got the U.S. Nation After
attacking Spain's colony of Cuba
in 1898, making U.S. an "empire"
Approaching Dayton Ohio
where Wilbur & Orville Wright
watched birds & made bicycles
The Strange Frogs of the Leaves
        ill yellow and clacking brown

in the hwy lightstream
April 22, 1915 near Ypres, Belgium
the first poison gas used against
humans, Chlorine, canister
bombardment by the Germans.

"Right is more precious than peace!"
—so said Woodrow Wilson like a fool.
Another child of Cake-smashing demons.
"Big Darby Creek State and National
Scenic River" 332m 3:25am Central
Urban America was electrified in
the 1920s. Prior days were candle lit &
gas & oil lamps. By 1929 the
majority of American homes had
electricity. "Olentangy State
Scenic River" 270 N 353m
Northwest of Columbus. BILLBOARDS
SPROUTED IN THE 1920S. Credit's
advent in the 1920s: by 1927
3/4ths of all household goods were
bought on credit. 71 N 356 m
4:47 AM central—Exit 122 pull off
to gas and sleep just north of Columbus
[I sleep in the driver's seat
put the steering wheel all the way up
and wrap up in my Patagonia jacket and
blue fleece blanket and u-shaped neck pillow]

Wake 8:15 am Central—9:15 Eastern
8:22 got large coffee and donut
at BP (British Petroleum) next to Shell—Shell
is good safe comfortable parking lot to

sleep in, at BP got "gourmet"
coffee w/ real half-n-half come here again,
have slept here 2 or 3 times already.
IT'S HOLLuhWEE. Sunny.
Warm. In fact I have seen
bug splats, or maybe they are small vampiric
moths
or the flies electrified to life by Renfield,
consider
the day. Mt. Gilead
State Park and a lovely creek. "I Got
You, Babe" on the radio. It has got to be
one of a few perfect songs. Trees
rather bare here. Oh the leaves
are blowing here:
shallow yellow maelstroms unchaining
across the bright highways. The
rapid hip hop music is delightful
to watch these leaves by, Dawg. I am in fact
from the far blond wheat fields
          of Minnesota.

I miss that Minnesota:

When I was a child, I was young,
and the lakes I had been to
and the lake I had been in
were petrol blue in the evening
and stray smells of straw were on them

and nearby the maple docks
the attention of the carnivores
was bound in the gooses

all these living things
on the lake home
when I was a child, I was
wild upon it, the tennis court by the lake
strange how the animals
enjoyed their wings

some of the small live things were swollen,
others tiny, some were windy

there was a squirrel who was windy
none had umbrellas
and for a while when I was 12
my parents did love the lakes, and all of us
and themselves

Thomas Campion will be added
to Mark Ritchie's independent study
bibliography. Mark Ritchie, a Republican
student of mine, w/ shaved head and
leather jacket wishes to study the affinities
between poems and songs, he will do Bob
Dylan,
Dylan Thomas, Annie DeFranco, John
Donne.
Others. He is a senior at
Illinois State University. Dark woolen blue clouds
to the West, rumpled heaven bedding,
wind from east, Paganinic leaves
the farm Pond's surface in this wind-stressed
Milk-&-Apricot light
of Ohio in bare leaves, Northern Ohio,
Medina, Seville

w/ the arrayed Penske trucks in
that Parking Lot in the distance, the
surface of that pond is cold & lemon
silver. Horses, Appaloosas in that paddock,
blue watery sky
more leaves now. Here I am in Akron
just before noon, bare trees & brick,
and the shadows in the ditch are Johnny Cash
black. The above Paganinic: Nicolò Paganini
(died 1840). Paganini, whose unpredictable
music is the ancestor of these capricious
leaves, was born Oct 27 1782
A crash of orange wind frogs now, about the
size of
a Roman shield, launches from the right ditch,
my car,
an erasing javelin, blasts apart the orange
shield–word
of leaves. Lake Milton
498 m 11:30 am Eastern.

Meander Reservoir 507m
Partly Cloudy. A 6" metallic
chop is on the water.
Mahoning River, industrial
Gravel quarry. Strange Storage Rental parks.
The very
weather rented   Warren Ashtabula,
80 east
Nimbostratic clouds. Many wind frogs.
Pennsylvania border. A Skunky
cream sunlight, Shenango River
and the Sadness of light

at the Gordon Ward Interchange
with Feed Corn standing, at Lackawanna
Township,
How do the floating leaves
get so high? They touch my windshield.
Warm, upper
60s. The weather: is it
an athlete's philosophy?
Paul Harvey: is he
not A Nazi?
½ Way 12:20 eastern

As I got older, fools increased
till few were wise. The sun
is hard here at the great
valley of the Clarion

Christians, I know,
do not practice love
but law.

"Well it's freaky Halloween out
there," a pompous baritone discjockey near
Knox PA
opines, "So make sure it's a
safe one; keep that safety in
mind." Hear the dumb American
ideology of Fear:
Hear the ruination of a whole day for the lithe
of spirit
and the fat children nod: we cd be a
happy people, a loving people, a giving a
caring

people—but Hey we'd rather be a Safe people
—no joy
in chaos[34], no understanding that fearlessness
and compassion
are related if not the same. Our nation, of all
nations,
is afraid, longs for "safety," has for 40 years,
and
as such it slowly loses compassion, Rest Stop
609m 1:10 eastern
No delight in Disorder, a Smallness
grown to a smallness
which cannot find a house in fidelity
cannot find a home in philia

cannot find, won't find a—
we can find a—shed maybe
we can find a shed in anxiety—
There is
a puce ladybug loose in my car
it is glorious to drive thru Pennsylvania
when the leaves are snowing in the mild light
of Autumn
StOPPing in Lamar PA, coffee,
gas, food n bathroom 2:28 eastern
2:52 back on hwy
is not capitalism gambling?
Be a leaf gamble not

You will fall whether you have
burrs on you or not, leaf

---

34 "I have a great belief in the fact that whenever there is chaos, it creates wonderful thinking. I
consider chaos a gift." —Septima Poinsette Clark

Every leaf aspires to be a seed (not true)
R B Winter State Park is part
of the Bald Eagle State Forest
Hills big now sun
enkindling twigs, stroboscoped
oak trunks cause a cascade of blue shade
and vanilla sunflame : it is the height of the
trees and the time of day that
shoves the tree shadows
near Mile Run to fall picket-like over the road
There were many women
the smoldering gorgeous one
and tired of that had then had one in Sunbury
and smartly gone swimming after one in a
pool in Clarion and now what is it that fogs
up your memory of her figure, or her tongue out
in passion

or at least resign to never know
such face and hip again
at 3:45 I am approaching Lime Ridge
Berwick PA direct from the west
at the end of the road before it bends
slightly south are the twin gargantuan
cooling towers under a hoary
steam plume milk-lit in the
late peach sun—and then the wide
Susquehanna its green midge-blue sheen
the corrugated lips of two great Allegheny ridges
and before them tan dry standing corn
cattle feed. If you think
FDR did not assassinate Huey Long
you're a fool

and a typical American. 81 n 4:05 estrn

The leaves around Nanticoke
have not turned, but dried
brown that way. Scranton
the valley of Scranton laid
under a late peach sun
is smoggy today.
84 east 821 miles from Normal 4:40 estn
Whole hills cast shadows now
Now nearly all leaves down
The word "freedom" stumbling
wet and empty like
a masturbator from a shower
makes me ill. Sunset green peach
hue light filling the clouds
from horizon to horizon
4:55 eastern
4:59 pee 842 m

There is some green grass in the median here
and here
and now that the sun's gone down
and it's purple, I fear a deer may
cross and I will smack her
It is Halloween yet many bugs
so late are slamming at
the windshield. The candy bar was
introduced in 1912.
Crossing Hudson River 911m from Normal
Illinois 6:06 eastern : all car lights on
heavy red taillight chain away from me
& white headlight chain toward me

dense traffic CT border
Lovely Waterbury of the night
yr new cars, & white & yellow lights
Rhode Island border 1059m 8:25 eastern
Arrive Motel 6 Warwick 9pm

"What a fierce kind of lemonade is grapefruit
juice" says my daughter, age 6, as we sit
in stripmall Bickford's restaurant on the
warm November Sunday there in Warwick,
Rhode Island. Still there is nothing; tomorrow
a divorce hearing, I & her mother,
culminations of error.

Sometimes when running with my daughter,
as we did today on the Motel 6 lawn, it is like
there are no days, nor week, nor other time,
and she has no mother, and I
haven't one either—that we are somehow just
here; running, that we together compose 2
halves of Christ's, or someone's, distant
brother, laughing.

　　　[katabasis]

Nov 3 2003 Monday 11:52 AM
Passing Exit 13 S of Providence on
Interstate 95 S
Just left Family Court at 10:30. Am
quiet, as I usually am in the car,
but this particular quietness goes
pretty deep in me. I am deeply sad
Sunny day. Thin cover of altostratus. D

cried giving her testimony. D
hugged me afterward, ten feet outside the
courtroom she interrupting my lawyer next
me, her lawyer
behind her standing off, all around the
divorcing families beside us, the hallway
thrumming in poor and splitting
families, my lawyer nearby competently
waiting out her awkward and tearful hug.
Been this
sad before. Been this sad.
Have stopped
in Exeter Rhode Island
to call D. Just spoke
w/ her. I love her so
much I am in Connecticut
Now crossing New London Bridge
Now crossing African-American
War Veterans Memorial Bridge
the word bridge so close to bride

Cried on phone. D said maybe I should
get a psychiatrist, "a good one, a really good
one" I cried, and she thinks I'm "ill" when
I'm relieved to be away from someone's
constant need to belittle, hit, control. Bye bye.
Bye

bye Warm say low 70s
Crossing Old Saybrook Bridge
Take 9N to Essex to Hartford
Strange to feel the summer and
to see mild carrot of autumn

in those few trees that still
keep leaves
Now start the grumpy rocks
in the hills beside the road
metamorphic with granite stripes
Now here near Middletown passing
the Quinnipiac River
It is bright and warm as I
approach Cromwell & Rocky Hill
Pale yellow leaves
smatter the wet top of the Quinnipiac
In the back courtyard
of the Family Court building at One
            Dorrance Plaza

A ginkgo about 25 feet high
stood testifying of yellow
yellow as a lemon rind
and I looked at it, 91 South,
as my lawyer Don Moyer
was talking to me before we went in
to Family Courtroom 3-C
as Judge Jean or Joan Shaeffer
took our testimony, & granted the divorce,
which will take effect Febr. 3, 2004
I called D after
near the Connecticut border
and cried. 691 West toward Waterbury
Milldale Cheshire Cirrostratus
and Altocumulus   large
flowing bubble of starlings
at the junction of 84 West
The Rochembeau Bridge at the

Housatonic—the Housatonic
its cold river colors a
tonic Approaching Toconic Parkway
in now Hudson Valley: Marshes
Rest Area One Mile sun in
driver's window clear blue—
some cumuli. Rest Stop
Hudson crossed
5 bugsplats 5mm wide x 30mm
All the same color gray sun now in
windscreen a constellation
on the rt of windshield of 1, 2, 3, 4
splats from small yellow-winged
lepidopteran the dust enyellowing the
smeared contents of their bodies

dark blue smudge of crows in rt shoulder, a
manila sheen of sun on each
swart crow back. Mid-
afternoon, am in now the
shadow of a great lead-white
altocumulous. It is the shape of a
four masted flap-&-horn-sailed ship, it so
resembles a ship, the sun watery
behind it, I feel like a blue fish looking
up at it wondering what cargo it
does not bury in the water, speculating
whether it does carry a cargo of vanilla bars
Is there wind inside the turning tires
as they descend to the valley of the Delaware
through the Catskills
I smell the acrid scent of stressed
rubber and aluminum from the brakes

of the full truck ahead I cross

the Pennsylvania border, are
these not the Kittatinny Mts.
229 m 2:55 eastern
Sun strange low and the color of pillow stains.
Am in tree shadows and that
picketing effect of shade across
my dash and face is what I
associate with Pennsylvania. It is
stroboscopically lighting the interior
of my car w/ apricot marmalade light.
Stop in Tafton PA "Promised Land
Truck Stop" fill on buy
Parliament Lights, got 45 miles per gallon
on last tank, O Scranton
Mt. Pocono I come
I am in the hillshade, light in the hillstone
opposite pearlescent

N of Scranton south of 81 direct
into sun bugsmears pearlescent
sun prismatic & rubiate in
my frames of brown plastic eyewear
electric portable roadsign left shoulder
"PM Sun-glare Use Sun Visor"
green grass in the median
green bushes it is November & there
is green the afternoon leaves
translucent "Aggressive Driver
High Crash Area" Smog &
haze in the valley of Wilkes-Barre
Moon up in the Southeast 5/8ths to full

80 W will take sunglasses
off soon 4:22pm
Lights on 4:26pm getting hungry. The mix
of lights at day's end raises
something in me, a nurturant melancholy

That great orange yo-yo of the sun, when I
cannot look elastics down
under the trees and then coiling
up again to my right distant in
some lovely gloaming and woodsmoke
happy cows, holsteins, are walking in a line
farm of wood smoke and barns so red
the susquehanna river 5:10pm eastern I wd
call this
official sunset
near Mile River PA. Write a poem that rhymes
"mortified" with "mortar fire"
5:51 having eaten at McDonalds
I make the road
Moonlight 7pm at my
4 o'clock

Stop to call C___ 7:05pm
She had a good day
and was doing her homework when I
called. She wore her Halloween Costume
a white lace princess outfit with white parasol
all Saturday and Sunday with me to the mall
and the movie and
a total lunar eclipse November 8 make
an appt w/ psychiatrist
8:10 eastern : 550m = 1/2 way

I shd arrive at my apt on
Kreitzer & Grove in Normal Illinois
at 4:10am Central
        Shenango River's now just a
sign, green sign in the dark: too dark to see
her comforting mud lip body
ohio border 571m
        Youngstown 12m
Mahoning River
Meander Reservoir 588m will
take 89/90 across northern
Ohio, Indiana, & down fr
Chicago 80w 588m new route
stop to get ticket

The Airs smelled of cold woodsmoke and
river when I unrolled my window to collect
the ticket. Mahoning River again
598m. Little traffic
When my ankles left the thistles
there were musics in the airs
and in the music hung a clattering
because it was stuffed with big
clear dragonflies
it was like they were balsa crafts
w/ walnut heads
        Rest Area (Service Plaza) 610.4m
And the music brought to mind the
        memories of breasts
Cuyahoga River
Children children children
how I love them, their little hairs of hay
smiles of hey, knees that shuttle

9:46pm Legs and lower back aching
Oberlin College use next rt—home of <u>Field</u>
magazine that panned my book
fog as I approach Cleveland
Th. Edison's birthplace and a Lake Erie island
legs and lower back no longer aching
after taking 4 ibuprofens 10:45pm
I always found Field a really boring magazine
If you go carrying pictures
of Chairman Mao, you ain't
gonna make it w/ anyone anyhow
FOG heaven Ohio mile marker
near Elmore
Portage River, Ohio—this is the ancient
portage where
large men rode the
floating pumpkins. Much better
radio stations up here than there are down in
west central Ohio

Toledo next 3 exits 733m I love
this fog up here near Fifth Third Field
and Toledo Zoo so I opened up
the air and let the bad window out
It went. It took the curtain w/
the curtain took the chair the
chair took the room the room caught
the hall the hall grabbed the foyer
and all the house was towed
arroint a tunnel of air
the air, a towel, the hair, the chair
a rug, the mops, the hall, the cup, the foyer
                and anvils—all the all

to Wichita now   on a gust
of window Midnight 790 m fr Providence
and C___, Melpomene and D
12:12am Pay $8.30 toll
end Ohio turnpike end of Marriage end of
family

Indiana border 806 m
"Animal Present when Flashing"
stop gas coffee pee 837 miles
near Howe Indiana fog lifts
somewhat. Coffee and small hamburger
at Hardees, moon in Transylvania clouds
up there in the west 12:55am central pat toll
$4.15 80w 941m
No such soul. Return to Sender.
55 south at last 993m
2:18am Des Plaines River 998m
(eta 3:40am at Kreizer)
Kankakee River no fog this time

strong east wind car pulls to rt
Anybody here seen my old friend Martin?
McLean Co., home of Normal, border
3:14am 1056m
Mackinaw River 1066m
Glow of Normal just over "hill"
South of Mackinaw
Money Creek 1071m
Streetlights of Normal at horizon
Exit 167 my exit 1076m 3:30am
Washington St 3:37am
leaves, wind frogs   my old friends the frogs

still here
lt on Mercer 3:38
rt on Grove
rt on Kreizer 3:40am exactly!
leaves everywhere!
blowing in the night of Normal
Anybody here
seen my old friend Martin?

I remember that there are maps in my closet
Carried from some motels in Kentucky
And an Ohio motel with pool, the last
summer with my daughter

Are there not more stories for the father
More maps for treading
There are more maps surely

The cold is free. We can always have it
The cold is the map of all to come

12.20.03 –12.24.03

[anabasis]

4:35am Dec 20, 2003 DARK 10° F
Part of what was insisted in
divorce agreement is C___ not
spend any "major holidays" w/ me
thus not Thanksgiving, Christmas
Christmas Eve, Easter, New Year
Halloween, nor birthday her. Too poor
to oppose this. Hoarfrost on car.
Am very ill as I travel now to spend 21, 22, 23
with her, to have our own Christmas
in the Motel 6 in Warwick moon gibbous
sliver, dirty silver space pie, lit
by hard iceborn light in its lower
left. Set odo 73,452 depart Dunkin
Donuts on Oakland, have fever
2 old fashions a large coffee w/ cream
2 apple juices. w on Oakland
Left at Oakland n Center 4:50am
4.8m 74 east junction 70mph
4:55 AM moon 4/5th the way
up my windshield direct above
the steer wheel Indiana now n not yet dawn
6:10am

The Sea of Faith
Was once, too, at the full, and round
earth's shore
Lay like the folds of a bright girdle furl'd.

But now I only hear
Its melancholy, long, withdrawing roar,
Retreating, to the breath
Of the night-wind, down the vast edges drear
And naked shingles of the world.
Ah, love, let us be true
To one another! for the world, which seems
To lie before us like a land of dreams,
So various, so beautiful, so new,
Hath really neither joy, nor love, nor light,
Nor certitude, nor peace, nor help for pain;
And we are here as on a darkling plain
Swept with confused
alarms of struggle and flight,
Where ignorant armies clash by night. Arnold
was that lovely

I quit smoking dec 18. It is not true, the idea
above, that our world holds no joy or peace,
nor even love.
Arnold's wrong. I knew once a help for pain
and I will embrace it once again
when to Normal I return:
it is vipassana, I will begin again to practice
this ancient cultivation.
There is a dawn lurking behind
the reticulated veins of the trees
bunched here, blueback, and there in the
moving land & under now & again
the red blink of a
cellphone tower. Let me remain
under everything—subferre—as

Thérèse of Liseaux suggests one do.
It is a Saturday. I have the flu.
Woke at 4am after yesterday's all day fever
spent in bed at Maria's
have fever now
woke at 4, tho ate Nyquil and antidepressant
Trazodone. Snow patching

pale blue frost specked to pink
on roofs winks of dark
nodules crisp on
all manner of poles that rear
in silhouette like masts out of
barns farrow sheds and stupas of grain
bins tied by black pipes run
horizontal—all against the cold
lemoning band glinted w/ jets.

No blizzard of snow gnats yet.
Too cold to snow. "Some blessed hope
whereof he knew, and I was unaware"
Stop to Pee 145 miles 7am depart reststop
7:05am
Sun up radiant yolk
        1/2 ball erumpent

Thérèse of Liseaux
died at 24 of tuberculosis
on her deathbed she said
"I have reached the point of not
being able to suffer any more
because all suffering is sweet to me."

I recall that this is what is learned
in the practice of vipassana too. It is enough,
she said, to realize one's nothingness

On Housman's biographical maths
in *A Shropshire Lad:* 3 score years
& 10 = 70 yrs. Cannot, Housman
suggests, go back to 20-yrs old.
Wd he like to? "Take from 70
springs a score, it only leaves
me 50 more," means he wd not live it
again if a demon came said Nietzsche
and told us we were to live
the day the very life over and over over
wd we laugh, he asked, or what He said
what if some day or night a demon tiptoed
after you into your big crib, your hardwon
solitude or your favored spot under a scented
bridge or as you turned a corner from seeing
your lover in the hallway and said Demon said
to you: 'This life
, just as you live it now and have lived it, you
will have to live another time and even
innumerable times more—and there
will be nothing new in it, but
every sorrow and every happiness and every
notion and indeed every cough and all things
indescribably small
and important in your life will without
exception revisit
you, all in the same sequence and order, even
this moment, this road, and I myself.' Would
you not pitch yourself on the grass or haul

your harmed mind
to a bar or would you curse the demon
for this? Or how well disposed would you
have to become to yourself and to
life and to fate to desire such a test and badge of
triumph?

I-465s 7:20am Indianacity
90.1fm in Indy = NPR
70east 7:25am Ambassador
Al-Brahim, A woman w/ A
plum upper crust British accent

There are things in the fruits of
the dark—whole, impatient
orchestras; small emperors w/
special blue butters from the
milks of birds; tender

kingdoms, and she, your mother, is there
and here name is Al-Brahim.
Someone talks of Saddam Hussein's capture
70east 7:35am
            Last night I recall I dreamed
as I woke, About the German word
"Zug," which means "train"
and the English word "tug," to tow

Anthony Creek is white and cold
and the landscape is almost creaking
under the pale brass of the frost-sopped light.
227m 1/2 tank gone cloudy now
    Altostratus.

251m Ohio border—parabolic blue steel
arch
sunny now
sun 20° to rt. snow flurries. Each
snow glint a white & gold chip.

Buy on the rumor, sell on the news
there again the
constant graphite-grey sheen
on the Shenango River 280m

snow now on the air like gray-green jewels
beautiful yellow bridge cloudy
again 315m North wind
blows me right
                    270 N 343m

10:13am STOP on I-270 NW of
    Columbus Ohio to purchase gas
and food. 9.959g
Their very morally raised daughter
ran about weeping in the wheat
that terrible December 13th
and we didn't condemn her
we put 7 stones in the field
    upon which we placed Bibles

2 bibles to each stone making
14 bibles but this did not appease or fix her
it was
Sunny toward & now away from
Columbus. Much more snow here
Do I not have in my shelves

at home the complete works
of Aristotle—owned once
by Willie Unsoeld? Willie
Unsoeld the toeless? The guy who
w/ Someone Hornbine was the 4th
team to climb Mt Everest—but the 1st
to climb it via the West Ridge
long hill. Unsoeld taught at alma
mater The Evergreen State College
OF WHICH I AM AN ALUMNUS
Light of weak yellow
bumping in the snow 76e Lodi
   Akron 451.7m 1:13pm eastern

A barn there at the junction
has cracked w/ weight of snow
Ohio is the opposite of
                    Valhalla
Bare tan stones in the hills
—sedimentary class
at the 76 & 77 junction
117m 1/4 tank gone 1:30pm
Sun   low & in rear rt window
Salt   1:55pm STOP TO PEE
   Youngstown rest stop
2pm exit ill-designed rest area
Lake Milton a broad plate
of pewter crossed in its
midsection on a pontoon bridge

is clear of ice. And then
Meander Reservoir in the pines
& swollen w/ shadows in the

waves. 514 m STOP at "Travel
Center" on 80 east to buy
map light as I have forgotten
mine at home. Was that the Shenango before
because this is the Shenango here
my friend the Shenango River (don't
understand why I feel so tender toward this
river) a brown green bed of light as if
the river water lay on top of buried sunlight or
racks of luminous mud
but free of ice—now a
pond of ice—a white scum
of altostratus above us as
I and an oddly mechanical gaggle pass
thru east Lackawanna township

No more the red wine hangover.
Now snow. Teeth sized snow
near Fridley.
                    Now snow
        is the size of knuckles   At
OD Anderson Interchange [35]

---

[35] **THE GENERAL ASSEMBLY OF PENNSYLVANIA**

HOUSE BILL
No. 1304 Session of 1993

INTRODUCED BY KING, GRUITZA AND FARGO, APRIL 21, 1993

REFERRED TO COMMITTEE ON TRANSPORTATION, APRIL 21, 1993

AN ACT

1 Designating the interchange at Interstate 79 and Interstate 80
2 in Mercer County as the Orville DeWayne "O.D." Anderson
3 Interchange.

and appears to streak horizontal
against the brown cupboard colored hemlock
forest silos & stubby brown, but rather white,
hills.
          Now, find me one
derogator of western Pennsylvania
whereof I mean the landscape thick
of corduroy
Because of the wind
        and the coldness of the macadam
the snow does not stick here
on the bright and fresh blacktop
I love the wide majestic valley
of the metallic and chocolate Allegheny River

as if the Allegheny from
white pine from hemlock were
made of chocolate that were made in
turn of metal
the snow big as eyelids
snow thick now, a marmoreal wall of fog and
flakes
a shroud of white winking eyelids at
the Cook Forest State Park—wind buffet
and
road waft Allegheny

```
 4  The General Assembly of the Commonwealth of Pennsylvania
 5  hereby enacts as follows:
 6   Section 1.  The interchange at Interstate 79 and Interstate
 7  80 in Mercer County is hereby designated and shall be known as
 8  the Orville DeWayne "O.D." Anderson Interchange.
 9   Section 2.  The Department of Transportation shall erect
10  appropriate signs to indicate the designation under section 1.
```

National Forest
near Shippenville, trees a strange petrol blue,
marmot-filled forest now
passing over high bridge now
below under a scrim of flurries
through a scaffold of sepia light
the Clarion River marbled w/ top ice
deep valley. Now white-out
1/2 mile visibility BIG FLAKES
at Corsica PA are the dinnerplates of
dragonflies 3:45pm EST   250 m 1/4 tank
            608 miles from Normal

such messy dust smearing windshield a froth
of salt sludge on road, flakes big
each is in a sledge, Growing Darker, 4:15pm
snow dust squall drift
snow spindrift, 3 slush moraines
from tires
Dead deer on center line that almost glow
This glowing snow dusk shower
reminds me of the smell
of tortoiseshell and vintage fountain pens

West branch Susquehanna River
bridge 1/4 mile vis snow
squall. Thimble-sized flakes
massive sneezes
rack my chest
rt nostril bloody from sniffling
666m afternoon slate-colored
heavy snow 4:45pm
Stop Pee 4:52pm 673m

very slick @ rest stop
heavy snow—but only 1 mile
down rd (at Snowshoe) no
snow falling

5:10pm 684 miles from Normal darkness
finally come from the hills and
it's dusk, the rd shining
w/ wet, brake lights of the semis
in front smear the road red
snow dots streak in my headlights
descending now road all dry
dark blue night hills, brown blue sky
There like a grim
prodigious periwig
are the cuppedcake of cliffs
these are the great Siluro-Cambrian
magnesian limestones, charged with globs
of brown hematite iron ore
and they hang as on a great moon-broad
hanger in a licorice air, very dark as I cross
the Susquehanna River I-180 lopes off to
the southeast.

Nose situation disturbing
6:10pm Stop Danville, PA Gas 752m

6:45pm am experiencing chills
from a fever, have eaten
a cold cut trio submarine w/
swiss cheese on wheat am
using the map light to write
84e

at 841m in the very terrible air
a whale of snow dust
dark as a sneeze from a glacier
snow flecks: then they are albino houseflies
NY border 878m

Wallkill River clear skies, stars
smeared in it. Hudson River
917m 9pm EST
954m CT border 9:45pm
As I am east Rhode Island above
I-95 there explodes
Very bright Shooting Star at 11:50pm:
this star is as a flaming yellow mop dragged
one thousand seventy-nine miles fr Normal
Apponaug. It is the name
of the town.

　　　[katabasis]

December 23, 2003 12:34pm
Rhode Island time. 26 miles south
of Dunkin Donuts on Hope & Rochembeau
where I dropped off little C___
and where I collected her on the morning
of the 21st in a cold wind, tin light, and
among some snow moraines
on Hope. D refused a Xmas gift then but
took the ones for Melpomene. When I dropped
C___ off just now D was wearing a
yellow sweater, red corduroys. She
looked big faced, square jawed
sm nosed & beautiful as usual.

My sense was that she seemed to stare
at me a long time v. sadly as we said
a cursory goodbye as if she was thinking
this may be the last time we
see each other as husband and wife
(that is what I was thinking anyway)
[and it was]
Now I am looking at a truck that says
"Wheaton World Wide Moving."

CT border 40.5m. The wide world
is moving. It is the same every day
as Thérèse of Liseaux says
we must suffer everything.
I ain't afraid of yr Yahweh
I ain't afraid of yr Allah
I ain't afraid of yr Jesus
I'm afraid of what you do in
            the name of yr God. This on
the radio.
You don't get faith from belief &
worship, nor from baptism—you
get faith from testing things
out yourself. Faith is not a state of conviction:
it is instead a state of openness to experience,
a state of empirical engagement. It is a state of
directionlessness. CT Hwy 9 North
73.5m fr Hope & Rochembeau
I pass Beaver Meadow Road
very blue sky. The bare trees
flicker w/ light that's honey like
I think I "became" a "poet"
because I saw that it was

one of the few social roles
in which my apparently frequent
propensity to ignore rules

wd go unremarked. And to be
fair, I don't ignore rules that
matter—such as parking rules. I am
now passing thru the home
of Wesleyan University
I have cut my own hair since
I was 20. 2:30   A series
of traffic jams in the sun
Driving into the sun in a traffic
jam, nose hurts, left nostril
especially, sun in my tissues,
tissue lit. Haven't reached even
Danbury yet. Pretty Danbury w/
its St Mary's Hospital, which
I love b/c I imagine it's

filled with babies! I am now in
New York and I do not
remember driving thru Danbury
Connecticut. Rest Area on A
Mountain 173m—very few
urinals & heavily used rest stop
Many people traveling today
b/c it's the day before
Christmas Eve.

Governor of New York George Pataki
did today pardon
comedian Lenny Bruce posthumously

for Obscenity. He died
        43 yrs ago.

Penn border   sun   low in front
& like a big yellow cherry
hung about w/ manila colored cream
smeared thru clouds—C___
calls me "book boy"
Rest Stop 332   5:52pm
v. dark.
        7:19pm Stop fuel
$16.63   9.669g

"We won't have destroyed anything
unless we destroy the ruins too."
—Alfred Jarry
577m Ohio Border   9:55pm
Rain has turned to snow

Some time I wd like to talk w/ people
—friends, colleagues—about
the utterly strange fact: that we are here;
that there cd be <u>nothing</u>. And not:
that we are here & that "God"
created us—but that we
are here. Period.
Snow still falls N of Columbus
It has fallen now straight since Pennsylvania,
I think. At one pt the rain just did
turn to snow.

It snow less now, like how a ringing
of bold bright bells might be heard

to heat the airs
My many many 5 minute ideas
An bell is a Weebelow scout of the Air
And the Air is a squad of monkeys!
Let me drag A pumpkin from
            its meadow
And make it a vegetable puppy: I would
love to be that loving: to be friendly toward a
                              vegetable
Now not snowing not raining. A pumpkin
is a little bell of vegetable flesh
and has no clacker in it. A vege-t-bell
Past midnight, v. dark, am, v. v. dark
west of Columbus at 782 m fr Providence
1:15 eastern   Fuel 9.498 g   2:15am Brookville
OH 853m 2:37 am Indiana Border

am Indiana in, but just now
a New York plate. Got coffee, god I am
loping from the coffin, at night, the Aches
of Mild headache of earlier today
which lingered as clapboard relics
of the bout w/ this weekend's flu
have now dissipated: even my nose has
almost ceased smarting I recall I saw
a shooting star large as a
bird as I entered the hard Rhode
Island state late Saturday night
Now it is easy Wednesday morning
in Indycity am I

east of the city. Its blinking
pointy. Later I pee at 4:30

Illinois border. Vermilion
River. A missile of aspirin
Me like stoicism. I pee
4:15am Central time
We heard a wrinkled man
whistling softly in the wheat
as the snow-laden air grew dark
w/ geese. Let me be then
A big bonneted bosomed
woman, heavy in my jowls
& haunches gooey.

Kumbaya, snow
bring the snow, I would like to order
21 snows. Kumbaya, do not
bring me chains of cat bone, now am
hard thru Piatt County neighbor of
McClean County
McClean County I am
very tired. Le Roy, Kumbaya
I am grateful to you
town of Le Roy

McClean Co home of Adlai Stevenson
an highly competent
bald man
I am grateful to you
McClean Co
who hold my bed

319

2.19.04 – 2.23.04

[anabasis]

5:10 am am at apartment home curb
in Normal, Febr 19, '04 Engine warming
dark. Not dawn yet. Odo set.
C___'s ill, drive to see her. Gas up three
point three eight four gallons at Mobil 74e
5:23am 74east. Mid 30s. Warm day
Yest'day very springy. Brewed & brought
cup of Good Earth tea
A secret purple riding the east cloud
above Farmer City. Now
Champaign and Dawn. Am
bound for Nova Anglia my C___'s ill
who y'stday I found out's sick w/
Mononucleosis. Peach and Grape sky
above Homer. 70 miles from Normal
Kickapoo State Park. DUCKS

on the frozen middle fork
of the Vermilion River. Northeast sky
frothed in orange cirrus &
thatched w/ ripplings. Thousands
of rooks about Danville
gnat the sky rowing south
southwest. It is a muscular,
specky, blabby flight the flight
of crows. The rooks now
as I cross to Indiana at 6:35
row Southeasterly. Are they

seeing what did in the night.
There the bald head of the orange
mother appears in the skirts

of the day: sun up: or in
its hem, the grey brown hem
of the tree line 20° to the
rt of the road. A person is
a road, in a road, which, various
aspects of a road
may ride, Approaching
now Indy 7:25am
STOP Pee 8:22am 198m
Sunny, about 35° slight South
Wind. 205m 1/2 tank gone
2 bacon, 1 egg, 1 cheese biscuit
34mpg—why bad mpg?
What is wrong with Diane Rehm's
voice? [spasmodic dysphonia] Ah Ohio
border's bold blue arch—bye bye ignorant
Indiana like an dumb teen in the rain

I find myself thinking this
morning about my daughter's illness
and her smaller energy and
wider sadnesses of late: her
voice damp and little through the phone, 2
more US soldiers killed by
An roadside IED (Improvised
Explosive device) 60 m west of Baghdad
today. 540 odd US soldiers killed
ten thousand or more seriously
wounded (lost limbs, concussed

brain heads) and 10,000 to 100,000 Iraqi
civilians murdered probably a 200,000
wounded I approach the deep
valley of a river—on the
        old morning sun—

the "Great Miami River"—Now
the old morning finds me
at Mad River. It near
the Air Force Museum. Poor
Supine slain woodchuck in
left shoulder, head thrown
far back to Northern
sky, forelegs down now at
yr sides resembling arms
wrists bent down, damaged
brown, little hombre, such
an sun on you, & then cool
shadows, tinder blue, wreck
w/ car roar over you. You

La Z boy furniture of
ditches. You dead raccoons
you departed possums, you are
the further and minute furniture
of roadsides Why
did come here, little friends, to
explode? Panera, a loaf
of home. It looks like at
mid morning a very sad & old day
almost smoggy, like the palest
orange timber smoke has been
slathered behind the trees and

above the everywhere tan
there's a MOBIL at exit 15
on I-270 N 11:44am
Check oil—it's high! so
I happen to see a Sears
Autocenter—I go in—have
check—oil is A Quart high!

Have them remove A Quart
& am on hwy again at
11:45am—really 12:45pm
Eastern time Zone now in Ohio
Now that all is well, lay
the rug on the booze, chuck
the cups out to the snow,
what mellow tires, what sun, what
grease is on the light, & what a
dignified goose is that winging
in the dust (it is not related
to the demon goose on the golf course
that bit me) STOP eat 1:35 eastern

my engine hold 3.6 quarts
temp seem upper 40s
76east near bright Lake Chippewa
2:00pm then that flickering
of tree shadow I approach
the tree line at the end of the Midwest
around Youngstown. My daughter tells me yesterday
she's got all skinny—D had not
told me she'd lost weight from her illness,
the DIVORCE made official 13 days ago:

"Easter is born—crying aloud,

                                    Divorce!
          While
the green bush sways…." fr. <u>Paterson</u>
A fruzzed waterfall in the stones
has turned to slush but still grips
the brown rock wall a stubborn cold octopus
of ice, Airy ice partly hard water. Hi,
brown & dusty patina on
that dunnage on that
flatbed of that truck from
          Cortland, Ohio

A Transcraft trailer, new &
solid, passes thru Tallmadge
from the hwy near co. rd.
31, I see a business I've not noted
before—expansive steel bldg
incongruously in a graveyard bearing
broad & somewhat rude wood sign:
"Daily Monument" it is A
by God a gravestone manufactory: One
blonde crude wood track for a gantry crane
comes/pokes out loosely into the large yard
of raw and tall, two-man sized blank stones
who stand in a mud lot pied with thin snow
135m since filling & 1/4 tank gone =
45.38 mpg I hear

Gustav Holst now
in mid Ohio Afternoon

his "Saint Paul Suite" It makes
this part of dim Mahoning County
glorious. Milton Lake has
puddle pockets passim on its ice
Oh, Mr. Holst I get you:
this is Saul on the road
to Tarsas. 510m Meander Res.
Adopt A Highway. Truck Law
Restrictions. "Kalyn Siebert"
on that truck's mudflaps. Holst
I think was fascinated by Hinduism
Opus 29, no. 2 Richard Hicock's

It is yucky here, for are there
many trailers parked in the broad
macadam lot there but now
past the reservoir there are
fewer uglinesses in a pale
dimmed sun (the same as before
due to altostratus, alto-
cirrus which I have historically associated with
headache weather ick)—there are fewer
uglinesses, Shenango River, gritty & medium,
I think that of all the rivers on
this trip, you are my best friend.
The sun briefly was very hard &
crisp under the Beaver Valley
Expressway. Westminster College
Where D interviewed in
2001. Quaint Pine Township
w/ the ratty Amtrak tracks
under the bridge I cross

May I never be again a butler
to the anger of some other person
which I was so long of recent
a butler in the employ, in the servitude
of an anger of someone I long knew
and now know not. That was an hawk! Dead
in the road! clearly a hawk
w/ mottled wing
dead on the road. Its head planted in the snow
as if it had darted itself soot-fletched fire
rooting to the shoulder snow at rt

And also at the rt on a
mountainous snow-wave of an
west Ohio hill beyond a bare-leaved
picket of blue hickory in the
twilight swash of slush light
in a tree house in the middle
of a hill all alone—and a
mop in the tree standing there
where a boy should stand—the
tree there a porter
bearing ladder & rope
its boughs. There are riotings
in Haiti tonight & Bush is
calling for Jean Bertrand Aristide
to step down—I imagine

the CIA fomented those riots
oh the great Alleghany I
can barely see you over these
cement gunwales of
this bridge. 89.1 90.1 88.5

89.9 Pennsylvania
Clarion River down below in the
late blue light of the valley
is wider by a 1/2 again & it too
like Milton Lake bears gray-bottomed puddles
on top its softening dark ice. Road
filth polluting the snow either side
Former Enron CEO
Jeff Skilling. I hope he is
not feeling today that
pastoral optimism his money

has so long lent him.
Are his eyes nothing but balls
of lint on the television. North Fork Creek
under high cement stilt bridge
like all previous Pennsylvania I-90
bridges. Forgiveness, Redemption,
Reconciliation core values in all
the world's major religions, Now
Mr Skilling, Enron, Cheney and
the boys of Mammon may nt redeem
themselves, even at 5cents per bottle-heart
CA, IL, WI, OH. Stop to Urinate my pee 255m
& call C___, left message
4:50-55pm EST.
Near the SR1009 overpass
in the mts of Pennsylvania
American troops have been
murdering Iraqi civilians

for eleven months now
A 2nd dead hawk

also all shuttlecocked on rt
shoulder, flap no more, wings
flung to stiffness at death
it grey flight feathers long as my fingers
275m fr fill & 1/2 tank gone
= 46.22mpg, Bad day for hawks.
Got coffee! Am drinking 1st
cup coffee in many weeks
5:22pm: the veins on my hands
have expanded & rippled up
swollen twigs under my hand skin
this coffee stuff blows up our blood

I just heard an ad on NPR
for "Private Financial for Lutherans"
"Serving nearly 3 million members.
Values for Living." Either
side my head above my jaw,
in the muscles, at the temples,
veined blood bubbles. Today
John Kerry was endorsed by
the AFLCIO Labor Federation.
A bouquet of silhouetted cranes
big-hooks levitating
10 to 6 & "blue time" as C____
calls it: that indigo gloom that precedes
twilight: the finding of ourselves
in the penumbra of the earth's own shadow.
Darker but still
day, I'd say, or maybe

Just over some fence to night:
at the great dromedary hills

to the left I noticed back
last year when I lit an American
Spirit cigarette last March at
ten minutes or so after 6pm
the quality of light, the snow, was so
similar—right here 687miles fr Normal
91.5 FM. It's 43° in Altoona,
This is the silo valley!
A farmer there burns his
trash! The fields & hills
are snow blue. The
fluorescent & crisp bonfire light
                is a sparkling gel

under a dome of now opening
space—small package
of yellow apple light. WHAT
A kitchen of dusk is that valley
Mobil station at Exit 192 on I-80.
I have reached the annoying
pavement marking
test area at 725m fr. Normal. It makes
my car jiggle and buzz in a bumbination.
89.9 FM = NPR now.
"The war on terrorism is a
growth area."—from a Halliburton
pamphlet (really).—"That there
are men in all countries
who get their living by war,
and by keeping up the
quarrels of nations, is as
shocking as it is true; but
when those who are concerned in

the government of a country, make it
their study to sow discord,
and cultivate prejudices
between nations, it becomes the more
unpardonable."—Thomas Paine, "The
Rights of Man", circa 1792 Susquehanna
River. It's funny. When I arrive at the

Susquehanna River in the daylight
on the Road West, it seems

so far of Providence &
now I feel reaching the glorious Susquehanna
so close to Providence.
There seems to be milder, more
flat chested country east of
the Susquehanna. "Alcoholics have
the tremendous characteristic
that usually is common to all:
lots of pep—
& no judgment."—Father Joseph Martin
Susquehanna again 765.6m
Past—Mercy. Present—Love.
Future—Providence.

STOP Fuel at BP in Nuangola
PA 7:40-7:55pm. Get 6" sub
& candy (Starburst, peanuts,
Fritos, Mike & Ikes) & A
get well card for C___.
"Be faithful, weary Pilgrim,
our King is on the Way, and
the days are growing vile."

—88.9FM, "Pastor Rogers"
outside Scranton
"We're not looking toward A hole
in the ground. We're looking toward
cleavage in the Sky."—actually said by
radio evangelist "Pastor Rogers"

Interesting metaphors, Pastor
Rogers - 84 east 823.6m
8:24pm eastern Time
"Benign Anarchy"—Bill Wilson
re AA. This is where
the flaming Stupa fell upon
my car last year, for I am
in Matamoras, PA 873m
New York border 9:08pm
"I know people who have terrible
problems, but they feel better
than people who have no problems."
—Clancy.

Though nothing is wonderful
after you get used to it
And nothing is
horrible after y're used to it, I wd
seek to retain wonder while
jettisoning harrar. Bye to all
harridans and meanies
of the last 7 yrs
I cross over the Hudson River I-84
The prison on the right
w/ sodium lamps "A voice calling in the
hubbub (Why else are there newspapers,

by the cartload)" thus I quote fr Paterson
URINATION 10 pee-M 928m
Lots of icefalls in the dynamited roadway rock
at rt after East Fishkill NY Really bad string
of potholes in lt tire track of rt lane for 4
miles after rest stop

¼ tank gone 135m fr. fill Connecticut
border Clancy's granddaughter or dotter is
the chairman of the dept of creative writing
at the Univ of New Mexico. Her name is
Mary or Marcy Then is then 691 east 10:55pm
984m. If you hate someone it means, like, you
still have the capacity for love for Quinnipiac
River them. Odi et ammo,
               more like it Then 91n so dark 993m

Mattabesset River, which I never see, 1000
miles from Normal. 11:08pm Not to be rid
of emotions, but to keep those emotions from
becoming obsessions. Walnut St Silver Street
—the streetnames of Connecticut Are as
White, Roberts Street, As the rivers are Red
Beaver Meadow Rd near Haddam O thin men
 of Haddam Tat tvam
Asi

Thames River & US sub base If you want to
know how you're doing, you can also examine
those around you CIRCUMSPICE (as it says
on the seal of Michigan) if the people
around you are doing ok then you're ok; if
they're messed up, then maybe you're messed

up Rhode Island border 1062m 12:05pm
Dear Alan Davies, you said the river right:
"The hills are black mollusks
against the sweating sun
and the river is iced slate—
however we speak of April
we mean that we're passing through"

[katabasis]

Goofy and I are in Prospect Park 2.22.04 on
the hill overlooking Providence
behind the colossal marmoreal statue of
Roger Williams who founded the
city in 1636 and whose dust was put
beneath his monument there. He
is holding out a hand in blessing and
guidance over the city, the time was 1636
and the young minister left his wife and
children to avoid deportation to England
by George W. Bush and the Puritans leaders
of Massachusetts Bay Colony
for preaching wackism such as separation
of church and state, religious freedom
and buying the land from
the natives for a fair price instead of taking
it so Williams set out on foot from Salem,
Massachusetts, in the winter of 1636 with a
young kid named Thomas Angell and after
months of walking they crossed the
Seekonk River and settled on the bank of
the Moshassock. It is bright today. Goofy and
I are waiting for D. Just dropped

Sweetpea off w/ D. Her red hair & 1960s
hornrim sunglasses of tortoiseshell upon
which glasses all seals and spice and wax
and clips of light seemed to assemble. Her
bright red coat. Set odo. Down Congdon
street rt on Steeple Street passed the oldest
Baptist church (such white wood) in the US
now ten miles south on I-95 sky robin's egg
blue Upper 30s, 12:15pm. 95 in
Rhode Island a corridor of trees many
Evergreen near Exeter. The Connecticut
border just after noon passing the
Mashantucket Pequot Reservation Captain
Ahab's boat may as well have been named
"The Jews" it being christened the "Pequod"
cresting
a hill
buffets of north wind
car yawing. Great blocks
of limestone, tan, bed in the hills that bed
beside the roaring road the Mohegan
Reservation is
passed by a white Camry which
I follow passed the sub base &
US Coast Guard Academy

On an engine sized block of grey purple
rock rt side done in dark sprayspaints:
"Lightning Mittoo DE" The trees
here at Old Lyme charcoal-colored, not
broad, the blue of the sky fretted in their
rigging or at least their dark grey-brown
ribbing up thru the blue. 9N

71m. Now granitic rocks
sun picketing in the left near
Deep River CT, metamorphic rock
veining the limestone. Apple colored
sunbeams puckering the clouds. Wind seem
loud against the car today. This part of CT has
gorgeous big grained rocks called
pegmatite, an igneous (granitic)
compress of large grains (over 3 cm's)
bearing commercially valuable mins such
as beryl, emerald, tourmaline,
aquamarine, eg. Used to be tens of
pegmatite mines here, now just the quarries
of The Feldspar Corporation, which mineral
is used for ceramics, glasses and the mica
for wallboard Snow on the bald purple
stones near Chester
that is slate now on the left

Roaring wall of yellow birch
above the left slate. The stroboscopic
effect of the tree shadows
in the car interior, just post noon,
near the Godspeed Opera House
is fulgent, crisp, its flickering
the light in yellow boards
it wd not shock me were it audible
as a riffling. The yellow & black
of the slow vehicle lane sign is
appropriate not incongruous in the
day's pallet. Ice floes on the
Quinnipiac are thin & packed
against the northside of the

bridge pylons near Middleton
The river's mostly open water tho.
91s 100m 1:35pm
691w 17m A smearing of
chalky and tan stratocumulus
in the west.

Sawn looking cliff holding
an old fashioned watertower
Approaching Middlebury. A leaf
roars around the road near
Southington: A frog of brown.
rusted limestone at the Quinnipiac
near Cheshire, a near powdery,
deeply rusted rust. Wind
west northwest now. crow.
84 west I have driven now
under the marmoric stratocumulus that I
saw on the horizon at the
691 w junction 116m. 1/4 tank
gone, 135 m = 45.38 mpg
The highly metallic calm and
lowkey Housatonic
glisten in your little stick dots
w/ tiny towns of snows on the
small slopes above you

Do you have Waldeinsamkeit,
Middle-sized Housatonic?—the feeling
of being alone in the wood?
NY border   157 m . Bob Marley.
All around us the mighty wood. We are on
an island, Bob Marley. We are, on, every last

one, this Road Island. Ache
in rt junction of neck &
shoulder. East Branch Croton River
Ferrous limestone in road cliffs
rain leaching out iron, rush streaks
Head ache. 3 aches in my jaw
Molar related. That old
Republican sonofabitch walking
the edge of the world, far beyond
the cakes, is my father.
The final concert Bob Marley
played was 1980 in Pittsburgh.
Crossing the Hudson, glad light
on the Hamilton Fish. The trees,
hills, water, woods, all
blue & distant. Dead white torn
vinyl bags hang in the trees
glistering and tattered.

The snow in Southern Tier of
New York's been recent thawed
& frozen again. It looks like
old foam: The Air pushed
from it & conformed
in places from around tree bases
the tan grasses crusts thru
where there has been some
melting from the sun's heat
radiating off the dark tree trunks
or where too the snow's been
thinned & scattered by the traffic
of squirrels. The low sun marks
the many snow pocks w/ shadow

337

Crossing the Delaware 228m
into Pencilvania

3:53pm. It is called this because it was drawn
with pencils in the 1580s. The hills above
Scranton which are very breast like hills
are bare. No houses
just trees & snow. And sunlight
striking fr. the west
at seventy degrees. Here I
am then in Nanticoke, A
smear of cirrus embloomed
w/ a rusted orange spray of light
from the sun. The rocks here at Nuangola
are greased in Bitumin. There seem
a shade of coal even in the
green of the hwy signs
Susquehanna River: is it not
bingy-bangy!

It is a metal river & clear!
It is A sister of the Housatonic!
There are 2 great rivers on
this journey: No, 3: The
Shenango in Ohio. It is
glorious! and humble. The Sus
quehanna in PA. And the Housatonic
in Connecticut. First time
now, 343m from Providence,
near Bloomsburg, near Buckhorn
the Susquehanna (will I call her
the Suzie Q) run, along the road
—rt side—for one mile & I

I cross her
again at 344.

I am in the valley of the
Susquehanna! Sunset Sunset!
It is the sunset of the sunset!
It is 5:37 pm I am
underneath Schoolhouse Road.
The sun's the size of my middle
finger fingernail & as it sits
on the steering wheel—and it is
direct in front of my CAR
And there are 2 great VISTAS
on this journey: one West
of the Hudson (the valley of
the silos) and one at
Nuangola. I cross the

Susquehanna again at dusk, 366m, the
sunset fretted
w/ roseate horsetails
Above ink blue hills. Car lights
come sparkling white. I pass
an old dark barn & smell woodsmoke
along the road houselights are on
(no more horses in the decades)
Mobil Gas at Exit 192 on I-80:
I miss it. Also at Exit 185. I stop here
391m 6:19-6:30pm
Buy Starburst & bonbons
(sour tangerine manufactured by
Altoids) in Loganton PA
& as I exit station

I must wait for 2 Amish
buggies w/ lanterns & orange
reflective triangles. In the
dusk sky, which is green & purple
(the color of a starling) in the
west, are, in the west, venus, silver
and the gibbous sliver
of the moonball:
"Time moves from present to past."
                    —Dogen Zenji.
The moon is a horsefly of light.
My life is one continuous mistake.
"The awareness that you are here...
is the ultimate fact."—Shunruyi Suzuki
I shall call Suzuki the Susquehanna Roshi. Is
the moon in the west or is it
in the south or is the southwest in
the moon blah blah

It doesn't matter. I am the fish
behind its boat. Now clouds
are in the way of the boat blah blah blah
I cannot see the boat as I
(the boat's ass) leave Chesapeake
Bay Watershed. 7:40pm 472 m fr. Providence
STOP EAT—fish & chechen.
Small coke $4.23 497m
8:06pm. Inquire about
Flex money for mouth surgeries
120 m 1/4 tank gone
I buy isopropyl alcohol
for tank let's see how
much out of next 1/4 can get

Clarion River 516m
Alleghany River 532m

It is dark here at the O D Anderson
Interchange. Actually it is dark
all the way to Seattle now or
maybe San Francisco is
having a dusk as it is 9:15
here & 6:15 there. What I
have found is that when I
meditate, all of you
also meditate.[36]

Now: Shenango River 574m
9:27pm 70mph. I saw a tree
,as I climb the hill on crossing
the Shenango, silhouetted against
the sodium glowing sky
over Youngstown

12 miles in the distance—
Ohio border 576m. That
tree outside Youngstown was a
basic old tree. It was A
tree out of the special times
out of the old basic special
times. It was a very plain
tree. Meander Reservoir
"When we realize the everlasting
truth of 'Everything Changes' and we

---

36 Chala sadhaka chalata rahe, desh aur pardesh;
(Keep travelling, O meditator, in your country and abroad,) — S. N. Goenka

find our composure within it,
we find ourselves within Nirvana."

"In Buddhism, it is a heretical
view to expect something
outside this world."

"We should find the truth in this
world—through our difficulties."

Rest Area 608m 9:58pm
10:03pm on the road. This
morning Goofy and I woke up
in the Motel room, she in her
little bed & I in mine. And I
hopped over & snuggled w/
her & she examined my face
and hair and morning beard
with her small hands. She calls
my hair "Sticky up bangs"
and my stubble "little dots."

"We should begin w/ enlightenment,
proceed to practice, and then
to thinking."

Christianity, if it is done right,
is Buddhism.

"People think *they* are
doing various things but actually
Buddha is doing everything."
Tell C___ that when someone

yells at you, she is not
really yelling at you, she is
yelling outward from herself.
250 m 1/2 tank gone =
          42.02 mpg
71 S 654m 10:45pm
bird
and fish
are fish
No clouds—if I say
          no clouds

I mean many stars
but only if I say it in the
countryside
270 west 743 m 12:05am
753m stop gas 12:34am
Last tank 42 mpg
Got coffee b/c tired.
Also am irritable & woozy
70w 12:40am 760m
Darby Creek National
          Scenic River is but
5 trucks, 5 trucks are but
10 headlights

When w/ my electrical brain I
perceive the blinking of turn
signals, or when a bird fly
past w/ head smoking
because it has just flown out
of Abnego's pocket himself alert
and walking in the fire, when

w/ the rosebush of circuits
of the nerve–nut I see the
hair of the fire, I see birds
not in feathers but in hair
I see dogs not in fur but in
feathers I see horses in
hair and in wool & a lizard
in a skin of a young woman on
its lonely little tailored
body, a lizard in fact of
hard chests adorned

My thighs
Are hot with coffee, you can't
solve or remove or understand
suffering, you really can't
understand anything. The best
you can do, 1:49am, while thinking is see
similarities among particularities jesus
what the shit am I talking about, best you
can do is to keep a loving heart 79000m Odo
844.7m fr Providence Tractor & trailer
in the ditch. Pee 2 AM
Newsflash: I don't need

to get anything from the world.
There wasn't a day went by
, I think, when I didn't say
to my little sister she was
stupid. I remember
I saw Pastor Dean's hands and
his mean wife
on the German Church Rd. She

ws dumb and broad of butt
and muttered of the Nazarene.
She said to me this…
Snow like white sticks
in the headlights.
Morpheus on the hood.

Am puddy tired.
If I die on the rd ever
tell little C___ I love her
Someone apparently blames me
& tells someone, someone tells me,
that it's all my fault, this divorce thing
Sometimes the rd looks
like the great face of a
frog or something, sometimes the
rd's eyes, the high road lamps
outride on the road's face
are like those of a sea crab.
Illinois border 1014m
3:28am Central time sea crabs are
sometimes cute I have mentioned
this to C___ before in our nightly stories about
Teddy her teddybear

3:40 AM—Salt Kettle
Rest Area inside Illinois
border a ways I like
Illinois I pay taxes
Piatt Co. driver side
window down last 45m
to keep myself awake
the interior of the car

is a whirlpool of frigid air
got the heater cranked up
to warm my feet
De Witt Co. window up
Farmer City window up
Lights of Bloomington-Normal
enthronging the cloud w/
urinic hue.
Downs 1090 miles window up
Hats. Fruit. Trees. Signs
   = Spring.

February is winter. Kickapoo
creek. Dimness & suffusion
of yellow haze hung by
the clouds above Normal
The green of my dash light
woolen yellow of my writing
light that snake-necks
above the passenger seat
from the cigarette lighter hole.
4:47am central 1,099 miles m Exit
hwy. Clinton & Grove 1102
4:53 No breeze. No snow
dust & dirt moraines at curbs
4:55 at apt curb on Kreitzer.
All roads are letters.

4.12.04 – 4.17.04

[anabasis]

April 12 2004 4:45am
at curb in illinois upper 40s
north wind. dark. 81 thousand
14 miles on odometer. It has
been six weeks since I traveled
to see C___. A birthday's travel. This has been
very hard on us I enter the hwy dark
at 5am on Junction 74 east & set
trip odometer I ride up to 70 mph
& hold it I have stopped at
Dunkin Donuts. I have bought an
old fashioned & an Boston Cream & an
small decaf Goofy & I have
been v. lonely for each other
The North Wind

annoying & stiff. It is still dark
a cloud fuzzed moon 1/4 gibbous
coathangers above a red blinking radio tower
as I pass Downs Illinois this rd
is flat but I don't mind the
Illinois prairies of flatness
and never did really since arriving
in August 2002—helps to have
a good job at Illi nose State Univ
it took me out of a storm of an
hard relationship Illinois did
I got sober here I am fond

of this place I woke this
morning at 4 And showered. And
shaved. And got up to drive 18 hrs
I am wearing very used wool gabardine
            trousers

I have been on the rd 18 miles
I will try now a Boston Cream
After I finish my Boston Cream at 5:25am
I inspect the Sky, to the east north east
A purple scab of light has appeared
faint, and from it bleeds a
bruise of pale aubergine. I enter
Champaign County. 8 miles west
of Champaign Illinois I pass the
origin of the Kaskaskia river one of
these days I will inspect
the origin of the river. I once inspected
as a boy of 8 in moccasins the origin
of the Mississippi River in Itasca Minnesota
and I thought it was a jip. In
Champaign now I pass an
egregious display of cheeseball
religious Americana—the

vapidity of plains Protestantism
A great new white church
in its own little spiritual stripmall
caked in deep stucco (this is on
the right) that says in old "black-letter"
Gothic Gutenberg script
"CRUSADERS CHURCH"
20 miles to the west along this same

road a town called MAHOMET stands
and I'd wager frankly few round here
know that's an alternate spelling of
Mohammad Or maybe at some level the
Christians of that idiot church do know why
they chose to moniker it after a series of
religious murders and army barons OK: A
dawn that is Pink and salt blue comes 5:55am
There are dogwoods at Danville
Illinois that are flowering like a sea of
sharp pink periwigs under the
pink drawn jug of the dawn air. And they
pass into the quaint and foreskin-small valley
of the middle fork

of the Vermilion River where
many of the trees look like wrecked
large hardwoods carting on them
no leaves but a bud fuzz
I am in the valley for no more than
15 seconds. It must be a hidden cultural
requisite that in order to become a radio
evangelist you've got to have
a round bloated voice that sounds like a
melon too long in the sunlight
101.3 FM: at Indiana border
NPR 6:15am 84.4m. It's the
station from L_____ where I
used to live w/ C___ & D & Melpomene
in a firework sun where C___ was born
of sunseed, along an April Wabash.

¼ tank gone 100 m =

33.61 mpg—abysmal mileage!
90.1 fm 138m
I stop @ Lizton, IN rest area
7:06am 139m
Indy 7:25 156m
I tell you, b/c we are both sad,
we should get involved in picnics
We should buy Patti Smith albums
She is the poet laureate of Punk
We must get involved in picnics
Because they are collections of
Decency and Socialism
Fallujah in Iraq has

for the last week been the
scene of A strong resistance
uprising—American Marines have
fired on civilians shooting
children bombing residential
areas, they bombed a mosque.
The hospitals are full of
civilian wounded many families
have been burying their dead in
their gardens. 70 US soldiers
& "reportedly" 600 resistance fighters
have been killed Several cities
are sites of fighting in
addition to Fallujah: Ramadhi
Baghdad, Basra, Ohio
border: 246m

Dead hawk inside Ohio
one wing raised in hello

or heck with you. What is the deal with dead
hawks in western Ohio?[37]
That pale tin cap of cloud
of the Altostratic Variety
The Great Miami River is
glorious today. The Mad River
is a rooty-banked river
of the tender and cute variety
of A tender twenty foot river
338m I see the clump
of Columbus sky scrapers
HWY 270 N circles Columbus
Then 71 points to the NE
and passes through the
corporate harbor of Dublin's
glass bldgs on long green lawns

I pass
from Dublin I see An herd
of buffalo. Must get gass.
   They eat gras
Who hath woe
who hath sorrow
who hath wounds without cause?
They that tarry
long at the wine. Proverbs 23:29

You will be as one who lies down
in the midst of a Sea
Thine eyes shall behold strange women
thy heart shall utter perverse things

---

37 I suspect the Air Force poisons them.

but still yet they will rise in the morning
and seek it again. There
is an broken backed barn
at junction 71north / 76east

Now I am in Akron Ohio
It is 1:30 on the afternoon
Central time. Akron
secret Akron. Home of Dr. Bob Smith

There now is the curious graveyard store
called "Daily Monument" w/
hewn gantry crane of
blond wood. I imagine
it is made of filthy grave variety wood
unlike the clean baseball diamonds wood
of boys spry from suburbia. Now it is
Northeast Ohio, the sky is still
altostratic. The river I am come to says
I am
rural and I am auroral

The brief, the grey, the brown the bold
the dark the bright
the great the old
young and woody
Shenango! River!—you are
not dirty!—I wd expect
yr fish were clean and happy, yr bunnies
happy, the brains in yr
bunnies joyous Some men
of the working variety
are shoring up the bridge at the

O D Anderson Interchange
The bunnies of Shenango River
have come straight from the
picnic.

Where they were feted by
human babies—large human babies
dancing, dancing to fete them. The mothers
of the large ugly babies go
to take off the babies' diapers
so the babies can dance unfettered
by their waterabsorbing garment
and the mothers command
Fete the bunnies the babies
brush the moms away leave them on
the babies say we are large babies
we are the babies of the picnic And the babies
begin to say
that's the way uh huh we fete
the bunnies that's the way uh huh
we fete the bunnies
and the large babies said
bunnies

Do you feel feted
And the bunnies did not
answer, the bunnies backed up
Do you feel feted, bunnies
, the large babies asked again
, and the bunnies backed up further Then
the Moms alarmed at the
rudeness of the bunnies

stepped forward to control
the bunnies Bunnies the
moms said The bunnies
turned & looked & backed away
rain turns to slush in Central Pennsylvania

638.1m—begin jam 4:04pm
end jam 4:23pm 646m
Jam opposite direction 125m marker
to 127m marker
The Mommies continued to
approach & the bunnies cont.
to retreat Then
A large mom stepped forward
"I am the Mommy I am the
large Mommy!"
Such is the Proprietary Nature of Momism.
Jam 759m 6:08pm

The various mothers, their eyelashes big
as windmills, pots of snot jangling in their
noses, their brassieres made of maple lumber
the ugly clutter of their buttocks and their
panties bunched in the main fault, their facial
lips doing gymnastics out of which spill
lisping, blubber sounds, b's that babble in the
wind, their tongues, when making Rs,
sounding as a boulder thudding under the
froth of a river
bed. Their noses like hoe-cut crocus bulbs:
They have come straight from the Crucifixion,
each one claiming to be a Mom of Jesus. The

beds of these women are regulated with
longlasting thermostats. These mothers eat
nothing but sparrows

But the lads who ran the rain were glorious
                              children.
The rain was bright with gray or gray with
                              bright.
Nor were the raindrops the right weight: they
were as drops of whelks, as reservoirs
themselves, each teared ball a terrarium

That man there the sound of his anus is the
clattering of the Congo

Logs of lightning drop on their babies. Logs
like fattened axes. The lightning singes their
eyeballs, which are young fish. The puddle
water is pus. It is shining flatly, each puddle
like the stiff back of a nickel

The deer's penis is heavy as a bottle of coins.

Yr genitalia, this beautiful
hinged pedagogy, the cloudfolds hang
a moth at the bottom of yr torso.

I am passing Wilkes Barre at
7:15 eastern pm & light still hangs
This is unusual
last I passed here w/ light
, last summer, my daughter was w/ me
in the car. Heavy

rain since mid-Pennsylvania
I have gassed in Nuangola
I NOTE A lone Smallary of Ice
near Mt Cobb & Hamlin
on 84 east: it is spongy
& melting in the rain
on rt side of road. It is April. I am
hydroplaning. On this hill
slipping as I climb

So I cross the Hudson on the
very rain.
Now I am on the Sergeant
George Ross Dingwell Highway
near Waterbury CT, the rain
since noon has not lessened
—A 1000 miles from Normal—
10:29pm (est)—entering
9 South—The Chester Bowles
Freeway, While I am the rooster in
the rooster tail Chester Bliss Bowles
was a diplomat and "economist"
who made good Hobbesian
mots as "There can be no real
individual freedom in the presence
of economic insecurity."
Haydn's Liturgical music was
often criticized for being
too upbeat and almost comic.
His excuse, he said, was that
"When I think of God,
I'm happy."—the comic
and the divine. Probably the only

liturgy to employ comedy in 2000 yrs
There are mass graves now
in Fallujah, deaths of civilians
, murders, caused by US citizens, Rush
Limbaugh said we shd drop a Neutron Bomb
on Fallujah, leave the bldgs standing
but destruct the "terrorists"

[katabasis]

8:35am April 16 2004 I
cross the swollen Pawtuxet River
south into Warwick on 95-S
have just dropped Princess Mary Animalia
at her moms, Goofy was so sad
her hair & face small
as if she'd swallowed herself
I said goodbye to her at the curb.
She seemed smaller, her hair
seemed more unkempt. Her
big little blueberry eyes very round
D wore tan cords. A
bright blue blueberry sky, cool morning
Sun all over the porch
a sad bright grease

It is hard to write or even think
right now but I expect these kinds of
moments, those on the porch, for
my daughter, are moments of wounding
on which her little memory
will build a garage of emotion
and bring in the gritty weather

to park, but in the weather
will be happy gooses who will smile
and be cozy. We have a lot of fixing to do.
Meriden CT
Quinnipiac River. The
production of one gold ring
a wedding band, say, displaces
20 tons of earth in production
and a dreat geal of arsenic poured to streams
The grey roofs of the houses, all,
in the morning hills of Middlebury are
elephant colored & small
and they are tall.

Jam 145m near Bethel Connecticut
NY State border 158m 11:15am
Another jam 160m. Bethel was a town in the
Bible where criminals and all lost
souls cd go be safe, a place covenanted by
Mercy. The hills at Poughkeepsie are grey
w/no perceptible bud-green, nor along
bud fuzz though in some near trees
near Fishkill Creek buds
lay in chains along the finger boughs
The skydiving grandmother
lost her dentures somehow
above the picnic she fell through
packs of geese and doing so smiled
at one before breaking the way
of another in its wing & somehow

in there exposed the interior
of her mouth to the feather truck of the air

tearing from her flabbering cheeks
her prosthetic chunk of teeth Near
Matamoras Pennsylvania just passed the
Delaware River
I begin to accrue clear and green
bug splats—the first bug smears
of the spring
If I knew a man
was coming to my house
w/ the conscious design
of doing me good
I wd run for my life. Walden
"I never knew, & never shall
know, a worse man than
myself."
"Our manners have been corrupted
by communication w/ the saints." Henry
David Thoroughfare

"Like
pygmies, we fight with cranes."
A thin hipped uncle
The Susquehanna near Lime
Ridge is off its banks & brown
bubbling at the weeds. It is
bubblesome. It is warm
sunbasket, mid 60s. ETA: 1:45 am CST

Once I sate last year at a picnictable in
                                    Loganton
and it was trenched w/ pocketknife swastikas
and I pass now Loganton at 70 mph the radio
air is rutted and overrun with "focus on the

family" evangelical radio. I have
just seen a groundhog
12 feet up on the rt. hill side
at 430 m fr. Providence, near
Loganton, in Central Pennsylvania
I am listening to 91.5FM
Joseph Stalin called jazz
cheap—and depraved

Kruschev said jazz gave
him gas, who cares Kruschev,
you were a butcher just as
William Henry Harrison was
these men will
never Bring the tuba to the picnic)except
Jimmy he will(. What William Henry Harrison,
9th president of US brought to the picnic of
the Shawnee in 1809 far beyond the frontier
at a native trading hamlet on Nov 7th in a
place now called Prophetstown Indiana 20
miles north of what is now Purdue University
was a whole lot of killin and did not kill
Tecumseh til Oct 5 1813 and that on the
Thames river north of Lake Erie. How many
native picnics that man disrupted, Wm H
Harrison fr Virginia was an awful
man. But come to the picnic
Bring in laughter all the best children
Bring the good moms
Who liked the dads from the sea
Bring the uncles whose ears
are hairy padlocks
453 m begin Jam 123 mile marker

Bring them all, that we may love
all who perished beside
the olden rivers, without their mommies

Clarion River sun 30° horizon 5:30pm
Beautiful day Alleghany River 533
THERE IS A DEAD COW IN THE
                                    MEDIAN
It looketh like an immense apricot. It ith dried
decayed shrunken. First dead cow
roadkill I ever seen: 544 m fr Providence
about midpoint 89.1fm NPR 533m
73° Fahrenheit
A tin colored sunlight is
deposited into each mucoidal streak of cloud
each one a long island–muffin of sunlight
each one a funny sea–colored island of tin
HERE IS MY FRIEND THE FLUFFY
AND GLAD SHENANGO RIVER 575m

600 miles passed into Ohio
goodbye the joyous and just Shenango
The east way I was
traveling this way (WEST!)
in this patch of Ohio at
this point in the evening
w/ the sun in the trees was
the late summer 2003
an age ago, a marriage ago
I am in now Akron
Aged brick & industrial clocktower
at the corners of Willy Wonkaesque factory
of Akron

An blue shadow rich suburban light
washed in the late even sun as elevated
hwy comes briefly thru an cheap Akron
                                    suburb
RTLM: The Radio station in Rwanda that
in 1994 fomented n dictated the Hutu
genocide committeed by the Tutsis
at 671 miles in a
blue dark field, at sunset,
on the rt of HWY, A large
brown horse pulls a seated
man in A camel colored straw hat
w/ a beard. It is an "AMISH" MAN

Sunset is barn music.

If barren ignoble roosters
make in their gizzards
barky old hymns
they do so like geeks of disease
or as used boys in the Old Greece of the time
of discuses
My Grandparents, German and Frances Lien
met in a barn dance in 1918.
German was playing the fiddle
He was the dancing music that night
8pm & I am in that 8pm sunset part
of Ohio Above Columbus
where I first had an epiphany
while listening to Etta James

The sunset is a barn
It is dark now or green

It holds horses of cloud
purple just north Columbus
I start the circuit HWY
270 around Columbus
The ragged bad roosters
come in red coats

out of the neck of Dick Cheney
out of the neck of Lynn Cheney
out of the necks of Laura Bush
the necks of Humbert Humbert
they come out to the teeming picnic
where are the children of the world eating
and the women are tut-tutting in goodness
The bad roosters from
the necks of the evil wag
on the large prairie picnic grass
the scrotal skin that hangs
from the brittle beaks of the chickens of cruelty
the sputum of mayhem and death
pending in strings from their beak-knobs
and
into this display of shadow-of-the-barn
masculinity and evil the aforementioned
Grandmother falls
in her prim jumpsuit
matching parachute descending
w/out dentures onto the
undignified roosters splashing their musculature
everywhere this

the GREAT GRANDMOTHER of
Goodness

becoming a discoball of fists
kill'd all the roosters of evil
without teeth but of kung fu and of crushing
and the children loved it
for the She of Goodness
saved their sugar from sorrow
possibly caused by chickens of evil.
MICHAEL SAVAGE
the HOMOPHOBIC "talk"show
radio bum is calling for
an carpetbombing of Fallujah

Indiana border 853m we are beset w/ evil
men in our radios and televisions
10:50pm—big fat
cross on low hill a
hundred yards to rt: Jesus Christ Incorporated
It is a 40 foot by 20 ft cross
outlined w/ lightbulbs
and laid upon the grass
beneath a sign reading
"New Creations Ministries"
Then the forest of "Tom Raper" signs
ushers us toward the
Sparkling champagnelike city ctr of Indy
927m
11:05pm

I ignore the Eli Lilly bldg
Home of Prozac that causes us
not to feel the Consequence of Our Actions
(Kamma) Seems to be an Ostrich Ranch
at Exit 58 on 74 west

959 miles from Providence.
A battalion is 600 soldiers.
In Illinois again 12:30 CST
I screw down window in Urbana
Warm swirling ball of air enters car
sweet smells of rich cow atmosphere
reminds me of camping when 15
at Iowa Conservation Commission
in Des Moines

1:40 AM 1099 m leave HWY

1104m 1:47am Apr 17, 04

7.5.04 – 7.10.04

[anabasis]

July 5 2004 Normal 7:23am
Depart w/ Goofy back to RI. She just spent 2
wks w. me, now bundled in the backseat
asleep Clear morning. Onward winds
the dreary way (tennyson), altocirrus
hazes the upper sky
Return my daughter to D. After spending
part of summer with me
Dear Dr. Heritch—You'd
suggested I drop a note
and let you know how I'm doing
w/out the trazodone. In
short, excellent. My appetite
and sleep pattern both
remain healthy. I practice
vipassana each morning for
an hour before breakfast and each
evening just before bed

Altocumulus in Indy's Apolis
Robert Ader, fellow alumnus
of Cornell, in '74
at the School of Medicine & Dentistry
in the University of Rochester
proved the immune system can learn
Dr Redford Williams at Duke
studies hostility's damage
to the heart. (Interesting the Duke family

made its money on tobacco) Being prone to
anger was as strong a
predictor of dying young
than were other such factors of risk
as smoking, punching oneself in the throat
and high cholesterol
A Gray-blue Cumulonimbus
north of Columbus

July 6 9:45am departed
Holiday Inn @ Clarion PA
with Goofy
9:30am got govt rate on rm
C___ & I swam last night. In the pool
were beautiful fat mothers, a thin
mom, and a blond sad
republican family. Thought
I forgot my Evergreen t-shirt in
rm FOR I AM AN ALUMNUS OF
THE EVERGREEN STATE COLLEGE
Today Democratic Candidate
John Kerry chose John Edwards
as Vice Presidential running mate

The Assumption of Threat
or Hostility in Others is
The Hallmark of the Bully.

"It is a fact that
suppressed people show
more humor than the
people who rule or

are at home."—Isaac Bashevis
Singer

We have come into the world to work
together.

If all people are damaged and suffer—if,
                    that is,
damage, flaw, hamartia, is a given—I think
humor is a means of
dealing with damage by
appreciating suffering
as just another form of change.[38]

Humor seems to be
a method of equanimity.
It seems to be a means of
practicing and exercising that kind of
equanimity some people call detachment.

Seems to me the clown and the saint
are really close in having this detachment
from their own wounds.

(Doesn't the Yiddish word "Zelig," as
in the Woody Allen movie, mean at once
Holy and silly?) The ability to
"be at home" (in re Singer's quote above) is
what we see in "Zelig," and

---

38 "A person who has learned the skill of sorrow paradoxically will be lightened by kinship and
communion with all beings, and will spontaneously speak in phrases of empathy and saliency."
—Paul R. Fleischman

it speaks, to my sensibility, to a kind of ability
to "be at home" in an
existential sense too: if we are all damaged,
including the tragic protagonist bound in his
"hamartia," the problem of humor
amounts to
what we do in the face of that imperfection
and damage. If we can be
silly in the face of it, we can be holy.

Seems to me that blatantly
flawed people, whom Wm James called
"sick souls," have been forced by
circumstances to get some distance on life, to
appreciate constant change as both
a benison and a fact.

I mean, a clown is someone who
purposefully and theatrically
makes a show of debasing herself
by showcasing that innate damage: a
clown takes on and "owns" her own flaws
and wounds—and flaunts them
so triumphantly that we, the audience, feel
on the one hand superior to
the clown and on the other we
vicariously appreciate the courage
of that clown for being so triumpant and
skillful in the face of said flaws (big
nose, funny moustache, whathaveyou—yet
funny, awkwardly brave, and
finally buoyant).

In the case of a verbal clown [humorous
poet], that "flaw," that damage, comes in the
form of buoyant nonsense, anarchic
satire, tawdry rhyming, or incessant non-
sequitur:

In other words, maybe humor is a triumphant
display of detachment toward
the inevitability of damage.

It's a simultaneous owning and detaching
from one's flaws (and the fact
that they are inevitably and incessantly incurred)
that I think
makes an inspired clown useful.

Pay attention America persons you
are in need of psychosocial
adjustment this nation has lost all
sense of compassion not only
for other peoples but for its own.
It is in great need of a great
psychosocial adjustment.

July 10 2004 Saturday
I have left the normal route and
I am in the state of Maryland
But it is okay because Maryland is like the
state of Rhode Island
in 2 ways: it is small, its name ends in land.
on I-70 westbound. Glorious Saturday
like a Sunday of Sun. A Saturday of Sun
Altocirrus brushed up

Crossing Antietam Creek
& now Antietam Bridge
& now Antietam battlefield
only 59 miles from DC

Walked in the Potomac yesterday
w/ William Hayden, long time friend and
bouldered there, along it, mostly he did. Saw
many helmeted kayakers in the froth. Will
follow I-70 to Indy.

Onthemedia.org's
Robert McChesney is also
AN ALUMNUS OF THE EVERGREEN
STATE COLLEGE, as is my friend
Wm Hayden
Let me be a mini seagull

Ask D for School Photos of C___.
Refuses at first to give.

I have seen a bridge built near Dayton
that bears a bas-relief mural in concrete
of fighter jets and Soviet-like astronautical
machines.

Today in the Congo the
pygmies are being affected
in "Africa's World War"

Our biggest problem, said the Buddha, is that
we want not to have any problems. This is the
root of my misery. Because inevitably when

we fix one problem another arises to take its
place. There are three necessary realizations:
1. That all this crap is participating in the law
of constant change, 2) that this moment is
enough, 3) that I am enough

There are 3 kinds of Dukkha, or suffering:
1)   pain
2)   change
3)   being (what will happen to me?)

What we call "person" the Buddha called
"stream"

What I really need and want
will never appear as an object to my mind
This is v. important for me to remember as
regards fountain pens—I must stop
searching
for the perfect fountain pen?

We are always late. But we are never too late.
They who say to us in our lives that we are
too late—these people are always wrong.

In fact:
Redemption and Reconciliation can only
happen in a condition of belatedness—and
that condition is always attended by a sense of
one's efforts being too late. That is the
condition—the only condition—in which
redemption can happen: in the illusion of too-
lateness. If we are staring at the past and

thinking of the future, we feel late.

These things around me, in me, of me
were not once
and they are
and will not be
One day Kent Johnson and I
will look for fish on the Spoon
River—wet road, a gray low-cloud/heavy
colored day

I cannot make my mind not crave, or not tilt
toward something at least not directly, but
when I am in the moment, the mind stops
tilting.

Samuel Johnson said we more need to be
reminded than instructed.
Am I speaking to help myself and others wake
up?

If I am wise I will withhold judgments.
A field of pale pumpkins next to the highway
they are patient globes strewn over the field
wanting to be declared heads
The Buddha said this, which is a more helpful
version than what the Christians got: Do not
do unto others as you would not have them
do unto you.

Avoid doing what makes division and
contention
Promote harmony and peace

let this be my guide
right action: selfless action
be my guide. Harmony, joy, good will
peace of mind. Right effort is conjoined
with right view, means simply being in the
moment. We must first see what we can
control and what we can't. The more I try to
drive away
thoughts of M the more those thoughts
increase. Instead I will observe my fragmented
mental state & see it for what it is rather than
judging it or indulging in it or trying to shoo it
away. Our goal is a non-obsessed mind.

"It is by holding onto this notion of self, and
we hold it most dear, that we live in defiance
of reality."—Steve Hagen

Substantiality cannot be found
in thoughts or feelings

There is nothing in the world
that is solid there are no
selves there is only flux all
things arise together what sustains
us is already in place we must
note what a deep ache
is in our hearts. We must witness our
confusion and ignorance. There is nothing out
there that will ultimately satisfy. There isn't
anything that we must acquire or repel.
Attend to immediate experience. Cultivate yr
mind in meditation. The last words of the

Buddha
Be a light unto yourself
Betake yourself to no external refuge
Hold fast to the truth
Seek no refuge in anyone but yourself.
Work out your own salvation with diligence.

Truth is the only thing that quiets the deepest
ache of the heart.

What words are these have fallen from me
Can calm despair and wild unrest
be tenants of a single breast
or sorrow such a changeling be?

For the cultivation of kindness
of lovingkindness

use real individual, one person at a time, a
neutral person at first, then the ones we are
fond of, then work toward those we dislike

Compassion must be joined w/
an experiential understanding
of impermanence
and when we realize
that there is a way for others
to avoid suffering, our
compassion will become even
stronger
When we generate true compassion
during the cultivation of our hearts, we should
simply hold

on to it, experience it
without applying thought or reason
and when the feeling begins to weaken
we then apply reasons to
restimulate our compassion
We cultivate a sense that all beings
are equal, the equality of
all beings
That all beings are equal in
their pursuit of happiness: their
attempts at achieving it and their
rights to it
That my experience has depended
on countless beings
(even our success and fame relies
upon other beings)
That All beings have been my
mother in the past
That I should view all beings
as I view my self, exchanging my self
for others
That everything about us has
been created by the hard
work of others
That even those who cause us
hardship are providing us
w/ the opportunity to develop
tolerance
The Tibetan word for meditation means
to familiarize
In the Buddha's teaching empirical
knowledge is higher than theoretical
but reliant on theoretical nevertheless

10.15.04 – 10.19.04

[anabasis]

Oct 15 2004 4:50 AM
outside Apt—RAINY Leaves
turned bruised & flames 10
days ago Odo 91611
Getting Dunkin Donuts
2 old fashions 1 large coffee
I rise onto I-74 east at
5:07am & set trip odo
Here I come my little bird
my daughter DARK wipers
one second intervals
susha hug shusha
        huh shusha hug
Indiana 85.3.m

I feel Fortunate I get to drive through days
of rain. The dawn comes up with the color
of tin the road is smeared in the oil
of rain Ray Charles is dead June 10 I drive to
spend an early Halloween with C___
as D demanded in the divorce
agreement that I am to spend no
major holidays w/ her

I am now in the Wabash Valley
where a Muse was born, some yrs ago
101.3 FM is where I find NPR in this valley
at 141.7 miles I stop to pee

at 7:13am in a heavy rain I have
finished the peeing.
STOP Gas PEE 207.4m 8:10am

Wind on the Ohio border at 9AM 250m
At 262.2 miles I see again
an large hawk standing in the median
facing west, like an little soldier he stands
His little feathered knees in the grass of the
median The grass in the median
is the color of wheat
The hawk stands, morning's dapple,
dawn-drawn falcon
Great Miami River bright w/
mud, spacklinged in October
neon leaves pee 10:45am CST 369m
10:51 back a hwy
scudding cloud racks, cobalt dishrags
blue dark sky smoke stiffens
scudded clouds, kaftans made
of berry smoke
such water rags smear across orange and red
Ohio hills rain since Normal
Sun since seven
1 pm eastern stop eat

Wind on Pennsylvania border 536 m
Dead hawk rt shoulder
O little Hillock of air meat. Thiel—
Westminster College 550m—D.
was interviewed there in 2001
Shippensville PA—I was
interviewed for a job at univ there

in 2002. We got neither. We got
divorced. Trees are nice.
All Gray in sky. On wind shield
rain crackling. There are
crazy bright periwigs, the trees
orange red yellow pink periwigs
PA is a forest of wet
multicolored treesized periwigs.

Fire at fire & clock in the alleghenies
lenticular banner clouds leg the air
Road is rut-lit, shining, spray shrouded
gloaming. That red buick
pulls a bush of spray
The road is a clock to the alleghenies
The terrible day of election is upcoming
Been 4 yrs since last such
election day horrible
Such not day election hopeful
susquehanna wide mirror
in sepia tone Freiabend

Signs of a Great Canoe
The small mice in the fields
are exploding
Something is sad about this
Great canoes make lights
            nests, gnats
Where are the great canoes
They are behind the immense rind
behind yr head behind yr girlfriend
behind yr item yr other item
Somehow it got dark—it has

rained since Normal I am
860 miles from it, in the rain, in
the dark, in eastern PA It is
7:40pm est.
Stop pee 7:42

Behind the rind is
friendship
compassion
sympathetic joy
equanimity toward others
is a little place
to transcend oneself
as an act of compassion toward
all other beings,
in the yoga of compassion.
   528 BCE—in Spring
    yr he achieved
   "yatha buttha"
   Arrive midnight
     Motel 6
       Warwick. It's still raining

    [katabasis]

18 Oct 04 Bright fall day
of Providence. Rippling Quadrangles
of sun splashing from the
Dorrance Plaza Sky Scrapers
the windows of which stand
like horizontal pool water
Just dropped Goofy at MLK School
The children thronged her

plastic Halloween pumpkin candy bucket
(we had Halloween two weeks early
in the hotel 2 nights ago)
D. was late by 15 min's
No clouds & little traffic as the
forest of Rhode Island scrolls
heavily by with pines. Few trees, until
Connecticut, stand as autumnal bugles
toning red. Must be the difference
of 50 miles that causes Rhode Island
to lag in its leaf change
proximal to the sea

I am come to Connecticut
at 70 miles an hour
I am wearing a blue Patagonia jacket
Pawcatuck North Stonington
Rest Area one minute
I am come to Connecticut
my pants are greencorduroy
D looked beautiful
and my daughter looked sad.
Bobbety had
scraped her eye
a day or 2 ago.
She & I swam a lot
in the Marriott Hotel.
Her eye,
her loveborn eye—tore she a scratch in
stretched an 1/8th inch scab
from her brow down her lid
n onto her cheek top—poor her

so sad in
that scratch.

10:10AM 61.5 m fr. Providence
A traffic jam, a moraine of traffic
WHY IS IT PLEDGE DRIVE TIME
ON NPR NOT GOOD TRAFFIC JAM RADIO
Abates 636.3m 10:30am
I set the trip odometer at
Sweetpea's school
A stellar blue jay
from the fiery foliage
framed in my windscreen as it flies
it is glued in my memory
there in my windscreen
Another traffic jam 102.8m at
Junction 9 N & 91 S. 11:06AM
Abates 11:19am 104.8 miles
35 mins thus far wasted in
            traffic jams of connect
icut

The Housatonic reminds me
of Maria Helena Schmeeckle
bright, shining, friendly:
A thin park at the shore
glimpsed from the bridge
A rack of cloud in New York State
When a woman is so beautiful
one feels like swallowing her hairdo
—and then one loses her
Christianity is a personality cult.

It's an idolatry
Which is more important: to
look for A Woman, or for
yourselves—so asked the Buddha.
In PA, 378 miles from Providence I pass
A white Saturn Station Wagon,
well washed, w/ signs n
Mottos upon it read

(on bumper) "Keep God in America"
(on back window) "Reverend Cannabis
For President"—a cannabis frond
painted in green on driver's door
Above which: "Jesus is Coming Very Soon"
on which bled onto
back door "Don't Bogart that Joint"
Under which "Reverend Cannabis 4
President 2004"
3:30pm CST I stop to eat & gas &
see that above described car
& photograph it. Then I went to
(this is in Loganton, PA)
to gas up at A Mobil (their gas
has more detergents in it, I'm
told) & the man

Who looked like Mr. Rodgers
parked nearby (in the lot
where I have slept 5 or 6
times on cold nights of winter
while traveling to save my
partnership when I was partnered
w/ D or traveling to see

C___ after I ceased to be
partnered w/ D) & after
gassing on my 9.6 gallons w/
which I drove 408m I drove
up n unrolled my window
as he smoked outside his vehicle
in the gray wet air n said "I admire
yr car" n he "Thank you
Wd you be able to help w/ gas"
n I yes n out w/ 2 5s.

He thank you n told me had
been driving to the debates but
had missed the one in Arizona
I told him I took A picture of
his car n he said to show
it around, lot of people have,
sd I wd. Will put it on
my blog. I did not ask him
what his car "meant" nor "why"
he did this peculiar thing
only that I was grateful
for such abnormality. He
for the ten said "bless you"
n I "take care" I feel I
have met that man before
and that I will meet him somehow again
somewhere

DO NOT DO UNTO OTHERS
AS YOU WD NOT HAVE THEM
DO UNTO YOU.—The Buddhas
version of the golden rule—note the

negatives. "Remember me
as one who woke up," Is what he said.
Sweetpea v. sad this AM & last night
at Dinner in the booth at table in
the Bugaboos restaurant in Warwick. This AM
in the dark just-uncurtained hotel room I told
her the "secret" of how
to use sadness: First one
should feel it & welcome it
say HI to it: Then use it as
a Way of understanding
the sadness of others: and 3rd to use
it as a way of Helping

others w/ their sadness & this
is called "Compassion," I told her &
she said she already knew
this secret & I said she was
A very wise & kind & smart girl
And then we went to the car
And I took her to her mother
Rainy driving the sky
of dirty milk, since 20 mns after
seeing the odd cannabis man
I do not understand why people
smoke the marijuana.
"Democracy it doesn't come
from tanks. Democracy it
doesn't come from killing people."
—Syrian man on US in
Iraq on NPR 4:41pm CST

THE INVIOLATE LAW:

Separation from those we love
will, and does, come to all.
I told C___ that all people
have been sad, and that
all people will be sad—that
we cannot escape sadness
by not wanting to feel it. I
told her that all people
get separated from ones they
love, all her friends at school have
and will too and that we have to
be full of love in order to help
with all the sadness. Separation
is the law of life.
Getting dark 6:45 eastern time
24 m fr PA/OH border
I will get in at 3:30 tomorrow
morning. A sad evening. It is a dark
greased rain at the OD Anderson
Interchange & the

low clouds are brown
and weakly luminescent w/
residual light—
near night—trees silhouetted
& featureless, as if a great dim lamp of mud
were hung on the back of the world
and everything else
were handkerchiefs. Road a
        smear mirror.
Shenango River which
to night I did not see, then

Ohio Border
"Genuine peace of mind is rooted in
Affection and Compassion."—Dalai Lama

(1)   Limit what I want
(2)   Not have-what-I-want but
want what I have
   (2b) develop, that is, contentment
(3)   have a sense of self worth
-        dignity & self worth come from
my self-self here meaning my
sense of a self composed of other selves &
connected w/ others
Approach my daily decisions
w/ this simple question:
     "Will it bring me happiness"
The basic nature of all
beings surrounding me is
gentleness.

Compassion is the way out of
loneliness. It also reduces fear.
It creates openness with others.
States that are closed, irritable,
indifferent: opposite
states to compassion.
Jct. 71 S 660 m 7:20pm CST
The woman's name was
Keesa-Kah-Tommy (spelling?)
who sought from the Buddha
a cure for the death of her child
"Unhappiness, I saw then,
comes to each of us

because we think ourselves
the center of the universe
because we have the miserable conviction
that we alone suffer
to the point of unbearable
intensity."- Jacques Lusseyran,
survivor of Buchenwald

How to deal w/ the notion that
my suffering is unfair:
(1)   Suffering is a natural fact of
existence
(2)   It arises fr past negative actions
[or theologically, god has a plan and
there is some meaning behind this]
(3)   Rational objective analysis—
revealing there are other factors at play—
showing that some or all of the suffering
has nothing to do w/ me personally.
(4)   Examine how my own actions
helped create this situation.
(5)   Realize that all things change
(6)   Shifting perspective
         (6a) What are the advantages to my
given situation—to this experience of
suffering?
I-270 W, N of Columbus, 750 miles
8:45pm — 340 miles remain
ETA : 5.5 hrs = 2:15 am
May my suffering be
A substitution for
The suffering of all
Sentient beings.

Suffering is the most basic
factor we share with others.

1st imagine my own future suffering
then with an attitude of compassion
take my own future suffering
upon myself RIGHT NOW
2nd realize that negative emotions
have no true foundation: they
are always the result of
basic misperceptions of reality.
Love, compassion, good will
are all based on solid
perceptions of reality.

862 miles from Providence I
reach Indiana border

"People are ordinary and
existence is natural."

—Diki Tsering,
Mother of the Dalai Lama

It is 11:10 at night. I have
driven since this morning
I've 3 plus hrs to go. I went
to RI, Again, to see C___ my
daughter the little Pomegranate
from the Tuscany of Joy
She was sad this morning
and sad last night
because she didn't

want me to go. Ystday
, Sunday, we went to the
Boston Zoo. I'd never seen
gorillas outside of a
television before. They were bigger
and had depth. Traffic jam   922.5 m
11:35pm—bad accident
2 trucks—semis—smeared
like 2 great deer
Goofy and I enjoyed our Halloween
in the Marriott Courtyard
She dressed as an Arabian princess
and I dressed in a thick all polyester
royal blue and gold Marching Band
Grand Marshall's costume
tight as a wet suit frock
coat w/ tails reading "La Mirada"
across the chest diagonally &
"Matadors" on the shoulders

Fog since Columbus now west
of Indy. At Attica fog gone. The zoo
the Boston Zoo: I am saying goodbye
to the day
in which my daughter and I
went to the sad zoo
of Nova Anglia
We saw dancing storks
peacocks, swimming ducks up close
lions, Bactrian camels (3)
an vulture,
an vulture in fact did wish the air
as if it were a champagne hung

upon a cup—a vast beak,
A vast mess of knuckles was
that vulture we saw in Boston. Severe and
full of foam it seemed—
like the rotten lung of a saint
was in its chest—

it had old jellies from
the beach in its toes—
the beige gray jellies of snails,
the special snot jellies of
the dams—About this
vulture hung the death of
meats. As we watched it in Boston
and knew the comedy of Death
and then I tickled her because
she farted. 1/2 tank gone 262 miles
2:30am exactly 44mpg 1112 m
fr. Providence I exit hwy—
seems my new tires are smaller.
Am having chest pains—left side—
no pain in arm.
                    Arrive apt.—leaves thrown
by trees on curb—bricks on
porch, I have tried 2:37 am

12.17.04 – 12.21.04

[anabasis]

Dec 17 04 Depart 5:17 AM
American frost islanding windows in Dark
Dunkin Donuts in white light
Indian men own it
My trunk is full of gifts for C___
19° F. 40m fr Normal 45 minutes
into journey
The beats rhythms and subtle rhymes
of the great mid 1970s hit song
"Blinded by the Light" by _____
probably I believe deeply influenced
the development of my "poetic ear"
sun up at Linden/Crawfordsville
Sarco Metal Recyclers: dumptruck
"Chatauqua: 'A Funny Word that Means
Regional Airline of the Year'"
Chatauqua in fact a word from the Mohegan
people that means meeting place

"On Harlem Heights in '76
Washington fought the British pricks"
That crushed and destructed
barn at the clover leaf of I-76
off 71. It's dry snow-crisped
rafters the ribs of a last
deflated n unfolded fish
No ice on Lake Milton
Allegheny & Clarion Rivers

both iceless
The white water tower at Brookville
PA in the tangerine & tin light
of a late afternoon in winter, the white
watertower of Brookville stands like a
belly of light against a glaring rack of cold
clouds

frothed w/ sweet yellow, teat-milk blue
and child's-forehead pink. Now what is it
of mother-and-child
that is infused in the very barns
of the Alleghenies? In 1570 (I think)
the Pope Pius the Fifth excommunicated
Queen Elizabeth w/ a bull and
then, in same Bull, laid a
curse on her—and declared in the bull
that Anyone who assassinated her wd
not be committing a Sin but
wd be doing God's work
"Ropes of Sand or Seashine
leading to the Moon."
—Queen Elizabeth on treatises
and arcane questions of Theology

Queen Elizabeth's court
annually consumed
20,000 sheep & lambs — 600,000 gallons beer
more than 4 million eggs
No clouds tonight
        Stars coruscant
Waterfalls still
    in hard gray ice

17 hours 43 minutes
after departing I arrive
Warwick RI Motel 6
Midnight exactly   12.18.04

[katabasis]

Dec 20 2004 Caught in
snowstorm and mansion of snow
on I-95 in east Connecticut
standing still on hwy—by New York
v. scant snowfall this winter
& clear skies High
Winds tho—v. strong head wind
since east CT
   Old fort or fence in wood between
mile markers 10.5 & 8.8: in uninhabited
woods on rt—old fort?
    old fence? of stone
delapidated brown fieldstone wallwork
under the empty rattling boughs
and islanded by
the rolled leather of leaf piles

C___ and I celebrated Christmas
in the Courtyard Marriott Hotel
We swam in the pool
She mostly swam
I gave her my watch[39] to throw around
in the pool, and she dove for it
with Teddy watching by the pool side

---

39 A Timex Indiglo "Expedition" whose leather band decayed in early 2004, which band I
replaced with a black Velcro strap.

I brought Anthony DeMello's book
to poolside, the one on Awareness
which I read last year too at Xmas here
when I was sick with fever
She has glasses now, oval ones
with hair longer than I have ever seen it
her brown hair clumping
She is so glorious
My little daughter
whom I don't know as well anymore
She brought all of her Secrets of Droon series
by Tony Abbott, her favorite author now
I bought her this series last summer
She's read it 5 times now through,
each book hundred or so pages
24 books in the series
She is glorious smart
and wants me in the pool
We are the only ones here
and she shouts and claps
at her own echoes

5 hrs 37 mins I pass
A little red Ford
bearing an old white haired thin man
along under a baseball cap
And an outsized bumper sticker
in ALL CAPS reading:
    GOD BLESS
    THE WHOLE WORLD
    NO EXCEPTIONS
This to counter, future reader
the powerful selfish

ubiquitous back-car sticker
seen since Sept 11 2001 that reads
with idiots driving
God Bless America

C___, when you are older
get involved in picnics.
Get involved in the secular picnics you see
in the park, the ones with kids in them
with big headed moms
ones with the dads who are sad
and drinking in cars—those picnics. Get
involved in those kind of picnics that have
quilts and cheap arts, and ants and
eggs—and if there are girls
whose curls stand
as capstans on them
brightly, okay, but
if there aren't those sorts of happy
children there, go dutifully there anyway
and bring some
cheer though it is hard to give cheer
sometimes,
so go there where there are moms
who don't need pills. Or moms who
do need pills, it is ok, go there.

You will be there at the picnic perhaps years
                                    hence
and they may speak w/ certitude
of yr father, or of some other
person or curio
from old times: know that it is well

Be joyous. Be beneficent
toward yourself (too)

Also
Be like those fructifying gales
that among the archipelagoes
bear from island to island
not only weed and seed but
fat dazed fowl glazed in sunlight.

I intend to spend the rest of
my days in such picnics

Let there be rainwater in your hair
when leaving the picnic
you are actually coming to the picnic.

Do this because one day all the grandmothers
will be gone. There will be no grandmothers
anymore—neither next summer
    nor at the churches—they will be gone
from the porches. And there will be an
                                autumn
without them. With none of their old hard
                                hair.

That type of grandmother in the gravel,
the gray kind, the which we knew, you and I, so well,
she will be gone.
            Nor the new ones in their sandals.
Nor ever again
a grandma at the darkened lake:
of the old and normal ways.

They will not be the mavens of Sundays
                              anymore.
They will not be the matriarchs of cakes.
They will not be the ladies who saved the
children from the hunchbacks.

Because I know that you have not liked
worry, though your enemies might say so
                    to dismiss you.

Because somehow you wound up with
enemies. Because you tried to do good. You
will deserve these picnics, tawdry
as they are.

Because we are such a winch of small skin.

Because the dark umbrellas creak in the
sunlight.

Because you feel you must think
like your worry.

They may talk of some curious and intricate
features of an impending explosion, of
governments and stupid policies and the
death of congressional officers, of women
walking around in
yellow low-priced small dresses: you may
encounter
these disturbances. Is there a mastodon who
has stood on yr foot? Or is one who has a
mighty bowling ball sized dung smashed

into
his haunches refuged in yr garage?
                You may encounter these disturbances.
(Is there a threat composting
itself at the edge of yr group or group
 values?
Suppose a baker has risen up?)

But if at the picnic you worry, and if I am
 alive then, neither I nor anyone else will
advise that you cease worrying. Rather
we will allow our ease
to suggest this by example.

And too,
Some who left the picnic already.

And okay, so, before I go
beyond a final
border,
                        before
little sparrows stop for me—
I bet you and I will talk of scenes at a cliff,
clean dragonflies,
or how hues packed the leaves—

Okay, so you have heard
that getting involved
in picnics is a good thing. The weather there
is just as the weather here. The here there is
the same here as the here here. The warm
and the height and the hurry there—the
same calm and hurry here. We can generally

drop the hurry and
get thus to the picnic. And further No No real
dropping of anything is required. Take then
yr time getting involved
immediately in the picnic.

Equality, Community
Simplicity, Harmony
⠀⠀⠀⠀⠀:

These are Quaker Ideals
These are Buddhadhamma Ideals
These are Shaker Ideals
These are good ideals

⠀⠀⠀⠀⠀⠀⠀⠀⠀⠀And
Now, with a lake beside you, fish beneath
⠀⠀⠀⠀⠀⠀⠀⠀⠀⠀you
And an air behind you, I acknowledge you,
⠀⠀⠀⠀⠀⠀⠀⠀⠀⠀small child
There is no hair that may recover after you
⠀⠀⠀⠀⠀⠀⠀⠀⠀⠀touch it
No fog will not catch fire when you
⠀⠀⠀⠀⠀⠀⠀⠀⠀⠀skip in it and through it and
because of it.

I have always liked, Sweetpea, that fog
makes you dance.

I have always admired how you found
goats cute to pet.

You are a thing for goats to know and
for boats to carry round and round.

One day
Providence
will be far behind you.
Work out
your happiness
with diligence.
Rely on no external
refuge.

Know
that I
am okay.

As
everything
always
is.

9 hrs 51 mins dark the
car white w/ salt
& piebald too w/
wind shaped brown glaze
of iced grime like a bulging salve
slavered on my doors
composed of road cream & chloride froth

Ten hrs 49 mins
the salt near Youngstown
on the macadam dried
to talcum so thick it blends
into ditch snow
Unlike CT and RI this AM
11 hrs ago no fresh snow here

bare leafed trees & conifers

inquire about Maria's
wisdom teeth—were
they extracted? She
has such a cute jaw
Am now in Akron 11 hrs
28 mins   Dr. Bob's house is
855 Ardmore Avenue Akron
MASSIVE METEOR!
BLUE STREAK! GOLD

AND YELLOW AND RED!
11pm exactly east of
Dayton—it came right!
out from the 1/2 moon n
went direct toward east
thru about 30° of sky → as if the moon
Crapped a Spark
v. cold tonight → 10° F
v. clear
THE WINTER SOLSTICE
THE SOLSTICE

Passing the Wright Bros
Air Force Base, solstice
15 hrs 13 mins The Indiana
        border, solistice

Dear Prof & Dear Comm
A belated thankyou for
the invitation to apply for
the poet position advertised

by yr department at univ of
Illinois at chicago
At 75 mph on ave I earn
38-39mpg. At 70 mph
I get 42mpg
16 hrs 49 mins make
I-74 in Indy: last leg
1:30am v. tired

Just had 2nd Mocha Starbucks Frappucinno
fr a bottle from a refrigerator
at gas station GOD BLESS ALL THE
GAS STATIONS
Illinois border 18 hrs exactly
It is
Not as Cold as Ohio was
No snow in Median on shoulders
Exchange keys w/ Maria
Make Maria my Literary Executor
Meet my parents
For long time last few hrs
Moon was dirty brown
And tan, luminous—tawny, a
Luminous Carhartt brown
—and now it's gotten burnt orange
almost OCHRE, like a sodium light but w/
more red—and now
it trips into bed beyond the west's
red tipped radio towers
Reply to Jim Bertolino's email
Piatt County. Ahead, high Above
that truck, The Moon again, it lowers out
of A black fold in the sky like

A great luminous buttock cheek
and I and I

19 hrs and 11 minutes after seeing C____
for the last time this year
I exit the great highway I-74
that bears such whorls across the mid plains
Decatur Bloomington exit 2:50am
v. tired have been driving
w/ window open since Ohio
to fight fatigue
The roaring cold, is 20° F
3am done
no snow here
just xmas lights

I am traveled today
in a hardened furrow
one 24th the circumference of the globe
one day i will say perhaps tomorrow
i have realized
life was this short
, and do not get sad. Somehow
I knew in lights
in dark
in joy: the day the night
and the very universe
even
, and how it coagulates
around us
around my daughter, large
windy, and I am a home here

in it
and may she also be
a sailor
crossing sorrow

APPENDIX

Do not naively confirm
The conventional categories
Of ordinary experience

Let you become one
W/ this dusted world

An ant rising
Out of a bowl
"Goes" ah baby ah baby
This life is good
So let us go
This life is good

"To a mountaineer a
sea voyage is a pleasant
and restful change."
—John Muir

"It seemed strange
that everyone more or
less afflicted [w/
seasickness] should seem
ashamed."

—John Muir

Strong, glad life

All of us in the brawling traffic

Sun-spanglettes in the ditch
Tumbling black bag, plastic, inflated
In an accident
Of wind
Rolls, dog sized, along
A tan of the concrete
Median barrier

The world indeed this moment
Is kind of a sloppy dock
In a broader, happy bay
Whose flotsam at night
Chips the sky
In stripes of flame

The taillights towing a chain
Of red fire through a tearing fog
The road a draggle
Of quadrangular quanta

"Go where we will, all the world
over, we seem to have been
there before."—John Muir

"The world though made
is yet being made
and this is but
the morning of creation."—JM

Paints fade
Patinas grow

Scratches froth

Muds puff

And we jig still

"Most people when they
travel only look at
what they are directed to
look at."
—John Muir

Beautiful mallard blue
& red feathers brown head down
Dead at confluence of on-ramp
With I-80 near Milton PA
Noon. Susquehanna River
V. high & turbid brown

Sometimes cresting a hill, the sudden
New view, our skin is made
Of sails, our thighs are girls, all
Those books we ever read are
Opened in a bright wind and remembered
—there is a bright bridge

"If totalitarianism comes to this
country, it will almost surely do so
in the guise of 100% Americanism."
—Huey Long

Christian Bök and I
built a fjord together

Marianne Moore sd

"It is an honor to have witnessed
so much confusion."

It is always an occasion for 2nd chances
Woke at 6 Five hrs sleep
ITHACA—Island Kingdom of Odysseus
This is a Waterman Phileas
Broad nib and Noodler's black
Noodler's Black ink is made by
An engineer for Ford named Nathan Tardif
Who lives in South Dartmouth, MA
As far as I know and
He is very patriotic, perhaps even
Nationalist, but he makes the best
Fountain Pen ink anyone has ever used
Makes it in his home can you believe that?
Guy's a genius

Also best price of any ink ever

7am on road ½ hr low overcast
Past dawn in April
Empty wet fields filled & seeded
Made espresso this morning
With fussy chrome espresso pot
Farmer City Gibson City

There is a group really out there
Called "The Righteous Brothers Foundation"
Supports the "This I Believe" show
On NPR. I reject the Augustinian
Formulation "Credo ut intelligam"
And recall Confucius's "A fool

Rejects what he sees for what he
Thinks
A wise person rejects what she thinks
For what she sees"

"Intelligo ut intelligam"'s a better
Formulation for me

Little white shack on left labeled
St Josephs Sportsmen's Club
Near HOMER Illinois

Is at edge of hwy & bunch of
Hay bales as a target wall
And a shabby shooting cage
There is a ratty mist in the sky

Danville home of Gene Hackman and
Bobby Short the piano prodigy
Who talks like he's from England
Lakota means "Alliance of Friends"
"Us folks" or "Plains People."

"They call themselves 'Indian'....
They say they do not want to change
Their way of life"—Wm Blackmore
The North American Indian, 1869

In the 1760s during the

French and Indian War
The Ottawa chief Pontiac almost drove
The British out of Michigan

During the War of 1812 Tecumseh
The Shawnee nearly united all the Indians
Against the Americans in the Ohio valley

But Sitting Bull was not only
A great warrior he was a
Holy man who had the ability
To see into the past and into the future
His name in Lakota Teton
Was Tatonka Iotakay

Considered by his people as a seer
A Weechashah Waukahn
He was born in 1831
Died in 1890. That same year
The US govt declared
The frontier no longer existed.

The Lakota name for white people was
Waséetchoo. Between 1862 and
1890 the US govt fought 11
Indian wars—About 200 separate
Military actions: Ambushes, Raids
And the chasing down and killing
Of fleeing family groups.

Some historians believe US troops
Killed btw 1776 & 1890 about
4,000 Native Americans by
Gunshot or fire or knifing or bayoneting
It is estimated by some that Indians

May have killed 7000 soldiers

And civilians during that same time.

Th. Jefferson believed white folk
Cd not live on the plains:
The Choctaw, Creek,
& the Chickasaw—& the Cherokee—
Were ordered removed from
Alabama, Georgia, & Mississippi
B/c the whites wanted their land
Which they owned outright
For the growing of cotton Oklahoma
Was to belong to them forever

Genl Philip H. Sheridan
Who devised the masterplan
And coordinated the systematic
Genocide of the the plains Indians
Wrote in 1878 "The govt made treaties,
Gave presents, made promises—none
Of which were honestly fulfilled"

"We took away their country and then
Their means of support, broke up their
Mode of living and habits of life,
Introduced disease among them—and
It was for this, and against this,
They made war."

This was the same
Soldier Sheridan who fought
So viciously in the civil war

Sitting Bull stood 5 ft 10 inches

Weighed 100 75 pound
Had red brown / brown red skin
Eyes brown large & white
In each eye nestled a great student
Each of his eyeballs was a schoolhouse
Sitting Bull was a highly confident man
He wore 2 long braids
He wrapped them in badger skin
A badger is a bad animal
They are hard to catch and subdue
And once you catch one
God help you
The subduction of a badger is difficult
2 hrs 42 mins enter Indy
His buckskin jerkin was ornamented
With strands of human hair
From hanks of hair of men
Whom he had defeated in knife fights
3 hrs 5 minutes exit Indy
1st erection 3 hrs 15 mins
3 hrs 21 stop pee buy vending machine
Espresso 50¢ 3:28 on hwy
Bright gray altostratus cool day
His battle headdress when he wore it
Had a hundred feathers in it
From the eagles of the Black Hills
And the Tetons but mostly he just wore
A single feather in his hair

Sitting Bull was a primate
A great ape
He once to a reporter in the west
"I see. I know. I began to see

Before I was born, when I was
Not in my mother's arms but inside
My mother's belly. It was there
That I began to study about my people.
The Great Spirit gave me the power
To see out of the womb.
I studied there in the womb
About many things.
I was so interested that I
Turned over on my side.
The Great Spirit must have
Told me at that time
That I wd be the man to be the judge
Of all the other Indians.
A big man to decide for them
In all their ways."

Warm Glow Candle Co. Outlet Store
Country Kitchen: "½ restaurant ½ store:
All Country." "Shelton Fireworks, Shoot
The Moon
World's Largest Warehouse"

The Lakota had rules of engagement
He never broke them.
If he had he wd have the lost
The respect of his people. The sight of
A sick child, any child,
Any such child—the child
Of a fat lady, the child
Of a white lady—the child
Of a fat white lady
Any such sick child, any child,

414

Brought tears to his eyes
Tahtónka Iyotáke

Have seen 3 Bush/Cheney stickers
In the two parking lots
And a new silver Dodge pickup
A Confederate flag bumpersticker
That says "Keep it Flyin'"

Few trees if any near Dayton
Have fully matured leaves
A wan unripe green yellow green

Poor Poor Kernel George
Armstrong Custer
For you hath been killed
By Tahtónka Iyotáke
And his regiment too
Little Bighorde, Battle thereof
Sitting Bull never attacked a
White settlement. Sitting Bull
Always released the white women
And the white children
In a notebook during the 1860s
Sitting Bull drew an autobiography
41 pictures using a crayon

Again with a white elder couple
In a maroon Buick
A burgundy Buick
What is it about that car
That demographic
The 41 pictures matter of factly depict

Violent events in Sitting Bull's life
His drawings were signed w/ a
Line connecting a seated buffalo
To a human head

Varment [sic] Guard 794 8169

In the Great Plains alone there
Were over 30 different
Tribal languages
Each w/ multiple dialects

50 miles north of Columbus
Few trees in leaf bloom
A whole field is stained
In blaring dandelions. Near a sign
For Schwartenberg Farm

Now I come
To the breast hip
Shoulder hills
Of northern Ohio
The woman hip hills
Amish land hip hill land, land of pig
Sausage, juice of loins land
Thick nipple women land
The superfluity of languages
Meant that for trade a
Common language of signs and gestures
Was invented by the plains Indians
Which became the basis
Of what is now American Sign Language
Tushunkah Weekoh in the

Language of the Oglala Lakota
Means Untamed Horse
But ½ breed interpretors
Translated his name as Crazy Horse

Often the Whites got things really wrong
When they were talking w/ the Indians
Such that the name "Man Whose
Enemies are Afraid of His Very Horses"
Became "Man Afraid of His Own Horses"
Thus placing in the names of things Indian
Slight denigration

Squaw is a word fr the Algonquin Meaning
Woman whereas the Lakota Word for
Woman was Wéeñahn. Whites
Referred to Lakota women as
Squaws.

In 1877 Sitting Bull sd
"What I am, I am." Which I guess
Was his way of saying
He accepts himself & is comfortable
With his position in the world
This is a Rotring Core fountain pen
When he was born the midwife
Covered Sitting Bull in bear grease.

Lakota parents did not boss
Their children or other children the children
Sleep when they want eat when
They want they were never put
To bed, never forced to eat "on time"

The Lakota never struck their children
Nor did they yell Lakota
Babies were not allowed to cry
For crying cd learn the enemy to them

Grey collapsed barn
At junction I-71 / I-76 now just boards
Heaped btw the 2 longest walls
In the 1600s when the French Jesuits
Encountered them the Lakota lived
In the parts of Minnesota
I grew up in, at, among other places
The headwaters of the Mississippi
Near now Itasca State Park
Which I visited as a boy
And thought a swiz

They were living
Then in timber framed houses
A Father Marquette sd
They do not attack until attacked
And they keep their own word
The Creek and Chippewa were
Their enemies and the French
Trade happened to reach the Chippewa first
The Creek first
Bringing them thus firearms who made
Then war (there again the Daily
Monument Gravestone Manufactory
8 hrs 4 mins) driving the Lakota out
Of the forests west & south
To the valley of the Missouri
The journey taking decades

And the Lakota separating into 3
Peoples: the Teton, The Santée, and
The Yankton groups. Oglala means
People who Scatter Their Own

Sitting Bull's family belonged
To the band called Itchy-Craw
Which means those who laugh
At each other. The Lakota
Languages contain no swear words.

By 1700 the Lakota reached the Missouri
8:18–8:24 Stop Pee, walk
8:44–8:57 Stop Eat
Shenango! River! 9:09
Former radio personality
Pappy O'Daniel former gov of TX
Was the 1st media personality in US
To go into politics preceding
Reagan, Sonny Bono, and Schwarzenegger
As I pass under bridge 13 m into PA
Near Lackawanna Twnship
Mid 60s, Sunny, a Large
Woodchuck lies on its side
Curled up & hugging itself, its
Head in its paws, fetal position
It obviously fell from the bridge
& curled up in pain and died

"You—on the road—

Must have a code—

That you can—

live—by—

So you can grow

Teach—

yr children well"

"Work is for people
Who don't know how to fish"

Allegheny River 9 hr 54
Near Sign: "Welcome to Pennsylvania
Wilds" just across Allegheny River bridge

James Brown made a career
Out of apoplexy
I wonder what that dude's
EEG looked like

I believe it is the Hitchcock film
"Notorious," starring the Glorious
Ingrid Bergman in which a young
James Brown is filmed as a nightclub act
Whose onstage apoplexies are
"Patronized to" by an eyerolling
Obese whiteboy businessman who does not
Understand what James Brown is doing
The sublimation of Rage
The affrontive subversion of Minstrelsy

"Bad Bad Leroy Brown" An
Example of Modern Balladry
3 characteristics of a ballad:

1) Impersonal narrator

2) Simple plot

3) Often based on real events

I pity Leroy Brown when he
Loses the knife fight
Even tho he was so formidable
I pity Leroy Brown
His loss of life in the fight

I cross again the great Allegheny
And pass the smear of coal vein open
In the ditch hill on right
Surfing channels in PA:
In an important and somber tone
"It's a shame. This comes as
A disappointment to many
Pittsburgh Pirates fans. As it
Should be…" 6pm Eastern
10 hrs 48 minutes NO leaves
On trees—the small buds only—
At the highest point on I-80

Prior to Edward Bernays
A propagandist employed
By Woodrow Wilson, toast and coffee

Was the typical breakfast—but after
Wilson was paid by the AG industry
It was eggs & sausage

69% of all freight in US
Is moved by trucks
Right now there are 25 % fewer
Trucks on the road

This cd be an indication
That the economy is taking a dive
Tonight I will look at the
Trucks stops to see if fewer are there

Still bright at 12 hrs and
Sun behind me, low 7:40 eastern
The light behind me comes
Thru the car the color of pale
Maraschino cherry juice

Or the color of light
Through lemonade

12 hrs 12 mins the great cliffs
Sunset on them like an orange movie
They are near R B Winter State Park
The Waterman Phileas again
With broad nib

Strangely the majority of women
I have been lovers with
Have been Catholic
And the rest atheist

Wyoming is Lakota for "Large plain"

In the 1520s the Conquistadores
Brought horses to the Americas
Re-introducing the animal
Which had died out here 15000 years ago
In the Ice Age

Between 1640 & 1770 37
Tribes abandoned farming
And began to hunt buffalo full-time
With horses. Some of these came from
Outside the plains.

Lakota boys liked to paint
Scars on their bodies
14 hrs 43 mins NY state

August 17 1862 New Ulm, MN
Santee Lakota killed 700 whites

September 3 1863 White Stone Hill, MN
Cavalry killed 150, captured 156
& burned village (near Monroe)

A collection of rocking engines
Capture gold
A collection of shelves, squirrels
Churches, Storms
Collection of that stem
Collection of ointments
Of steam
That crooked thrown-out

Yodeller at trouts

In 1863 (?) near Killdeer Hills, ND
Sitting Bull fought whites for
1st time: 2000 soldiers
Led by Genl Sully

Then Sully went to junction
Of Missouri & Yellowstone River
& there built Fort Beauford
Fanny Kelly: Book
My Captivity Among the Sioux Indians

Col. George Armstrong Custer
Was a great ape
Formerly Maj Genl Custer
Gave a standing order to
His aide that if
Indians should attack when Custer was
Away, his aide was to
Shoot Custer's wife in the head
If her capture
Was to seem imminent

There was a fort at the
Confluence of the Cannonball
And Missouri in what wd be
North Dakota
At this fort (Fort Rice) for several days
Sitting Bull ran off its
Cattle and ineffectively
Harassed its defenses
But the soldiers responded

W/ cannon & exploding shells

A Cpt Rankin
At Fort Beauford MT
Shot his own wife
Afraid she wd be taken
As Sitting Bull harried
The outside of the fort
Sitting Bull never captured the fort

As a matter of fact no fort on the plains
Was ever captured by Native Americans
Cpt Rankin shot his wife too soon

"We must act w/ vicious
Earnestness against the Sioux.
Men, women, children:
Even to their extermination."

—Wm Tecumseh Sherman

After the Fetterman Massacre of 1866
Led by Crazy Horse
Both Sherman and Sheridan
Believed in Total War
The targeting not only of combatants
But of Civilians

RI: 1080 17:43

At one massacre, on the Washutah River
Custer killed 93 women & children
In Rhode Island & CT & NY

When you go to pass a car
The other driver will speed up
Anywhere from 5 to 15 an hr
To prevent you from passing

By late 1860s the 750 mile
Journey between NYC and Chicago
Could be done in 3 days by rail
Custer's job was to stop the
Lakota from robbing & sabotaging
The Northern Pacific Railroad
Which started in Duluth, MN
And was planned to extend
The valley of the Yellowstone
The way to Seattle

George Armstrong Custer
Was not unlike Geo. W. Bush
A very poor student he
Graduated last in his class
At West Point NY & once
Broke into a professor's office
To steal exam questions

Following a battle once he shouted
"I cannot but exclaim
Glorious War!"

Custer led haphazard charges
Against the Confederates
Assuring that his command
Suffered more losses than any other
Outfit in the Union army

[katabasis]

Iron in the limestone
Rust on the bridges
I just stopped in Southbury CT
For 2 Boston Creams and a latte
Someone seems less short-tempered around
me But is still rude: won't say
"You're welcome" when I say "thank you"
The boy general George W. Custer
Received Robert E. Lee's flag
At Appomattox and led the
Union Army at its Parade of Triumph
In DC. He loved loudly tailored uniforms
And ostentatious headwear
Very like Lord Cardigan

"Like a woman" he was very fond
Of his hair his hair fell to his shoulders
The Indians called him Long Hair
He designed his own uniform

Custer loved animals tho
And was filled often with a buoyancy
Resembling joy

He had a pet porcupine, pet badger
A pet wild turkey, pet beaver
A pet prairie dog and a fieldmouse

That lived on his desk
In an unused inkwell
And a pet raccoon

And hounds upon hounds upon hounds
Houndreds of them
Yet for all he loved animals
He hated human beings

Most specifically black people and Indians
And if any subordinates broke his rules
He actually ordered them tied up in
Funny positions
And exposed them to flies and gnats
Many leaves blooming
In the valley of the Hudson

His own troops called him Iron Butt
On June 18th 1873 he got telegram
While at Fort Abraham Lincoln
& Left for the Yellowstone country
With the 7th Cavalry on Aug 4th
Sitting Bull ambushed Custer
As he rode ahead of his main force
With a 90 man escort

Whitey took cover in a riverside copse
& Sitting Bull set fire to the tall grass
Custer's ammo ran very low
Before the main force arrived
In late afternoon

3 hr 30 min PA border

Lakota scouts first saw
The Black Hills in 1776
They pushed out the Kiowa

Felt the place was full of a life
Giving energy called Wákan
In 1823 Jedediah Smith first
White man in Black Hills. In 1873
Pres. Grant orders Genl Sheridan
(Mr. Total War) into the Black Hills to
Determine if gold was there as the
US was suffering from a mini depression
Due to bank failures & the idea was
More gold was needed but the
Fort Laramie Treaty stipulated this
Area as a Sioux Reservation
Snow making banana shaped dives
At my window
East of Scranton (in Catskills?)
Near Lake Wallenpaupeck

Because the Lakota refused
To sell the Black Hills
Pres. Grant decided
To provoke a fight w/ the Lakota

5 hrs 1 to 5 hrs 6—rest stop
In Pennsylvania
I see on the right an ancient
Dilapidated
Chicken house
In the rain
Use less, window less chicken house
Near Mainville / Mifflinville

Brown swollen grey-bubbled
Susquehanna

Berwick Lime Ridge

The Indian name for the Battle
Of the Little Big Horn
Is
The Battle of the Greasy Grass

The Lakota medicine man
Who would come to be known as Black Elk
Was there at the Battle
Of the Greasy Grass and he
Was thirteen

Near Limestone new graffito on bridge
On 2 pillars in white spray pain
1st pillar: JESUS
2nd pillar: IS GOD

My enemies are the kind of personnel who
Read abridged books
(—if I have enemies
—and if they read)
Or who
Try to make books of bridges

Custer's men & family (some of whom
Died with him) all shot themselves
In the head or shot or were shot
By their comrades

After the death of Custer, Sitting Bull
Was so feared by Americans that
Newspapers surmised he was

430

Probably white—for it was thought
An Indian cd not kill a white man

Newspapers conjectured Sitting Bull
Was in fact a renegade white man
Who spoke English, German, French &
Chinese fluently

It was first the newspaper
Editors who suggested
That the government should spread
Smallpox deliberately among them

Custer, like Genl Grant, from Ohio
A town called New Rumly
"The only good Indians I ever saw
Were dead."—Genl Sheridan

"We're making off for Sitting Bull
And this is the way we go:
40 miles a day on beans and hay
In the regular army, O!"

On May 6 1877 Sitting Bull
Led 889 people & 12000
Horses into captivity at Camp Robinson Nebraska
On bridge near Philipsburg PA
In black paint
"I LOVE SHERRY"

I loved sherry too, a cheap
Drink fr. Juarez Spain
W/ high alcohol content

But no longer do I—you
Can have her Mr. Bridge Painter

Next Bridge: mixed words from
Succeeding generations of graffitiists
But near the surface of the
Layers of tangled words this phrase
"Mad Dog Love" something something

7 hrs: 452 miles: 64.57 mph
Strange but patchy snow on ground
In woods to rt and sm. buds on trees

It was in this state, Pennsylvania
In 1871 that a tannery company
Found a way to make quality
Leather out of Buffalo hide
As leather was always in need
For furniture, clothes and drivebelts
(We forget that our rubber drive belts
Were once leather) and at
This time the real slaughter of Buffalo
Started. The term "sharpshooter" comes
From buffalo huntingkilling. The Sharps
Was a rifle, a big game rifle in that it
Shot a shell 2 ½" long
It could kill a buffalo at 1500 yards

Native Americans said of it
"It shoots today—and kills tomorrow"

THE IDIOT
Joseph Wright Moore killed 20500

In 9 years—a Record
Btw 1872 & 1873 the buffalo
Was wiped out of Kansas
Then they moved into Texas

The Society for the Prevention of Cruelty to
Animals
Was founded as a result of the
Buffalo slaughter
In 1866. The army encouraged
The destruction of the buffalo
Because it would hasten
The extermination of Native Americans

8 hrs: 507 miles: 63.38mph

Mr. Total War G W Bush Genl Sheridan sd
"These men [buffalo hunters]
Have done more in the last 2 yrs
To settle the Indian question
Than the entire regular army
Has done in the last 30 years.
They are destroying the Indian commissary."

And sd they shd all get medals
It is for this reason that Pres. Grant
Vetoed a preservation bill
Passed by Congress. "The sooner the Indian
Loses all his Indian ways, including
His language, the better it will be for him
And for the government."—Richard H. Pratt,
Principle of Carlyle Indian School, 1883
Tuesday July 19 1881 Fort Beauford MT

Sitting Bull surrendered with 187
Children & women

"I wish it to be remembered that
I was the last man of my tribe
To surrender my rifle."

The first white town Sitting Bull visited
Was Bismarck ND—August 1 1881
He ate ice cream in the
Sheridan House Hotel.

Genl Sheridan being the one who
Made the equation btw
Good Indians and the deceased ones.

My little daughter C___
Named after the muse of history
And of heroic poetry
Talks so much she is a
Selfdescribed motormouth

At 9 hours I cross the 6pm beautiful
Shenango River under

Dark swirled clouds mottled in sun
And the Shenango swollen brown
Puffy out of its banks.

The Lakota word for cattle was
Wohl-Haw from hearing
Cowboys say this:
Whoa (stop) & Haw (go)

The Bureau of Indian Affairs
Banned the Lakota from
Practicing their religions thus
Denying them their rights to
Religious Freedom, banned the Sun Dance
The motto of the Carlyle School
A boarding school near here, in
Carlyle PA was "Kill the Indian
To save the Man."

During the summer of 1855, 150 yrs
Ago this summer, Sitting Bull
Joined the touring show of Wild Bill Cody
Visiting NYC Philadelphia & DC
He gave most of his money
To white beggars in the cities & sd
"The white man knows how to
Make everything, but he does not
Know how to distribute it"

Strange long series of very white snow
On rt hills mid Ohio 685 miles
So late in April & warm
In the light's lee.

And then more very white snow
Near Mohican State Park
With orange light splashing sundown
Over everything from just above
The right treeline I am traveling south
Coins of apricot colored light
Are flipping on the ditch water
Why not be happy about whatever

Let it come, maybe. Go ahead
And approach, empty in spirit, all the days

At fairs in rain
At fairs in sun

"The gateway to the Buddha's
Teaching is sadness, sorrow, and grief.
He does not encourage these emotions:
He encourages awareness of these
Emotions....
The awareness of suffering & sorrow
Is the 1st noble step."

"The capacity to face pain has been

A virtue in every single culture—

Except for modern America."—Paul R.
Fleischman, MD

Acknowledgments

Thanks to Joe Amato, Karen Leona Anderson, Sayagyi U Ba Khin, Jim Behrle, Aaron Belz, Jasper Bernes, Christian Bök, Chris Breu, Franklin Bruno, Sir Francis Buchanan, Sitting Bull, The Nation of Burma, Ed Brunner, C___ _____-Gudding, Azure Carter, Brian Collier, Josh Corey, Ricardo Cortez Cruz, Jeremy Davies, Jordan Davis, Danielle Dutton, Kristin Dykstra, Carol Eagan, Tim Feeney, Paul Fleischman, Kass Fleisher, Gina Franco, Jerry Gabriel, Roger Gilbert, Lara Glenum, Johannes Göransson, The Respected S. N. Goenka, Henry Gould, Myself, Irene Gudding, Julian Gudding, Jorge Guitart, Elizabeth Hatmaker, William Hayden, Patrick Herron, Susan Howe, Tim Hunt, Tahtónka Iyotáke, A. D. Jameson, Rodney Jones, Sir William Jones and the Asiatick Society, Pierre Joris, Jim Kalmbach, Amy King, Ivy Kleinbart, Tim Lanning, Barry Lapping, David Lehman, Ginger Lightheart, Reb Livingston, Rachel Loden, Erin Malone, Sue Martin, Christine McCarey, Aaron McCullough, Didi Menendez, Tom McCulley, Amalia Monroe, Murat Nemet-Nejat, John O'Brien, Nathalie op de Beeck, Eden Osucha, Rochelle Owens, Karl Parker, Peter Ramos, Riban Riban, Martin Riker, Jerome Rothenberg, Gautama Sakyamuni, Paul Sawyer, Standard Schaefer, Maria Helena Schmeeckle, Zach Schomburg, Peter Dale Scott, Alan Sondheim, Mathias Svalina, Irene Taylor, Roberto Tejada, Mike Theune, Leanne Tonkin, The Toyota Corporation, John Tranter, Ven. Webu Sayadaw, Curtis White, Allyssa Wolf, Vincent, Kirstin Zona.

Sections, poems, essays from this book were first published in *New American Writing, Jacket, Aufgabe, LIT, Action Yes, MiPoesias, Salt Hill, VeRT, L'Bourgeoizine, Mandorla:Nueva Escritura de Las Américas, Spoon River Poetry Review, Court Green, Backwards City, Counterpath Online,* and in the anthologies *Poetry 30: Thirtysomething American Thirtysomething Poets, The Other Voices International Poetry Project,* and *Cadence of Hooves: A Celebration of Horses.*

Jorge Guitart's translation of "My Buttocks," "Mi Trasero," first appeared in *Mandorla: Nueva Escritura de Las Américas,* and the original appears in *A Defense of Poetry* (University of Pittsburgh Press, 2002), by Gabriel Gudding.

About the Author

Gabriel Gudding's first book, *A Defense of Poetry*, was published by the University of Pittsburgh Press in 2002. His work appears in numerous periodicals and such anthologies as *Great American Prose Poems: From Poe to the Present* (Scribner) and as translator in such anthologies as *The Oxford Anthology of Latin American Poetry, Poems for the Millenium,* and *The Whole Island: Six Decades of Cuban Poetry* (University of California Press). He has started three creative writing programs in prisons and teaches creative writing, literature, and poetics at Illinois State University.

SELECTED DALKEY ARCHIVE PAPERBACKS

PETROS ABATZOGLOU, *What Does Mrs. Freeman Want?*
PIERRE ALBERT-BIROT, *Grabinoulor.*
YUZ ALESHKOVSKY, *Kangaroo.*
FELIPE ALFAU, *Chromos.*
　Locos.
IVAN ÂNGELO, *The Celebration.*
　The Tower of Glass.
DAVID ANTIN, *Talking.*
ALAIN ARIAS-MISSON, *Theatre of Incest.*
DJUNA BARNES, *Ladies Almanack.*
　Ryder.
JOHN BARTH, *LETTERS.*
　Sabbatical.
DONALD BARTHELME, *The King.*
　Paradise.
SVETISLAV BASARA, *Chinese Letter.*
MARK BINELLI, *Sacco and Vanzetti Must Die!*
ANDREI BITOV, *Pushkin House.*
LOUIS PAUL BOON, *Chapel Road.*
　Summer in Termuren.
ROGER BOYLAN, *Killoyle.*
IGNÁCIO DE LOYOLA BRANDÃO, *Teeth under the Sun.*
　Zero.
BONNIE BREMSER, *Troia: Mexican Memoirs.*
CHRISTINE BROOKE-ROSE, *Amalgamemnon.*
BRIGID BROPHY, *In Transit.*
MEREDITH BROSNAN, *Mr. Dynamite.*
GERALD L. BRUNS,
　Modern Poetry and the Idea of Language.
EVGENY BUNIMOVICH AND J. KATES, EDS.,
　Contemporary Russian Poetry: An Anthology.
GABRIELLE BURTON, *Heartbreak Hotel.*
MICHEL BUTOR, *Degrees.*
　Mobile.
　Portrait of the Artist as a Young Ape.
G. CABRERA INFANTE, *Infante's Inferno.*
　Three Trapped Tigers.
JULIETA CAMPOS, *The Fear of Losing Eurydice.*
ANNE CARSON, *Eros the Bittersweet.*
CAMILO JOSÉ CELA, *Christ versus Arizona.*
　The Family of Pascual Duarte.
　The Hive.
LOUIS-FERDINAND CÉLINE, *Castle to Castle.*
　Conversations with Professor Y.
　London Bridge.
　North.
　Rigadoon.
HUGO CHARTERIS, *The Tide Is Right.*
JEROME CHARYN, *The Tar Baby.*
MARC CHOLODENKO, *Mordechai Schamz.*
EMILY HOLMES COLEMAN, *The Shutter of Snow.*
ROBERT COOVER, *A Night at the Movies.*
STANLEY CRAWFORD, *Some Instructions to My Wife.*
ROBERT CREELEY, *Collected Prose.*
RENÉ CREVEL, *Putting My Foot in It.*
RALPH CUSACK, *Cadenza.*
SUSAN DAITCH, *L.C.*
　Storytown.
NIGEL DENNIS, *Cards of Identity.*
PETER DIMOCK,
　A Short Rhetoric for Leaving the Family.
ARIEL DORFMAN, *Konfidenz.*
COLEMAN DOWELL, *The Houses of Children.*
　Island People.
　Too Much Flesh and Jabez.
RIKKI DUCORNET, *The Complete Butcher's Tales.*
　The Fountains of Neptune.
　The Jade Cabinet.
　Phosphor in Dreamland.
　The Stain.
　The Word "Desire."
WILLIAM EASTLAKE, *The Bamboo Bed.*
　Castle Keep.
　Lyric of the Circle Heart.
JEAN ECHENOZ, *Chopin's Move.*
STANLEY ELKIN, *A Bad Man.*
　Boswell: A Modern Comedy.
　Criers and Kibitzers, Kibitzers and Criers.
　The Dick Gibson Show.
　The Franchiser.
　George Mills.
　The Living End.
　The MacGuffin.
　The Magic Kingdom.
　Mrs. Ted Bliss.
　The Rabbi of Lud.
　Van Gogh's Room at Arles.
ANNIE ERNAUX, *Cleaned Out.*

LAUREN FAIRBANKS, *Muzzle Thyself.*
　Sister Carrie.
LESLIE A. FIEDLER,
　Love and Death in the American Novel.
GUSTAVE FLAUBERT, *Bouvard and Pécuchet.*
FORD MADOX FORD, *The March of Literature.*
JON FOSSE, *Melancholy.*
MAX FRISCH, *I'm Not Stiller.*
　Man in the Holocene.
CARLOS FUENTES, *Christopher Unborn.*
　Distant Relations.
　Terra Nostra.
　Where the Air Is Clear.
JANICE GALLOWAY, *Foreign Parts.*
　The Trick Is to Keep Breathing.
WILLIAM H. GASS, *A Temple of Texts.*
　The Tunnel.
　Willie Masters' Lonesome Wife.
ETIENNE GILSON, *The Arts of the Beautiful.*
　Forms and Substances in the Arts.
C. S. GISCOMBE, *Giscome Road.*
　Here.
DOUGLAS GLOVER, *Bad News of the Heart.*
　The Enamoured Knight.
WITOLD GOMBROWICZ, *A Kind of Testament.*
KAREN ELIZABETH GORDON, *The Red Shoes.*
GEORGI GOSPODINOV, *Natural Novel.*
JUAN GOYTISOLO, *Count Julian.*
　Marks of Identity.
PATRICK GRAINVILLE, *The Cave of Heaven.*
HENRY GREEN, *Blindness.*
　Concluding.
　Doting.
　Nothing.
JIŘÍ GRUŠA, *The Questionnaire.*
GABRIEL GUDDING, *Rhode Island Notebook.*
JOHN HAWKES, *Whistlejacket.*
AIDAN HIGGINS, *A Bestiary.*
　Bornholm Night-Ferry.
　Flotsam and Jetsam.
　Langrishe, Go Down.
　Scenes from a Receding Past.
　Windy Arbours.
ALDOUS HUXLEY, *Antic Hay.*
　Crome Yellow.
　Point Counter Point.
　Those Barren Leaves.
　Time Must Have a Stop.
MIKHAIL IOSSEL AND JEFF PARKER, EDS., *Amerika:*
　Contemporary Russians View
　the United States.
GERT JONKE, *Geometric Regional Novel.*
JACQUES JOUET, *Mountain R.*
HUGH KENNER, *The Counterfeiters.*
　Flaubert, Joyce and Beckett:
　The Stoic Comedians.
　Joyce's Voices.
DANILO KIŠ, *Garden, Ashes.*
　A Tomb for Boris Davidovich.
AIKO KITAHARA,
　The Budding Tree: Six Stories of Love in Edo.
ANITA KONKKA, *A Fool's Paradise.*
GEORGE KONRÁD, *The City Builder.*
TADEUSZ KONWICKI, *A Minor Apocalypse.*
　The Polish Complex.
MENIS KOUMANDAREAS, *Koula.*
ELAINE KRAF, *The Princess of 72nd Street.*
JIM KRUSOE, *Iceland.*
EWA KURYLUK, *Century 21.*
VIOLETTE LEDUC, *La Bâtarde.*
DEBORAH LEVY, *Billy and Girl.*
　Pillow Talk in Europe and Other Places.
JOSÉ LEZAMA LIMA, *Paradiso.*
ROSA LIKSOM, *Dark Paradise.*
OSMAN LINS, *Avalovara.*
　The Queen of the Prisons of Greece.
ALF MAC LOCHLAINN, *The Corpus in the Library.*
　Out of Focus.
RON LOEWINSOHN, *Magnetic Field(s).*
D. KEITH MANO, *Take Five.*
BEN MARCUS, *The Age of Wire and String.*
WALLACE MARKFIELD, *Teitlebaum's Window.*
　To an Early Grave.
DAVID MARKSON, *Reader's Block.*
　Springer's Progress.
　Wittgenstein's Mistress.
CAROLE MASO, *AVA.*

FOR A FULL LIST OF PUBLICATIONS, VISIT:
w w w . d a l k e y a r c h i v e . c o m

SELECTED DALKEY ARCHIVE PAPERBACKS

FOR A FULL LIST OF PUBLICATIONS, VISIT:

www.dalkeyarchive.com